SMART
WOMEN

DON'T RETIRE—THEY

BREAK
FREE

Dedicated to
Werner and Denny
and
the fabulous women in The Transition Network

FROM WORKING FULL-TIME
TO LIVING FULL-TIME

SMART
WOMEN
DON'T RETIRE—THEY
BREAK
FREE

THE TRANSITION NETWORK
and GAIL RENTSCH

Foreword by Lynn Sherr

SPRINGBOARD PRESS

NEW YORK BOSTON

Springboard Press
Hachette Book Group USA
237 Park Avenue, New York, NY 10017
Visit our Web site at www.HachetteBookGroupUSA.com.
Springboard Press is an imprint of Grand Central Publishing.
The Springboard Press name and logo are trademarks of Hachette Book Group USA, Inc.

First Edition: June 2008

Library of Congress Cataloging-in-Publication Data

Rentsch, Gail.
  Smart women don't retire—they break free : from working full-time to living full-time / The Transition Network and Gail Rentsch. — 1st ed.
     p. cm.
  ISBN-13: 978-0-446-58091-5
  ISBN-10: 0-446-58091-0
  1. Women—Retirement—United States. 2. Retirement—United States—Planning. I. Transition Network (New York (N.Y.)) II. Title.

HQ1063.2.U6R45 2008
646.7'90820973—dc22

                                                                          2007042480

                    10 9 8 7 6 5 4 3 2 1

             Book design by Giorgetta Bell McRee
             PRINTED IN THE UNITED STATES OF AMERICA

CONTENTS

FOREWORD

Lynn Sherr

It is the only thing we seem to talk about. "We," of course, are the women—women who have been there and done it—not all of it, but an awful lot of it, often under the most trying conditions and usually after kicking in a few doors to get there. "There," of course, is where we were never meant to be—not, at least, according to the rules of society, notably American society, with its back-to-the-kitchen mandate during the maddeningly traditional postwar 1950s. But thanks to many of us, the rules changed, not always peacefully, and new generations of women not only entered the workforce but swam to the top, becoming the voices and the faces and the brains and even the brawn of a newly energized and occasionally confused nation. We challenged the system and cherished the results, setting the pace for our daughters and theirs, all the while transforming jobs into careers and teaching the world that our place, that fabled and long-limited "woman's place," was indeed everywhere.

So now what?

Now that we, the groundbreakers, are at an age when we considered our mothers old but know that we are not, now that our employers don't necessarily agree, now that we are, or are about to be in transit, some removed from those careers by choice and some by fiat, with adult children long out of the house and spouses either gone from their own life's work or too early gone from the marriage, what exactly are we supposed to do—with our energy, our connections, our experience, our ideas? What exactly are we supposed to do with ourselves?

It is, as I mentioned, the only thing we seem to talk about.

A friend who was a school psychologist says she's glad she retired because she wanted more time—for herself, her husband, her passions. But it turns out her passion was partly in her school work, and she hasn't been able to replace that. Yet.

A talented film producer is ready to move on after a stellar career, but can't figure out what she wants to do.

A top-notch journalist who wrote and edited her way through much of the breakthrough 1960s is eager to have lunch so we can discuss "what's next."

Nowhere in the discussions does anyone mention the possibility of doing nothing.

And it's true for everyone, not only those whose pensions or savings accounts aren't nearly substantial enough to keep them going without a new source of income.

In fact, part of the lure is the possibility of doing more . . . for ourselves, for our families, for our community. If that means doing less of what used to seem important—pulling on the pants suit, putting on the face—so be it. Many of us have stared down disease or death too recently to settle for anything short of what simply makes us happy. Many just want some unscheduled afternoons to hang out with grandchildren while we can still beat them to the trampoline. And many crave the opportunity to play out at least one more act, to reach for the stars or burrow down within, whatever makes us feel alive.

But how?

We're scared, we're excited, we're eager, we're reluctant. And most of all, we are bewildered: how to face the reality of no longer having an office to go to, a job that defines you, colleagues to bounce ideas off of, and, oh yeah, a paycheck. You probably know the old joke about retirement: a woman marries a man for better, for worse, but not for lunch. Well, liberation has made retirement a gender-free option, and we are facing not only the notion of fixing lunch every day, but also of eating it alone.

Which is a large part of the problem.

"I know now why I went to work in television," a former correspondent confessed to me. "I get lonely. I like working with people." She went on: "When you're on TV, you never have to work on your social life. Everyone comes to you. The invitations are endless." And now? "I have to arrange things, make them happen, if I want to see anyone."

Others say they will miss the power, being at the center of the action, feeling that they matter. It is, and I don't say this unkindly, an addiction. My hero, Susan B. Anthony, who led the campaign for women's rights when much of nineteenth-century America viewed the possibility as a radical threat to the republic, candidly admitted to a newspaper reporter in 1905, "Work is my gospel. I am seldom idle." She was eighty-five years old.

Those sentiments are just a few of what I've collected in the last few years. This book compiles many, many more—concrete evidence that the angst of friends and colleagues is, in fact, part of a flood of concern across the nation. The good news is, we are not alone. The better news is, there are some answers here, or at least signposts that point the way to new possibilities. By exploring the roots, the issues, the anxiety over retirement, suddenly solutions emerge.

A few of my own friends have gotten there already.

"Don't be afraid," counsels a woman with a few years of postcareer experience. "Don't think of it as if empty time were the enemy. Let yourself lie fallow for a while. Doors will open that you didn't even know were there."

A close pal, a longtime lawyer, says she has her answer ready for anyone who challenges her decision to drop the casework, give up a schedule, and happily travel with her (also retired) husband, when she is not reading and thinking and otherwise engaging her still very fertile brain. What does she tell people who ask, "What do you do?" Easy. "I'm living my life."

Another has put together an exhausting montage of consulting, nonprofit board work, travel, and plenty of time to care for her aging mom and growing grandkids. "It's a life," she announces without irony.

Indeed. Living, breathing, thinking, doing—with respect, in control, on our own terms. I'm facing it too, asking all the same questions. *Smart Women Don't Retire—They Break Free* is a great start.

Lynn Sherr is a correspondent with ABC's 20/20 *and is the author of the memoir* Outside the Box.

INTRODUCTION

Christine Millen and Charlotte Frank, Cofounders of The Transition Network

As we faced the desire to retire from our jobs and leave the prestige and pride in accomplishment that each of us enjoyed from them, we struggled with the question What comes next? We wondered whether our identities were so tied to our work community that making a transition was even possible. After all, it isn't easy to leave a job where you spent much of your adult life, and to do it in our society, which is founded on a strong work ethic, idolizes youth, and equates success with money and job title. The question is even more difficult to answer when so many of these qualities have been central to your own life.

So there we were, confident, successful professionals who felt like teenagers trying to forge an identity. We could not turn to our work friends, since many of them were not yet ready for the discussion. And we saw few examples, guidebooks, or training manuals for a "retirement" that potentially could last for thirty or forty years. Out of our puzzlement we realized that we needed to do what we always did in the past when we faced similar quandaries. We needed to talk to other women.

We also thought that we weren't the only ones thinking this way. We saw the need for a national, even international, nonprofit organization that would bring women from completely different backgrounds together in small and large communities to examine this transition and imagine new possibilities for it. We envisioned a safe, supportive environment where thoughtful women could help other thoughtful women explore new opportunities and test out ideas. The women's movement of the sixties seemed to us to be a good model, particularly the idea of women talking to women in small, intimate groups. We quickly found other women who felt the same as we did. Thus, in 2000, The Transition Network (TTN) was born.

Since the beginning, TTN has attracted an educated, talented, and experienced working woman (whether or not she worked for pay) who is beginning to think about her many productive years ahead. She may be someone who has a clear retirement date in mind and wants to know what she can expect to encounter. She may have been downsized suddenly and needs advice and inspiration. Or she may be struggling with her retirement, which she thought would be an easy transition filled with endless bliss, and now wants to reinvent it.

The women in TTN range in age from their late forties to over eighty. Half are married or partnered, and most have children. Most work either full- or part-time, in a variety of jobs: as teachers, writers, human-resources specialists, doctors, lawyers, engineers, executives, therapists, marketing specialists, entrepreneurs, librarians, financial experts, artists, and more. Their major concerns are about the future, especially about how to be intellectually stimulated, meet new people, have fun, maintain an identity, and sustain a sense of achievement. And they are especially eager to find meaning and purpose in whatever they do. Many volunteer for religious, museum, and arts organizations and health and illness advocacy groups, and help people in need through charitable organizations. From the first, we sought innovative ways to partner with nonprofits by providing them with the talent and resources they want, need, and cannot afford, and offering our members opportunities to be of value to something worthwhile.

When we began TTN, we modeled it on professional organizations where women assemble to learn career skills, hear different viewpoints on building a successful career, network with colleagues, look for jobs, and enjoy being with others who share similar interests. But we never lost sight of the essential concept that as women we have the power and inclination to form communities to offer support and friendship to other women.

What our members value most are our peer groups of eight to twelve women who come together regularly (usually monthly) to discuss topics of mutual interest. The first TTN peer groups focused on the topic of transition from full-time work to "something else," all the while adhering to an informal "no whining, keep things positive" rule. Since then, new groups form regularly to discuss an amazing variety of topics limited only by members' imaginations. Just a few examples of current peer groups include Writing for Pay, Dealing with a Retired Partner, Exploring Dormant Creativity, Singles in Suburbia, High-Stakes Poker, Widowhood, Travel, Volunteering, and Chorus.

Yet, even as these peer groups are precious to the individuals in them, they represent communities of thoughtful women in the process of changing the social climate. These are women who were pioneers and groundbreakers in every aspect of American society, accustomed to influencing others and having some degree of control over their lives. And now collectively they, and we, believe we can overturn ageist stereotypes in our culture and advocate for older women by demonstrating that we really can learn to use the latest technology, look attractive, retain our sex appeal, and be productive members of society.

The title of this book, *Smart Women Don't Retire—They Break Free*, acknowledges that none of us are comfortable with the word "retirement," which traditionally has been associated with a withdrawal from society in order to spend the remainder of life in pursuit of leisure. The way we approach the concept of retirement couldn't differ more. It is based on the experiences of TTN women and friends who share their concerns, experiments, and excitement as they contemplate and pursue new directions. We hear from the preboomers, born before and during World War II, and early boomers, born between 1946 and 1958. All of them reveal their thoughts about this fascinating and tumultuous "retirement" stage of their lives. They discuss the alternatives they explored and they describe their ongoing steps toward creating a new brand of retirement. They also reveal how they reimagine what it means to be an older woman in society today. We listened to their voices at monthly meetings and in one-on-one conversations. It was Gail Rentsch, one of TTN's founding members, who came up with the idea for this book and has seen it through every stage of the publishing process. For two years she interviewed hundreds of women about their concerns and experiences and wrote about them. Each section of the book delves into a major area of special interest to these women. It starts by exploring why we are even thinking about retirement and what we can do to prepare ourselves for this transitional period in our lives. And because work is such an important and continuing part of our lives, it looks at what we like and don't like about it and some of the options we have to change it. Later chapters explore some of the exciting things we have always wanted to do with the freedom to be ourselves, and consider our changing relationships with friends and life partners at this stage of our lives.

Throughout the process of preparing the book, we were consistently struck by the perceptive insights these educated and accomplished (and some would say privileged) women contributed about the second half of their adult life. Certainly we recognize that these women do not, and cannot, represent the voices of all women everywhere. There are many women who are unable to reinvent the latter part of their lives because of economic constraints and demanding family needs. The kind of reinvention we consider requires a degree of freedom, access to options and the ability to make choices. However, we also believe that the experiences discussed in these pages will inspire all women and men to rethink what to make of the many years they have ahead and provide them with fresh ways to think about it.

We want to share our respective transition stories with you.

Christine: I was born during World War II and grew up in a small English village at a time when the butchers, the bakers, the newsagent, the grocery store, were all family owned and everyone knew me and my family. It was very peaceful and probably quite dull. But I had the sense that my mother and her closest friend were very happy in this quiet domesticity and postwar tranquillity. Education was a given in our family and I always assumed I would become a teacher, work in a retail bank, or join the navy. Along with nursing, those seemed to be the available choices for women. But good timing and great fortune took me to London University in the early sixties, where miniskirts, new friends from worlds way beyond my own, and the arrival of the commercial computer industry transformed my opportunities. I jumped at the chance to learn something new.

In those early years we were all discovering the computer industry.

Bright, smart people came from everywhere to work as programmers and analysts and in sales. We had no models or standards; we took risks, made it up as we went along, invented clever techniques, and pooled our ideas. My career in consulting and the transformations in the computer industry allowed me to work with a variety of clients, many of whom were in financial services and ready to take risks with technology to support the innovative products that Wall Street was developing.

I married at twenty-three and lived for a year in an untroubled Northern Ireland before moving to New York, where my daughter and son were born. After my divorce I was a single working mother for a few years, before finding Bill and his two children. So with the dog and the housekeeper and shared custody we lived a busy family and work life.

In my early fifties I experimented with ways to reduce my focus on work and have more time for myself. My children and stepchildren were in college and I no longer needed a structure that mirrored the school year. I was able to take a sabbatical that allowed me to spend time with my dying mother in England and bond with my sister as we shared those special days together. I came back and worked on a project in California for two years, and Bill and I commuted alternate weekends. I took on new roles, which led me to full-time commitment to client work and minimal participation in office leadership. I also decided to join a theater board and make that a priority instead of a "will help if work permits."

As I look back I realize that these were all ideas I was testing about what life would be like for me when I was no longer committed 200 percent to my career. And when the economy turned sour in the late 1990s and the computer industry was about to go through yet another major transformation, I decided that, rather than put all my efforts into revamping the career I had loved, I would move on. Which is how TTN came to be. Now, along with Charlotte, dedicated board members, and wonderfully active and committed members of TTN, I am building TTN into a national nonprofit organization.

Charlotte: I am a Depression-era baby, who grew up at a time when women were encouraged to get an education and then use it to further the career of their husbands. A premium was placed on raising lovely, well-behaved children and serving on the local PTA. My mother actually told me not to show my intelligence if I wanted to get a man. But my classmates blew my cover and voted me most likely to succeed, forcing me to pursue an advanced degree in political science at the University of Chicago and a career involving challenge and purpose. I chose government service and moved up the ranks in cutting-edge local, state, and federal programs. This included serving in the War on Poverty, with federal and local agencies dealing with employment discrimination, and in New York City's child-welfare agency, and, finally, heading up procurement programs at the city level and for the Port Authority of New York and New Jersey. I retired in 2002, after helping put the agency back on its feet after the towers of the World Trade Center, both Port Authority buildings, were destroyed on 9/11.

Although Christine and I had started TTN before I retired, to bring it into being without support staff, without money, without an office, with only a dream, was a challenge beyond any I had ever faced. But I knew my new retirement would not be a life of leisure. I have a great need to create something meaningful, to live a life of purpose, to be relevant and useful. My greatest strength is persistence. My greatest concern was being front and center instead of working behind the scenes. My transition was short. Within days, I was working full-time (this time without pay), but with extraordinary freedom. I reported to no one; my creativity was unfettered by bureaucratic restraints. I learned how to present our case. I found myself becoming an assured speaker (although I still do not love public speaking). TTN's growth and success were heady in the early days and continue to be so today. I love my transition. My biggest challenge is to maintain some balance in my life, making sure I carve out time for family (I never married but am devoted to siblings and their children, some of whom call me their cool aunt Charlotte), friends, travel, my interest in outsider and self-taught art, cultural life in New York, and reading.

We hope the voices in this book will inspire you to find your way and further prove that life after fifty can be a special and valuable time. To learn more about TTN and join our community, visit us at www.the transitionnetwork.org.

PART

I

THINKING ABOUT RETIREMENT

CHAPTER
1

What Is This Thing Called Retirement, and What Does It Have to Do with Me?

Retirement is a radical idea. It suggests we are about to be launched from something familiar and comfortable into an unknown or, some would say, a downright boring place. Many of us just can't wait for the big day to come. But lots of us feel a bit queasy at the idea.

As trailblazing women who have been pioneers in all aspects of our lives, we consistently fought against a status quo that limited our options and squelched our confidence. So why stop questioning and challenging previous expectations for who we are and what we will be now? But just asking and challenging what has gone before won't answer personal questions about what we will find ahead, including: What will we do if we no longer have the things we spent our lives fixated on? How will we feel if the access, status, and respect we realized become marginalized? What will it be like if the power and prestige we fought so hard to gain wears out? Just who will we be without our work identity? How will we function without the mind-bending, adrenaline-pumping energy work demands of us? What else will confer the same amounts of perks and connections we enjoy through our work? Where will our self-confidence shine as we prove once more that we are capable and productive? And what about the money! Can we manage without a regular paycheck? Not only that, God knows where we'll go at nine o'clock on a weekday morning, having to do without the structure, and all the contacts and friendships, we've so carefully cultivated. What's ahead for us?

Such concerns about looming retirement don't always jibe with what the already retired say—which is that they've never been happier, nor had a greater sense of freedom to be themselves. But we are skeptical and wonder how that can be. When Christine Millen, at fifty-seven, was planning early retirement from her career as a business consultant to global corporations, she remembers asking everyone she knew how they spent their days as retirees. She wanted detailed explanations: "So after you wake up and shower, you begin reading the newspaper. Okay, how long does that take? And then what do you do? And after you've been to the gym for your workout, what do you do next?" No amount of explicit information about how others spent their time assuaged her concern over whether she could replace the dynamic, high-energy, intellectually challenging career she loved.

> *When I stopped working, I felt emotionally at risk. Having given up a controlled environment for one that I had to create was terrifying. I was the only one who was going to put it together. It was totally on me and took all of my energy.*
>
> **—Allison**

Like most of us, Christine expects to have twenty or thirty or more good years ahead. And for that gift of time we are truly grateful. But receiving a gift usually means that we must give in return. In this case our giving back is using the wisdom we earned in the first half of our adult lives to make the second half into something special. Fortified by statistics that show we are likely to have many more years of continuing good health if we stay fit and eat right, we reject the idea of our late adulthood as a time of necessary decline and loss. Nor does the concept of incessant leisure thrill us. We have every intention of remaining vibrant, dynamic individuals for a long time to come. This is new ground we're trekking across, and we go with some trepidation because we cannot know until we've passed through this transition that anticipation is probably the worst part of the trip.

> *To be somebody, you must last.*
>
> —**Ruth Gordon**, actor

Since our mothers did not expect such bonus years when they were in their fifties and sixties, they never experienced anticipation angst. After all, they believed that they would not live much past seventy-five and knew from observation that anyone living into her eighties was worthy of kudos. Without the expectation of a long life, the question "What do I want to be when I turn ninety?" didn't occur to them. More likely they just slid into the existing model of years devoted to family and bridge. Would they have considered the future differently if they had thought they would be active and alert at ninety-three?

It dawns on us that we may be only halfway through our adult lives, with the bonus of extra years sandwiched between middle age and old age, effectively elongating the vital period we traditionally think of as the middle years. That realization has momentous consequences for us, and for society too.

Why Change?

Do we suddenly become a different person because we're fifty, fifty-five, or sixty-five? This question is posed by newspaper, magazine, radio, and television features about sassy seniors, ways to prevent aging, and the importance of planning for the future, especially financially. "Are we ready for retirement?" is a regular refrain, as if it were the inevitable consequence of our passing the fifty-year mark. Drug companies, financial institutions, and others produce self-interested spin reinforcing the message that pills and patches will keep us vigorous and professional money managers will ensure a secure fiscal future. Life in retirement, these commercial interests tell us, will be a blast, filled with gardening, traveling, hiking, and enjoying our partners and grandchildren.

Nothing is particularly wrong with this picture except that it is blatantly simplistic. If we absorb this image without self-analysis, then we buy into a cinematic dream sure to leave us feeling confused and paralyzed about what to do next. It needn't be that way. Sure, this is an excellent time for us to begin to reassess what we want our lives to be like moving forward. But first we need to ask ourselves, what does it mean to retire, and is retirement inevitably the best answer?

Because of our overwhelming numbers, wherever we boomers go, and whatever we do, we leave a big footprint. Regularly we hear about the repercussions of our retirement for business and society. With all this attention it's hard to avoid reassessing who we are and what we will do. Pressure to change comes from friends, spouses, family, colleagues at work, and human-resources departments.

Whether we are considering making a change or not, external noise adds to that nagging inner voice commanding us to plan now for our future. After all, we know about planning: growing up we dreamed about the ideal mate, having children (including what we would name them), the perfect home, and the type of car we wanted to drive. In college we discovered anthropology or engineering. After college we espied career directions and plotted paths to lead ourselves there. Even now, some of us have a clear idea of who we would like to be, what we would like to do, and where we would like to be doing it, and gleefully anticipate a future free from work that has grown tiresome.

Linda eagerly looked forward to her release from the structure, tedium, and politics of her job as an editor for a nonprofit organization. For her, the freedom from long commutes, endless meetings, and training yet another new assistant was not just welcomed, it was longed for. She knew exactly how she wanted to spend her time and talents and couldn't wait to get to it.

A lot of us aren't like Linda. We like working full-time. It's stimulating, and we want to continue for a long, long time, thank you very much! The only thing is, we also know few things are permanent or totally within our control. Perhaps we will be offered a windfall in the form of a golden handshake or a hefty inheritance, or we will be undermined by workplace ageism, economic downturns, unexpected health issues, or a change of heart. We know anything is possible.

So how do we plan for financial security and emotional happiness when we are clueless about what our future will look like? What will we do if we are no longer able to live as we do now? What if we no longer have a choice? How do we prepare for such a day, just in case?

Contemplating the Future

Whether we have a clear or murky vision, it is normal to fear initiating a seismic life change. Dorrie, fifty-nine, loves her job as the director of recruitment and career development at a major university. Her problem is that she loves her work too much. So she worries that if her job were eliminated for any reason, it would destroy her, because she knows from earlier experience that finding a new job is not easy. "I cannot imagine what I would do if I were not working. The whole concept is so foreign to me that I can't grasp it. All I care about is my work, it's my passion. I want to go to an office where there are other people. I need someplace I'm expected to be. If I didn't have that, why would I get up in the morning and get dressed?" For her, working is about not staying home. She enjoys weekends with her happily retired husband, takes yoga classes, enjoys reading and attending lectures, and would like to study another language. Perhaps her memory of her Depression-era stay-at-home mother, who hoarded everything she bought, contributes to Dorrie's concerns. "Part of my fear of staying home is that I'll fall into the same patterns as my mother."

Who Am I? and Other Existential Questions

Work gets us out of the house at a certain hour each weekday. Work also dictates how we structure our time, how we manage personal and household chores, what we do with family and friends and when, and why we decide to do certain things and put off others. Work is our identity, our label. It is how we reveal ourselves when we meet others for the first time; it is our defining elevator speech. Telling someone that we teach high school or college math, or direct a project for the government, is shorthand for what we can do, who we know, and how we fit into the general scheme of adulthood. What will we do when we no longer have such a label to fall back upon? And, even more frightening, how will we think about ourselves?

Jenny feels such an identity loss. She joined the Silicon Valley dotcom boom during a mid-1990s hiring frenzy, when there was an incredible opportunity to make a lot of money and learn an enormous amount.

But it was an extremely stressful environment defined by long hours of fast-paced work amid fierce competition. Then the roller coaster of up-turns and downturns began. Let go during one downtime, she was hired as a contractor by another dot-com, but more instability in the Silicon Valley economy ate into similar opportunities to work.

> When someone says, "I'm retired," it's tempting to say, "From what?" Basically, that's saying, "I want to know what you did before to see whether I find you interesting."
>
> —Hannah

Emotion wells up as she talks about her current situation. "I gave them my life for ten years. It was my home. My company even built its offices far away from civilization so we would eat there and use their gym. We came in at six in the morning and didn't leave the building until ten at night. All the companies did that; one had people sleeping in their offices." She says she is fine with what happened because she feels a oneness with the industry, in that enjoying success and then surviv-ing various downturns were what it was about. Only, the last time she was let go, "I knew in my gut that this was a battle. I kept trying to go back, because that was where I knew how to make it." It surprised her that interviewers considered her too old and technologically outmoded, although she had worked hard to learn new skills. Now fifty-five, she refuses to allow herself to be "beaten up by the high-techs anymore." Instead she is looking at new directions so that she can prove to herself and the rest of the world that she is indeed a survivor.

We need to feel comfortable about ourselves, and if our careers de-fine us, then thinking about "something else" to replace that identity and focus is unnerving. Catherine loves teaching emotionally disturbed students for a small city school district. "I have to be on every day. It's a great profession, very action packed. I get time off to refresh and think and prepare for the next year; I love fall, I love going back." She is also an adjunct professor at a local college, where she teaches classroom manage-ment and behavior. Catherine's plan is to retire in five years, when she is sixty, and she admits to feeling a "little nervous" about the idea. Self-described as "not an artsy-craftsy person," she is worried about what she will do. During the previous summer she took an education course, but that still left her with too much free time. "I don't know what will turn me on besides my regular job. I'm having trouble finding a passion that's my own and won't necessarily involve my husband."

On top of feeling pressure to find our passion, we believe that everybody else who retires is going on to bigger, better, more inspirational things than we are, like being on the board of a foundation to create world peace. That's one pretty tough standard to aspire to as we try to identify a postretirement life, and too easily sets us up for failure if our goals are anything less than saving the world.

In addition to struggling for inspiration and a new identity as we contemplate our transition-to-retirement navel, we fear becoming isolated. Work means other people—a community where we share small talk and find companionship. Even if our coworkers, patients, clients, or customers are not close friends, they engage and stimulate us, and we reciprocate. Complicated or easy, these relationships are a key part of what we think about and participate in at work. Mostly it's banter and gossip. But that is the very stuff that lets us know we have others' support, can count on their feedback, and have the emotional IQ to survive. If we retire from this work community, we worry about losing these connections. That's because we know they will not be easy to replace.

And have you heard the one about dying shortly after retiring? This is a myth, of course, based on early 1950s "wisdom" that is totally unsupported by data. Less cataclysmic but equally potent is the idea that we will lose physical strength and mental alertness when we retire. Well, there may be some truth in that concern, especially if we become couch potatoes or computer addicts without exercise to keep us strong and friends to arrest isolation and depression. This is the "use it or lose it" refrain, big-time.

What Is Retirement, Anyway?

With a great deal of passion and a healthy dose of common sense, most of us hate the word "retirement." Just look at the origin of the word to understand why. It is derived from the French *retirer*, which means "to go into seclusion." Any dictionary definition will mention removal or withdrawal into a private or secluded place, implying that retirement is a time for us to find a spot in which to curl up and die. "Retirement" is also defined as that portion of our lives when we are too old to work and too young to die. Without consciously thinking about it, we hear and see "tired" in the word. Absolutely nothing about the word instills optimism or enthusiasm. In discussions on the meaning of retirement, people usually cite negatives: "without paid employment," "losing my job," and "not being able to do the things I love." One woman said quite emphatically that she refused to use the word because it implies her life is finished. Similar distaste for it has prompted others to find new, more optimistic alternatives. We are advised not to retire but to "reinvent" or "regenerate" ourselves. Since terms such as "retirees," "senior citizens," and "elderly" also offend us by reinforcing the concept of decline and frailty, we are now called "third-agers" in our "second adulthood" or "third act," who engage in "maturity planning," "independence planning," and "downshifting."

Currently, "retirement" is used in several ways. It describes the event of leaving a job, profession, or business with the intention of no longer working. It also refers to the state of retirement, when we enter a sustained period of inactivity or leisure. And it refers to an age, usually over sixty-five, when we are eligible for retirement benefits. When economists speak of retirement, they mean withdrawal from the labor force, but we are more likely to think of retirement as separation from a long-standing career job, even if we are still in the labor force. So basically none of these definitions begins to address new ways of thinking about how we will spend the latter part of our lives. If we must work with the language we have, then let's just give it a new meaning and let previous definitions become obsolete.

> *Retirement is the notion of reshaping our role in the world, whether our activity is for money or not.*
>
> **—Ginny**

Retirement 2.0 is as flexible and creative as our imaginations can make it. It may mean the day we take our pension and leave work and then take a similar, encore job, or the day we head in an entirely new direction. And it turns out that employment in retirement is more common than it is exceptional, with more than three-quarters of older adults choosing to work past traditional retirement age. Vera is an example of this. She became a full-time independent contractor after retiring with a pension from a job with the government. "On Friday, they gave me a cake. On Monday, they gave me a new office." Despite the fact that she continues to work more than thirty-five hours a week, she thinks of herself as retired because she is taking her pension and because she no longer has the same authority and is no longer subject to the rigid regulations of a hierarchical office structure. "Retiring to me is giving up my career, even though I go back to work that is familiar. But being a consultant is different because it gives me incredible flexibility to work as much or as little as I want and call my own shots."

Retirement (the new edition) is having freedom to be ourselves. We can go for existing passions. We can discover new interests. We can re-invent ourselves. It is often a period when we think about starting a new business or launching a new initiative.

> *Now that I finally have some time, a few dollars, freedom from child-bearing, and a feeling that I don't have to prove myself or hope someone likes me, I'm gearing up for my next step.*
>
> **—Moira, fifty-nine**

Retirement is a fluid state, not a rigid target. It may be all things at the same time or something we do in successive chunks. As retirees we may have an encore job or career, *and* go back to school, *and* contribute time and skills to a nonprofit or governmental organization, *and* go to art exhibitions, *and* lunch with friends, *and* care for a frail parent. It is a shifting state through which we may pass in and out. It can be a period when we actively pursue a singular passion or combine a variety of interests and commitments. As retirees we can take a break from work and then become a returning retiree. We may donate our services as a volunteer and possibly receive a small stipend for our time and skills. Or we can take a seasonal job and retire again as the weather turns beautiful. Retirement is a changeable state that integrates education, work, and leisure, defined in terms that suit us. Let's just get past our aversion to the word and use it to mean what we want it to mean.

The new retirement is also an opportunity for us to break new ground in our social lives and in society overall. We have time freed up to retrieve old friendships and develop new ones that fulfill the person we are now. With our partners we look to rekindle the best in our relationships so that they will blossom into something special based on independence, mutual respect, and love. And within our culture we want to show that we are valuable contributors deserving of respect and opportunities to do more.

Why Are We Different from Our Mothers and Grandmothers?

Our grandmothers were not especially concerned about retirement. If Grandma worked at all, she "retired" early into the unpaid labor known as marriage. And if her husband died, she retired into widowhood, remaining home as long as she had enough income to avoid unskilled, low-paying work. Her retirement was closely connected to and dependent upon her husband, her brothers, or her sons.

> *I never had choices. It never occurred to my generation to think that we had choices.*
>
> **—an eighty-year-old woman**

Our mothers too had a perfect life road map, even if circumstances prevented them from reaching nirvana. Having a job might be in the picture, although they mostly waited until after their children were in school to get started. With few exceptions their pattern was to go to school, maybe to college, marry before twenty-five, and have babies soon after. Their primary career was to manage the household, children, and spouse. If they had a job, it was rarely thought to be of much consequence and often featured summer and holiday breaks, to coincide with children's vacations. When their husbands retired, they quit work to manage the household, even if they were not yet of retirement age. Affluent couples flew off to warm retirement communities to share leisure interests and activities. But living an adventurous, self-directed life was not a part of their visions.

> *My mother moved to Florida with my father immediately after her retirement. She went into the world of crafts, canasta, and early-bird specials. I guess, for her, this was "heaven," but it wouldn't be for me.*
> —Sylvia

How we look, feel, and think as we approach late adulthood is much different from how our mothers did. We say we are not as old as our mothers were at the age we are now. We may be in our fifties and sixties, but we feel as if we're in our forties. If we are fortunate enough to be in good health, we see the world through a lens of opportunity with few limitations. When our mothers were fifty, we thought of them as old, which is probably what they thought too. They dressed in styles deemed appropriate for "women of their age," and their conversations were laced with comments about limitations: "What does she think she's doing, wearing shorts at her age?" and "I can't travel by myself." The idea of taking on new challenges and seeking adventures was simply not in their mental lexicon.

WHY WE ARE BETTER OFF

Here are just a few of the reasons why we look, feel, and are healthier at this stage than previous generations were:

- Our mothers had better nutrition during their pregnancies.
- Public health improved, making our world a bit safer from disease and injury.
- Immunizations controlled or eliminated many childhood infectious diseases.
- Better education has been linked to better health and longevity.

- We smoke less and control other unhealthy behaviors.
- There is more medical attention to treating and controlling diseases such as hypertension and heart disease.
- We have new and better surgical procedures and interventions.
- We have newly developed drugs.
- We undergo regular tests to screen for diseases such as colon, uterine, and breast cancers.
- We have increased our commitment to wellness through exercise and good nutrition.
- We have improved standards for safety at work and at play.

The chasm between how we and our mothers perceive life is due first and foremost to the women's movement, which blossomed and gained force in the latter part of the 1960s. It was the catalyst for a monumental revision of women's place in the world. It caused us to reexamine normative ideas about women's roles and to rethink expectations. It spurred us to question previous assumptions, and it informed our vision of who we could be and what the world might look like. During this tumultuous time we developed an inclination to challenge everything and hone our instincts for reinventing outmoded rules of society. Such were the characteristics instilled deep within us.

Because of the women's movement, many of us embraced work as our salvation from shackles that would bind us to the home. Better educated than our mothers, we were accomplished, intellectually inquisitive, and capable of imagining the previously unimaginable. Our jobs were where we could search for achievements and accomplishments. They were where we could earn money, power, and independence. We looked to our careers to define ourselves, and to prove ourselves to ourselves and to the world at large.

Different Sizes, Different Styles

No two of us will handle how we approach and deal with our next phase of life in exactly the same way. Each of us will draw on inner resources to deal with external situations beyond our control. How we cope with change can often be anticipated by the way we approached and completed earlier transitions in our lives. Perhaps we glided effortlessly from adolescence into adulthood or became a mother without feeling overly stressed by our lack of knowledge and the enormity of new responsibilities. Perhaps some of us approached our thirtieth and fortieth birthdays with trepidation, while others ignored or embraced those milestones.

We are likely to repeat those past patterns when we deal with life changes in the future. The unexpected loss of a job, sudden health problems, a romance, and the offer of a buyout too good to be ignored are just a few of the things that can hit us when we think things will remain the same. How each of us reacts to them will be unique. Therefore, though we use "we" and "us" throughout the book, we recognize that "we" does not necessarily mean all of us at any one time or in every situation, although it often implies that a good many of us are thinking or feeling about something in similar ways.

> *Retirement is all about choices. People should be able to choose to do whatever it is that floats their boat.*
>
> —Irene

Who Are the Experts?

We are raising important questions that women everywhere are asking. We talk about our fears and concerns. We discuss valuable insights, share personal experiences, and explore possibilities. We think about what it means to be in the transition process. If we examine our lives up to this point, we see that we fought hard to prevent life from just happening to us by taking control whenever we could. Whether we set up a five-year plan on a spreadsheet illustrated with PowerPoint slides, or found a mentor at work, or took classes to open certain doors, we attempted to plan for the future. Even though at times we did not plan carefully or refused to make certain decisions, we have not led serendipitous lives up to now.

So why are so many of us feeling befuddled about what to make of the many years we have ahead?

This kind of transition is new to us as well as to the experts. Since we are without guidelines or role models to conjure up from the past, it can leave us feeling isolated and adrift. The process of tackling this distinct transitional stage puts us in new territory. We know we need to prepare but are uncertain about how to do it or whether it is even possible. As we examine others going through transitions, we see that a variety of role models are out there just doing it. Sure, we can seek practical advice from emerging experts, but the truth is that we must give equal weight to our own thoughtful insights that emerge as we talk to other women and as we observe women who are a few steps ahead of us in the transition process.

INFLUENCES THAT HAVE SHAPED OUR THINKING

We view retirement differently than previous generations of women did because:

- We are better educated.
- We know that we have many productive years ahead and feel a responsibility to use them well.
- We have been deeply affected by the women's movement.
- We have been pioneers who are used to questioning and challenging the status quo, and that mentality is now an integral part of who we are.
- We are used to confronting obstacles and finding ways to circumvent them or break them down.
- We have learned that we can compete and function on a wide variety of playing fields (even when they are not always level).
- We are the largest segment of the population in most countries in the developed world and are used to having an impact because of our numbers.
- We have confidence in our value and capabilities as women.
- We have learned management skills, including how to juggle and multitask our way through life.

- We feel equal to the challenges ahead, or at least to tackling them without dependence on paternalistic rules or guidance.
- We have the benefit of research into life stages and a body of knowledge about what it means to be "in transition."
- We have learned how to reach out to others and form groups outside of familial settings.

Within the following chapters you will find women's voices and their stories. Many of their insights were heard at peer-group meetings, where ten to fifteen women gather to discuss issues around transition. Most came out of the nearly two hundred one-on-one interviews conducted solely for this book. Where such voices or stories are attributed by first name only, their owners' real names and identities have been disguised. Where full names appear within the text, they identify experts we talked to or women who gave us permission to identify them and their accomplishments. In total these women's experiences help us better understand the full spectrum of the transition process, starting with those things that cause us to imagine new possibilities and how we can prepare emotionally and practically for our next stage. From there we take a look at how we make our choices, including how and why the emotional side of money affects our decisions, what our careers truly mean to us, and how we can find alternative satisfactions. We also explore different ways we can discover and add new meaning in our lives, how the nature and pleasures of old friends change, and why new communities are so important. And finally we look at how to keep our spouses from driving us crazy and what it means to be an over-fifty woman in society.

Why Are We Talking Only About Women?

It is useful to remember that collectively we experienced work life differently than men did. When we first entered the male-dominated workplace, we had to adapt to rigid rules for accomplishing tasks and equally rigid criteria for judging success and achievement. Those of us who began to work in the 1960s and 1970s had to accept and adapt to this work culture by stifling a part of our feminine side. As more women were successful in business, we opened up a slight chink in organizations' cultural armor and enlightened our workplaces about new approaches to creativity and team-based problem solving.

> *Yes, I will share my story—because each generation [of women] breaks new ground and we have a responsibility to help the next group coming into this experience.*
>
> —Joyce

At home, we experienced family life differently than our husbands or partners did, and certainly than our mothers did. We made strides toward reorganizing how home responsibilities are discharged, yet we were buffeted by a need to do it all, as we accepted a major part of home, family, and child-rearing obligations along with our work. These common experiences—dealing with an unsympathetic workplace and trying to be ideal mothers, wives, and homemakers—underscore the history we share as we speak and listen to other women.

And then there was a revolution. As we grew up we questioned the homemaker ideal and rejected "the way it has always been," because it just didn't answer our nagging thoughts about what is fair and unfair. All of us were affected to varying degrees by the women's movement. It inspired our vision of what the world could be. It motivated us to question and challenge the status quo, and we continue to carry those values with us to this day. Thus, this book focuses on—and emphasizes—how we as women are successfully plotting a course that leads from our career-developing, child-rearing, and home-building stage to a uniquely exciting next level.

In addition, women live longer than men, although the good news is that men's life expectancy is increasing significantly. What that means is that women and men must confront issues around retirement and aging. But women approach transitions differently than men do. For instance, we solve our problems best when we talk to each other, which we've been doing all our lives, and which men as a group tend not to do. It is through our mutual experiences and insights that we learn about ourselves. This practice of sharing, talking, and listening, known as "tend and befriend," comes easily to us, especially in times of stress. We are biologically driven during times of crisis and uncertainty to reach out to a close friend or other women who are experiencing similar feelings. Whether such connections take the form of peer groups, investment clubs, sewing circles, coffee klatches, or book clubs, we use groups to help ourselves tackle our most important concerns and gather support. This book draws heavily on the wisdom and experience of groups of women in various stages of transition who can tell us about what lies ahead and provide a preview of what we can expect. Their insights are invaluable as we attempt to redefine how our lives will differ from those of preceding generations of women.

Where This Leads

Many of us look forward to having adventures, experimenting with new ideas, trying out new careers, and learning new things. Most of us do not plan to retire early, and increasingly we say we do not intend to retire before seventy, if then. In some capacity we intend to work. Earning money and health-care benefits are incentives, but mostly we want to work to stay sharp, involved, and stimulated. In other words, to remain physically, intellectually, and emotionally at the top of our game.

We also see the retirement years as an opportunity to do something we've always wanted to do but were previously held back from doing by family responsibilities and fiscal obligations. What joy to think that now is the time to have a new career or a new business or earn an advanced degree. Or is it? Fear enters into this arena too. What if we no longer have the drive, smarts, energy, or connections to pull it off? What if the time isn't right, the cost too high, the risk too great? What if we can't summon up particular dreams? And if we find that our dreams aren't all that we expected, can we return to our former careers? If we take a step forward, can we go back?

> *When I was young I was a smart ass. Now I'm wise.*
> —**voice from a peer group**

Like trying to viscerally comprehend one-hundred-degree weather when the ambient temperature is twenty below, it's difficult for us to think about our future without making comparisons to the present. Now, for example, we get up at a certain time each weekday and know our day will have a specific structure to it. But how we think about our day when we no longer have that structure is difficult to anticipate.

And what if the decision to retire or continue working isn't totally within our control? What if we face workplace ageism, being downsized to cut company costs, or being overlooked for promotions or training opportunities? Voluntary retirees are usually happy with their decisions, but many of us who lose our jobs can be devastated financially and emotionally. These are legitimate concerns that will be explored in further chapters.

CHAPTER 2

Why Am I Suddenly Thinking About Something New?

Everyone remembers her fiftieth birthday. Maybe it's because a friend gave us a surprise party. Maybe it's because it was the first day we really felt over the hill. Suddenly the world seemed like a different place, or we felt like different people in it. Though for some of us, our leap into the second half of our lives may have taken place at another moment in time, or it may have been triggered by another occasion, something undoubtedly made us start thinking about how our lives would not always be the same.

Actor Goldie Hawn, in an interview in *AARP* magazine, said that sixty felt like a bigger milestone than fifty. It didn't change how she looked at the world, but it did affect how the world looked at her. "The sixtieth was the birthday where everyone goes, 'Wow, you still look good.'"

> *I am surprised to find myself thinking about retirement, when I hadn't before. I feel an urgency to enjoy myself more and act up. I want the freedom I experienced when I was in my twenties and I want it now, not at some future time.*
>
> —Lynn

Forced to Change

In the previous chapter we looked at the things that bombard us or gently nudge us into thinking about some kind of change in our lives. And, although the pressure to think about change often seems triggered by external events, the impetus invariably comes from within. It is why external noise and events resonate so emphatically for us now. It is why we are compelled to reevaluate who we are, why we're here, what we do, and what we can do. It is the reason we wake up and pay attention to certain personal events that had not affected us before.

At various times throughout our lives, we have paused to reassess our goals, our dreams, and our relationships. This was especially true in our teens and early twenties, when we wrestled with the question of who we wanted to be and how we might go about being that person. Our most recent spate of self-analysis probably occurred during our forties, a time when the terms "midlife" and "crisis" were often heard in unison—and a time when we began to move toward something new, which meant we had to leave some things behind. Sometimes the changes we made were relatively minor fixes, course corrections: we took on challenging tasks that led to promotions and recognition, or we looked for a new job; some of us took momentous steps by getting divorced, or married, or having a child.

> *Nothing in life is to be feared. It is only to be understood.*
> —**Marie Curie**

In our forties handling work and family also became a balancing act we struggled to perfect. It was when we either accepted who we were—if single, then single we would be; if childless, then so be it—or else aggressively campaigned to find a mate or take fertility drugs, with varying degrees of success. For Bobbi, forty-eight, it was the realization that she was spending the best years of her life working in the health-care field without getting any real personal satisfaction that spurred her to action. Putting in ten to thirteen hours a day, sometimes six days a week, in a laboratory, with an hour-long commute that started at three thirty in the morning, allowed her little time for living outside the lab. So she took a hard, realistic look at her life and went back to school for a degree in professional leadership in order to find work that would allow her to enjoy life more.

What Is a Transition?

Throughout our lives we go through specific developmental stages as we pass from infant to child, child to adolescent, adolescent to young adult, young adult to midlife adult, midlife adult to late-life adult, and on to late, late-life adult. These stages are part and parcel of the developmental process first identified in the mid twentieth century. They are understood to be eras of approximately twenty years (for the adult stages) that are comprised of stable periods, when we feel on top of our game and confident about who we are, and transitional periods, when we do what it takes to move out of our current life stage and on to the next one. This is why somewhere around our fiftieth milepost we find ourselves poised to begin a transition during which we will take leave of our midlife adulthood—and the many things that have motivated us and we have valued—and move on to our next stage, late adulthood.

> *I'm no longer as concerned about what people think. There were times in my earlier work career when it was important for me to have people think I knew it all, was ahead of the game, was right for the position and knew what I was doing.*
>
> **—Lois**

Each one of us will have to deal with our transition from midlife to late adulthood in our own way. Some of us will breeze through it with minimal angst. Some of us will feel whipped about by feelings that puzzle us. Some of us will get there early and others will arrive much later. Whenever it occurs, we will be on firmer terrain if we understand the process and how to prepare ourselves for it.

It is interesting that dramatic phrases such as "turning point," "course shift," "cutting loose," "sifting out," "separating," and "resolving contradictions" define transitions from one life stage to another. They reflect the truth that these times are not easy. Part of the process of being in transition is leaving behind certain dreams, beliefs, and concerns we considered important so that we can allow ourselves space for new or modified dreams, beliefs, and concerns to emerge, or to reclaim previously lost or abandoned parts of ourselves. There is a common metaphor to explain what it feels like: Think about transition as having to jump into a river and swim to the other bank—except that it's a foggy day, so we can't see how far off the other bank is, we have no idea how long it will take us to get there, nor can we know what to expect once we arrive. That is us. On the bank, in the fog.

Jumping into the water means that we leave the familiar for terra incognita, and the process is simultaneously anxiety producing and exciting. Some of us deal with the anxiety just fine, and some of us can be overwhelmed by it. Certainly, anxiety is an uncomfortable state to be in, and it's tempting to try to rid ourselves of it. We asked psychoanalyst and management consultant Laurence J. Gould how we might best manage such anxiety and remain open to possibilities as they unfold during our transition period. He is not a fan of the chirpy, cheerleader-like coaching and self-help books that push us to find immediate answers. "We live in a pragmatic, positive, *What Color Is Your Parachute*–tomorrow society and want quick fixes for our anxiety through medication, self-help gurus, and other get-over-it schemes. But that is psychologically naive and can even be quite destructive," he says. "That's because we need to *use* uncomfortable states as opportunities to learn and develop and grow. We need to ask the questions 'Who am I?' 'What am I?' and 'What do I want to be?' rather than use drugs or other means to deflect the discomfort or block altogether reflections about our experiences." It is when we forestall our discomforts, he suggests, that we are in denial about what needs to be done.

I had to face the difficulty, the hope, and the dread of going through this transition so I could move on to some other version of who I am— like pulling various parts of myself together and reshaping them.
—**Donna**

It is interesting to wonder whether the inclination of so many of us to plan and develop strategies to deal with this transition has been influenced by our grounding in business and corporate cultures, which emphasize strategic planning, goal setting, and action. Gould believes that trying to develop extensive planning intended to lead us through our current transition doesn't fit the facts. "It's simply not possible to look at our lives three years out and develop a picture. Whatever we get will be an imaginary image," he says. "It's like determining the end before you go through the process. It's totally backward." However, he acknowledges that planning does work for some of us who have some guiding experience that's already there and ready to flower. But most of us in transition are uncertain about where we are headed and need time and space to reflect and grow.

As in most voyages of discovery, the end points are never quite as we imagined them, and they are rarely the ones we originally charted.
—**Herminia Ibarra,** *Working Identity*

This is why being part of a community of others who are sympathetic to our transition anxieties and insecurities is so important to us. An example of how such a community can help occurred in a TTN peer group whose members had been meeting for six months and were comfortable discussing their transition concerns with each other. At the meeting one woman in the group brought a bouquet of colorful helium balloons and, in answer to puzzled looks from the others, told them the balloons were for helping to "let go of old garbage—the kind of emotional obstacles that hold us back and prevent new growth." She encouraged each woman to think about something she wanted to ditch from her life, and then write that particular demon on a piece of paper. A few of the women identified feelings such as anger or self-doubt; others thought about being rigid or dependent; a few focused on relationships. Then each woman attached her slip of paper to a balloon string and, with what was later described as childlike excitement and gales of laughter, went outdoors with the others to release each demon balloon into the night sky. It was an evening they say they will never forget.

HOW TO MANAGE YOUR TRANSITION

Although transitioning from one stage to another is inevitable, understanding the process can help make it easier to get through.

- Stay flexible and open to feelings that unfold. When you shut them down by denying their existence, you short-circuit the transition process.
- Give yourself time. Accept that your transition is not going to happen overnight. Most people need more than two or three years to complete the process.
- Stay open to opportunities. This is a wonderful time to consider doing something just because it sounds interesting, especially if you've never done it before.
- Accept that there will be anxiety and discomfort. Listen to it and use it to learn and grow rather than try to stifle it.
- Come to grips with unrealized career fantasies. Expect to feel some anxiety that goes along with mourning the loss of what you are leaving behind, including things you had hoped to accomplish and didn't.
- Let go of the past and accept that there are things you can't do, things that are lost to you forever or are no longer available to you. Regrets can be a stumbling block to moving forward. Idealizing the past and insisting that it can be recovered is often a way to avoid recognizing loss.
- Realize that a mild to moderate depression is normative for people in transition. Only a very small proportion of people go into clinical depression. Most do not.
- Be aware that a "can do" attitude and approach can be a defense against the anxiety and discomfort of transition. Be suspicious of advice that derails learning and growth.
- Expect to feel some social and psychological disconnection from your present life. This is often necessary before you can explore other options.
- Reach out to new people for fresh perspectives, insights, and

support. Talk honestly with others going through your particular transition.

- Don't become overly concerned about how you will identify yourself when you no longer have a job title. Instead, come up with a short, lively description that doesn't pin you down. One woman laughingly introduces herself as a "hedonist," which usually instigates a lively conversation.

- Expect good strategies to develop just from staying in touch with what is happening to you.

- Know that, like all of us, you enter this transitional period as a novice.

There was no way that the original thinkers on the topic of life stages, notably Erik Erikson and Daniel Levinson, could have anticipated the radical degree to which medical advances and healthier lifestyle would increase our life expectancy and our capacity to experience a rich life that stretches on for many, many years, effectively elongating our midlife stage and possibly that transitional stage as well. Gail Sheehy, who popularized ideas about the stages of our lives in numerous bestselling books, most recently in *Sex and the Seasoned Woman*, attempts to take into account our newly elongated midlife stage by considering how we change in terms of decades. The fifties, she says, are when we begin to search for meaning and pass from the idea of pleasing others to asserting our own mastery. Our sixties are a wonderful time when we enjoy maximum choice and freedom, even though we begin to deal with physical limitations, and it is also when we begin to emphasize our values and sense of purpose as we learn to "enjoy being loved for who we become." She sees our seventies as a time of growth and development when at last we are our own masters, which also makes us capable mediators and mentors for others. But she warns that if we don't commit ourselves to growth, it is also a time when we can easily drift into passivity or despair—something we must be careful to avoid. Our eighties and nineties, Sheehy writes, are danger periods when we must resist being overwhelmed by negativity that can come from family, friends, doctors, and the culture. To avoid it we must look inside ourselves for courage and stoicism about our physical limitations and stay focused on enjoying life's benefits.

The New Transitions

Part of the problem is that we have little information to guide us through our current transition. Just fifty years ago, women progressed from school, work, marriage, and having children in their twenties, to empty nests in their forties, and to the active pursuit of leisure activities such as bridge, golf, and charity work in their fifties and beyond. But such patterns have mutated for us. That course altered as we chose to work and marry and have children at more or less the same time, or as we actively chose not to have children at all. And we may have left school in our twenties, but education didn't end there. Continuous learning was a part of our lives as we attended job-training sessions or returned to school for advanced degrees. Building a career may have been a straight, winding, or in-and-out course. We married early or late—or both, or not at all. Many of us had our children in our thirties and forties. Sometimes we left our jobs for a short time, but usually we picked them up again, or started up a business that allowed us to combine our work and family. In addition, as we reach our fifties and even sixties, our role as nurturers extends for our late-born, adolescent or twenty-something children who remain at home. We have no choice but to reimagine traditional ideas about retirement to suit such a newly construed and elongated life. All we know is that the concept and the fact of it will look like nothing that has gone before.

Recent trends show that the rate of participation in the workforce is increasing among women over fifty-five. AARP studies, among many others, indicate that we boomers do not want to retire any time soon. Nearly 70 percent of us say we expect to work until sixty-five or longer. But one of the questions we need to consider is, can we take such expectations entirely at face value? Plans can change and many of us haven't yet reached the point where the triggers that lead us into our transitional stage have kicked in. Remember, for example, when some of us declared in our twenties that we did not want to have children. That was the plan, with few *ifs* or *buts* about it. Until, that is, the alarms on our biological clocks caused us to decide otherwise. Retirement might be similar.

Today we say we won't retire. Tomorrow a trigger that makes us aware of our approaching transitional stage might cause us to rethink our situation and act differently than expected.

"Aha" Moments

So, what triggers move us to realize we are about to enter or are already in a transitional period? As we approach our fiftieth and sixtieth birthdays, an "aha" moment can stir up feelings about how little—and how much—time we have left. That awareness that time is finite is a notice to reevaluate our lives. That was the case for Moira, who over the years had taken jobs as they ignited her interest. Previously she had worked as a teacher, an administrator, a social worker, and an actor. Now she manages construction projects for a large professional school. It's a responsible job, but she just turned fifty-nine and suddenly feels a sense that "it's time to get on with it." That sensibility shouts at her to take hold of her dreams now and not wait for sometime in the future. She has a sense of urgency she hadn't known before.

For many of us, going through menopause starts our self-assessment process. With hot flashes and multiple other symptoms, our bodies tell us we must be getting "old" because we can no longer birth a child. Although having a child at this point is not something most of us would find desirable, realizing that we cannot conceive is a rude exclamation point announcing that that particular vision of ourselves, as fruitful women, is no longer valid. It tells us we must mourn the loss and move on.

> *You just wake up one morning, and you got it!*
> —**Moms Mabley, on old age**

Partner Pressure

Even when we are not thinking about retirement, someone else can nudge us in that direction. Jennifer's husband, an artist who is able to work as he desires, is five years older than she. When his friend became ill, it stirred him to get going on things he had put off for the future—and these included a number of things he wanted to do with Jennifer. Which is to say, he wanted her to free up her time in order to travel and play with him. The notion terrified her. A mere fifty-seven, she was actively in a career-building stage of life and couldn't imagine herself without her work. Life was good; she felt in charge and independent. Why change things? So she did what anyone who has been married for a long time might do—she pretended not to hear what he said and hoped the subject would go away. But, of course, the idea was just waiting to pounce on her at inappropriate times, like the middle of the night.

According to psychotherapist Mary Beth Kelly, it is rare that both partners are at the same place at the same time. The impetus for growth is usually happening with one or the other of them. Usually it is one person saying, "I'm not happy," and the other person saying, "Shut up, I don't want to hear about it." But something has to give. Either one partner pretends nothing is wrong, or she or he takes the other's concerns as an invitation to growth. In Jennifer's case, her husband's remark initiated a five-year journey of self-discovery, during which she learned how to welcome change and become someone she had always wanted to be.

> *Get it while you can.*
> —Jerry Ragovoy and Mort Shuman, sung by Janis Joplin

Losing a Job

Getting fired or laid off around the age of fifty can send us reeling and boot us into a transitional period. Suddenly one of the major buttresses in our lives turns wobbly, and with it adolescent self-doubts return and uncertainty reigns. Though we may have felt good about ourselves a day before, the fact that we are no longer considered valuable in the workplace can seriously undermine our self-confidence. As we dive into the job-search waters and struggle with new styles of résumé writing and unfamiliar job-hunting techniques, we worry that we won't be able to find a new job because of our age or because the market for a comparable, well-paying job at our level is too competitive.

When Phyllis lost her job from a big bank at age fifty-two, it took her more than eighteen months to find another. Ultimately she went to work at a university for half the salary she earned previously. Seven years into her new job, she has respect, autonomy, and a bit more money, and she hopes to stay for another ten years. But she knows firsthand that anything is possible: "It wasn't as if I was caught off guard and didn't know I was vulnerable when I worked at the bank." While Phyllis gets praise now, she knows change happens. There is little employer loyalty. Usually a thoughtful and planful person, she realizes she has got to start thinking about alternative futures. Yet she can't seem to get around to it.

> *My job had become increasingly stressful, and, while I had toyed with the idea of leaving, I had not made any plans to do so. The ultimate trigger was a corporate decision to create a new managerial position on my team, which I felt meant I was being demoted.*
>
> —Sandi

Other Losses

One of the most painful triggers any of us can experience is the loss of a partner. Suddenly a future that had appeared stable and knowable is turned upside down. Frieda ran a program training middle managers in social-welfare departments about the meaning of welfare reform. When she was in her early sixties, her husband became ill and needed assistance. Her colleagues at work helped her complete the semester so that she could focus on her spouse's needs. Although it wasn't an especially happy time, it meant a lot to her to be there for him. After he died, she fell apart. First she got sick with bronchitis, and then she suffered an accidental injury. No longer married or working, she faced the need to reinvent her life.

Carol had a similar experience. Her decision to retire from her job at an international financial institution was initially triggered by her husband's death and then, within the next two years, by the deaths of her mother, father, and a good friend. "I was sitting there in my office writing a stupid report, and I thought, Life is bad, so why continue doing what I know? It's time to try something else."

The tragic events of September 11, 2001, made some of us realize that life is short and nothing should be taken for granted. When Moira lost her mother, it was a wake-up call in some respects, making her think about herself in terms of "Oh, this doesn't go on forever." When Carol's parents died she was startled to realize that at age fifty-five she was now part of the family's older generation. She had graduated into the role of "elder" that her mother had embodied for so long. A sobering thought!

> *You have to acknowledge that trauma does affect the next step. How could it not?*
>
> —Frieda

One of the most powerful triggers for making us take a new look at ourselves is a health problem of our own or the illness of someone close to us. A mammography exam with suspicious results might be just a blip on the screen, but the fact of breast cancer can forever affect the way we see our lives. Any illness that prevents us, even temporarily, from doing things we normally do has serious repercussions.

Edna, an active fifty-nine-year-old who has always been single, was temporarily unable to do simple things like climb stairs without pain after her surgery. It made her realize how important it was to be physically fit, "because everything else depends on it." Since regaining the level of energy she had before the surgery was her highest priority, she had to weigh her desire to work against the need to find free time for other activities. "It's this constant battle, not about how long I'm going to live, because when I'm dead, I'm dead, and who cares then what you do or what you miss. What's important to me now is how many good ones I have left. That's the only reason why I would leave work completely."

Expectations of Longevity

A premonition that we have a long or short time left will affect the way we see ourselves. A few of us can cite a history of centenarians in our families to support the belief that we'll get there too. Some of us don't expect to live much past the age at which our parent died young. Such beliefs are not particularly accurate predictors of what lies ahead, but they can have a profound influence on how we think about the future and plan for it.

Retired from a twenty-year career as a California-based environmental-law attorney for a nonprofit organization, Lorraine, sixty-four, wonders what her next thirty years will look like. She can tick off a long list of ancestors who lived into their nineties, and she anticipates doing the same. All the changes she has gone through up to this point—the jobs, the marriages, the children, the grandchildren—predict many more such changes ahead. "That's overwhelming and makes me realize I need to think purposefully about where I want to be in five years and not just day to day."

Alicia got to be the highest-ranking woman at three different big-city newspapers during her journalism career. Now sixty-five and a cancer survivor, she is acutely aware that longevity is not in her family history, "so I think about life in smaller segments." She worries from two sides of the issue: If she lives a long time, she might not have enough money to support herself. On the other hand, if she has only a few years left, should she spend her money on the bird-watching expeditions she covets now and not worry about meeting expenses at eighty-seven? Of course, she really can't know how long she has left, but she thinks about a short-life scenario as she makes decisions about what to do and when to do it.

> *Something happens to throw you. Something happens to disrupt that treadmill that you thought was moving you forward. It might be any number of things that happen, but the progress of your life is interrupted and then you've got to reassess.*
>
> —**Kay**

Good News

Not all triggers are about loss. Sometimes an amazing bonus comes along that can shift the way we think and launch us into a transitional period. There is always the chance that we will actually have a winning lottery ticket one day (assuming we buy one in the first place). Or receive an unexpected, or unexpectedly large, inheritance. Or the business we built up turns out to be a hugely successful IPO. Such wealth shocks invoke the ageless question, If I don't need the money, what do I want to do with the rest of my life?

Nor is all bounty about money. Fifty-two-year-old Sarah, an editor of a trade magazine, agreed to go on a blind date several years ago and now is in a wonderful relationship. "The ensuing transformation surprised me. I discovered the pleasure of having someone to care about and not just think about myself." She also joined a peer group to talk about topics around transitioning and says she "discovered how important it is to have the support and camaraderie of other women in my life."

Sixty-two-year-old Nancy also fell in love. A former senior partner of a midsized executive search firm, she was astonished to realize that a tiny, bald grandchild was having such an impact on her. "I have a whole new priority for what I want to do with a big segment of my life. Nonstop work no longer has the same appeal as it did before."

> *It's nice to know that other people have ambivalence.*
> —**voice from a peer group**

Updating Rituals and Retooling Time

Every culture has rituals for major life transitions such as puberty, marriage, and childbirth. We also have less formal celebrations for milestones in our lives. Sometimes at thirty, often at forty, and almost always at fifty and beyond, we celebrate birthdays that end in zero. And we tally up wedding anniversaries in quarter-century markers. These continue to be meaningful to us and may become even more so as we embrace the idea of growing older with dignity and purpose.

It seems that retirement rituals, once symbolized by the gold watch, are in desperate need of updating. The traditional retirement party to recognize our years of service with an employer or within an industry and presumably to launch us on a life of beach chairs and home improvement no longer makes sense. On one level, we want and appreciate the recognition. On another we enjoy the irony of retiring on a

Friday, only to return to an office on Monday as newly minted consultants. And on still another level, we feel uncomfortable celebrating an event that makes us so anxious, because we are uncertain about where it will lead.

> *I want to add more into my life rather than wind down.*
> **—voice from a peer group**

The ambiguity surrounding retirement rituals relates to the fact that time is a culturally manufactured construct divided into units that program what we do and how we do it. In the United States we have a five-day, forty-hour workweek, a two-day weekend, and a minimum of two weeks' vacation time. If we are fortunate, these time frames coincide with our natural rhythms and sleep patterns. Sometimes they don't.

Theresa, a retired Washington-based lawyer, spent much of her life adjusting to others' time rhythms. She is a night person who can't fall asleep until well after midnight. Because she had to be in the office early, she spent her entire work life getting by on something like six hours of sleep, five days a week, "because that's the way the world works." Now she gets eight, maybe nine, hours every single night.

Time is something we measure, name, and worry about. And how we think about it differs during each stage of our lives. Time can be slow or swift, free or scheduled, lost or productive, stressful and wasted or savored and enjoyed. It can be spent, saved, given away, counted, billed, justified, traded, telescoped, and extended. It can be used to meet deadlines, play, talk, shop, paint, read, eat, have sex, or watch television. For most of our adult lives, the way we spend time is determined by work, school, and family. Each weekday is structured by work routines that also have a powerful effect on how we use our "spare" time during evenings and weekends. They determine why we sit in commuter traffic or stand in line for morning coffee. They determine when we schedule dinner and get the laundry done.

During our working years we never seem to have enough time to accomplish everything we want to do. So we spend it carefully, ticking off items on our to-do lists. If we feel we've managed our time poorly or have been unproductive, we're uncomfortable. Wasted time can make us crazy, and free time can send us into a flurry of activity in order to fill it.

Between work and caring for a home and children, we generally have less than two hours each workday for personal leisure. Even when the children leave home, we can rarely claim more than three hours a day for ourselves while working full-time. As we transition out of full-time work, we suddenly come face-to-face with extensive leisure time. Theresa was curious to see how she felt about it once she stopped working. She intentionally spent the first few months allowing her day to evolve without scheduling anything. Some days she did absolutely nothing and got mad at herself for it. Eventually she created a "structure lite" that included going to the gym, taking dance classes, and meeting friends for lunch. It doesn't force her to get a lot done, at least not in the sense of her preretirement mode. Nonetheless, she celebrates the idea that it's her own schedule, and she can change it any time she wants.

Nora, single and fifty-seven, worries a great deal about how time will be different when she retires. She works twelve, fifteen, sometimes eighteen hours a day, five, six, seven days a week as an engineer for the army. She doesn't know what to do with free time. Time without commitments must be filled with any activity that will hold back "the wall of depression I expect to move in on me if I'm not achieving something or being productive." She is paralyzed by the idea of making decisions about her future. She also feels that by not doing anything, she is effectively wasting the time she has left.

Is It Productive?

Clara, sixty-four, used to work for a national media company in Washington and now sets up public-relations, special-events, and speaking engagements for select clients. Interested in a wide range of things, she feels there isn't enough time in the day for all she could do. She thinks of time as "the most valuable commodity imaginable, like a rare jewel to be treasured."

If free time is seen as precious, then how do we go about using it well? One technique Clara tried was to list all those things she would like to do and then consider each item in terms of what would be most important if she had only a year—or thirty more years—to live. It's not easy to do, after so many years of putting our priorities into a work context that dictates we do *x* amount of things in *y* amount of time. Too often we equate time with productivity and then evaluate whether we used it wisely. Put within that framework, how do we value going to swimming aerobics, playing with grandchildren, or taking a history course? For Amanda, who works in the defense industry, reading a book is an action item. Christine, who grilled her peer group about how they spend their time, now takes an hour and a half to read the newspapers but then feels guilty for having used most of her morning doing it. Maybe the questions to ask ourselves ought to be: Is it reasonable to weigh free time in terms of answering two hundred e-mails? Are we forestalling the transition process by trying to manage time too intensely?

Not only do things that we consider important, like time, change as we approach transitioning, they go on changing as we grow older. Clara, a sixty-year-old public-relations specialist, recalls how she invested most of her free time looking for and building relationships when she was younger. She remembers how "men took up an enormous amount of time," but at this point romantic-sexual relationships don't even come onto her radar. Ruth, who was divorced in her late fifties, feels differently. She invested nearly all of her time building a life for herself in a new state and the year she turned sixty made it her top priority to find a new companion. The next year and a half was spent dating men she met through an online dating service. It was the forty-first date that proved to be a winner.

Lost Time

If we truly get it right, we have the power to stop time. We've done it before, when we lost track of time at work as we met deadlines or solved problems. But that experience was usually stressful. There is a different, better, and healthier way to lose track of time. It's an incredible experience that occurs when our internal clocks shut down and time "stands still." We've felt it when we were fully engaged in doing something we really enjoyed or when we tackled something really challenging. Amanda remembers losing track of time as a child when she was dancing. Alicia loses it when she is reading a good novel. Others experience it when they play the piano or sew.

Changing our relationship with time is an important part of our transition process. It begins when we learn to be less judgmental about what we do and how long it takes to do it. It means being able to luxuriate in time without guilt or self-criticism. It means touching base with things that are important to us in the long term and cultivating them at leisure. Newly retired Christine announced to her peer group with some embarrassment that her postretirement schedule was so hectic, she had been driven to program "Do nothing this morning" into her calendar. No one said it was easy!

THINKING ABOUT TIME

Any self-analysis as you transition from midlife to the next stage must take into consideration your attitudes toward time. Consider the following:

- Why time is important and how it will affect your decision to make a transition.
- Whether you equate time with being productive, and how that influences your vision of the future.
- How you think about, measure, and value your time for play and leisure.
- How much time influences what you choose to do and not do.
- What structured time and free time mean to you.
- How externally structured time differs from your internal time structure and preferences.
- How you plan to deal with more personal time and less externally structured time.
- What you can do now to begin testing and understanding your relationship with time.

CHAPTER
3

Can I Afford to Make a Change?

Many of us handle our personal finances competently and manage our retirement portfolios effectively. We make sure that our investments are diversified, and we plan carefully for the years ahead when we will no longer earn income. We're in charge, and life seems good. If this is you, please feel free to skim this chapter and quickly move on to the next.

But the rest of us had better stay put. Because it's time we face up to a very serious matter that has everything to do with whether we will be able to retire sometime in the future and how we will fund our later years. Studies show that far too many of us think that our finances are in good shape because we have been saving but kid ourselves if we lack a long-term investment and spending plan that will take us well into our nineties. And then there are those of us who really don't know about finances and are just hoping it will turn out all right.

Although few of us believe that men should provide for all of our needs, some of us pre- and first-wave boomers still rely on our husbands or the gods of goodwill to make our financial decisions. We don't bother to save money and we spend it without thinking about consequences—often with credit cards—until excessive debt forces us to be more frugal. Or we pay attention to our finances but can't save money after we've covered monthly expenses. And even when we are saving and investing, we may slide into long periods of uninterest about how our money is invested, despite best intentions to the contrary. The prevailing philosophy seems to be that as long as we continue to receive a paycheck the future will take care of itself. And even those of us who feel financially competent are not immune to worry that we are not doing the right things, and may lack confidence to take action and make decisions.

Certainly, we don't talk with one another about it. Indeed, we are more likely to discuss our sex lives with strangers than tell our friends how much money we have. This isolates us from the support—the "we're all in this together" aspect—that predominates in so many other parts of our lives. And if someone does talk about money by blurting out her earnings or net worth, we often cringe at her boastfulness and insensitivity. Yet why, if money is equated with power and status, do we avoid admitting success and demean others who claim theirs? We prefer, instead, to dance around the topic rather than embrace it.

But we've heard this before and all the good advice and nagging hasn't changed us so far. So what is it going to take to make us alter our self-destructive attitudes and take practical action? In this chapter we look at the emotional side of money, including the lessons we learned as children of parents who were directly or indirectly affected by the Great Depression of the 1930s, to try to understand what has blocked us from making critical decisions and taking logical steps to control our futures. Because just maybe, by understanding what is keeping us from taking charge of our financial future and taking some specific actions, we can overcome it.

The Emotional Side of Money

Let's assume we are intelligent women, capable of understanding complex ideas and retaining complicated information. Why, then, is it so difficult for us to deal effectively with our money? Much as we may hate to admit it, our perceptions of money and our spending patterns reflect our innermost needs. Those of us who are compelled to acquire because we believe we *are* our possessions often refuse to see that our spending will lead to financial catastrophe. Penny, a sportswear buyer for a large clothing-store chain, didn't hesitate to use her credit cards to buy whatever appealed to her, a pattern she repeated until she was thirty-five thousand dollars in debt. For a time, she kept creditors at bay by switching cards, but when that caught up with her, she finally sought professional advice about how to curb her spending and develop a sensible plan to settle her debt.

Some of us, on the other hand, focus so hard on attaining financial security that we allow it to inhibit our ability to dream bigger or reach higher. Laura, who had headed up IT for an international investment bank, avoids buying things she needs or wants, lives below her means, and shops only for bargains. Everything she purchases is chosen to last, and her basement reflects her difficulty in throwing things away. She pays her credit card bills on time, claiming she would feel robbed if she ever had to pay a finance charge, which is not a bad thing except that she cannot bring herself to indulge in anything she cannot justify as a practical expense.

Our first introduction to the topic of money was through our families. Working-class families took money seriously but did not have much discretionary money to spend. Even in middle-class families, financial planning rarely went beyond having a savings account. Our mothers often managed household expenses independently or did so in consultation with their spouses, while some got by on strictly controlled allowances. A few were spendthrifts; others frugally doled out money for necessities, buying them at bargain prices. Some wealthy mothers, primarily widows, clipped interest coupons, but most clipped coupons redeemable for supermarket discounts. Fiscal heaven for the emerging middle class in the 1940s, '50s, and '60s was a savings account, a mortgage-free house, little debt, and a future supported by the man's pension, proceeds from a house sale, and Social Security benefits. Aside from a mortgage, the idea of taking on debt or living above one's means was inconceivable.

This is what we absorbed as we grew up, and some of those lessons haunt us still as we either repeat or rebel against them. Emily recalls growing up in a home where she wanted for nothing, but getting it was always a battle with her father, who used money to control her. She made a point of learning to handle money early on, determined that "no man would control me or my finances."

Noreen believes she inherited her mother's wild risk-taking edge, although she refers to herself as entrepreneurial with a "prosperity consciousness." Currently phasing out of her longtime job at a university, she is not worried about the future. That is partially because she has been financially independent since her late teens and so feels pretty resilient when it comes to making money. Her philosophy is "the universe provides." Despite intimations of a resounding confidence in such a grand statement, it's a cop-out that threatens to leave her struggling.

Marilyn, an artist who has been married for aeons, hates to think about money and remembers it as a great source of arguments between her parents. She says she leaves all money issues to her husband as long as he covers her credit card bills. Her coping mechanism is to be sufficiently abstemious about her spending so that money conversations with her husband are unnecessary.

> *I learned to "think poor" from my mother, whose scrimp-and-save approach came out of the Great Depression but is unnecessarily burdensome for me.*
>
> —Beth

Maria's mother never earned or handled money or balanced a checkbook. At home her father's salary was a secret. No one talked about money; it was as if it had nothing to do with life. Her mother felt that talking about money was bad manners, but of course she talked about it all the time: this one had a big house, that one couldn't afford a new car, and those others took lavish vacations. Money was the invisible elephant in the room, taking up lots of space.

Dawn thinks a dollar bill must have frightened her as a child. Smart, liberated, and independent, with a Ph.D. and a successful career as a college administrator, Dawn never managed money. Because her father wanted her to be an accountant, she took a bookkeeping class but vowed never to take another. During marriage, her husband handled the money, and since his death she has relied on her accountant and her sons. Basically, her money is invested in IRAs, bank accounts, and other traditional savings depositories. She looks at the bottom line when she must and questions her advisers about whether she has enough money. Although ashamed of this lack of involvement, she is simply not interested in the details. She admits to worrying more now because she no longer earns money, but she is content to accept family assurances that she is fine.

Dorrie, who works for a major educational institution where the pay is low, claims that the money is unimportant to her. Her husband pays their bills and manages the investments. At various intervals she scolds herself for not paying attention but then dismisses her lack of interest by saying, "I trust him and we get free financial advice, which is fortunate, since I'm not particularly good at math."

It is so interesting that some brilliant women have *a need not to know* about money, as they systematically cultivate ignorance. It is as if on this score we are still children relying on Daddy to take care of us. Even if we are ashamed of our lack of knowledge, that doesn't stop some of us from filing unopened bank statements in the bottom drawer of our desks. One day Maria asked her husband to tell her everything about their finances. She sat by his side taking notes and comprehending it all. But as she stood up to leave the table, she was unnerved to realize that everything she had just heard was gone from her memory, erased in a split second.

Are these behaviors examples of "money anxiety"? Sheila Tobias addressed the issue of why girls do not succeed in math in her landmark book *Overcoming Math Anxiety.* We spoke to Tobias about whether there is such a thing as money anxiety. Her take on the subject is that money anxiety is not due to math anxiety, nor are they necessarily related. She isn't sure that women are especially anxious about money unless they are actually in deep trouble because they can't meet their bills or pay off debt. Rather, she sees our attitude toward money as one of socialized indifference. "It's like anything distasteful that I don't have to do myself—clean my house, when I can get someone else to do it, or do the bookkeeping, when I can have an accountant. It's the boredom of it that we seek to avoid." Tobias cites her own attitude about money: "I'm not a dummy. I'm not afraid of math or calculations. For me my lack of focus on money is total indifference."

So, why do some of us find the topic of money boring or distasteful? Tobias thinks that our attitudes stem from having been socialized to believe that having our own money was not only unimportant, it was also crass. Instead, what was important was that we be liked by people, that we be good daughters, good mothers, and responsible wives, that we keep nice homes, dress well, and not become overweight. "We weren't socialized to consider money as a means of our survival or the survival of our families," Tobias says. She thinks that when many of us began to work, we made decisions based on early training, which rarely specified that we select an occupation primarily because it paid well. Instead, a large number of us chose low-paying jobs: we chose social work, we chose primary-school education, we chose writing and the arts. Being of service was important; financial remuneration was not. Men, on the other hand, were taught to seek out a high-paying field, and they will stay in a position they dislike because they don't want to give up their pensions or retirement benefits. Tobias observes that, in spite of feminist calls for self-sufficiency, many of us remain emotionally stuck with one foot in the prefeminist, precareer economic world.

> *I work for a foundation where it's my job to give away money. I'm good at it too. But I have no idea about my personal finances.*
> —Bryna

It's interesting that some of us who feel helpless about our own money have successful careers that involve the control of and responsibility for large budgets. Addressing the apparent disconnect, Tobias talks about women's approach to power and recognizes two kinds: there is the power to control other people and resources, and there is the power to control one's own life. "Just because a woman holds a powerful position doesn't mean that she's enjoying all parts of it. She may enjoy the fact that she's head of an organization that's doing valuable work or that she gets to interact with bright people. But you can't assume that the fact that it's a billion-dollar operation is what she is there for."

Time to Grow Up

So let's get over whatever it is that's stopping us from taking charge of our future. Statistics show that women are far more likely to spend their old age in poverty than men. It is insanity for us to ignore such a possibility by maintaining indifference, or to stake our future, for something so important to our lives and to those of our children, on another person. If we are single and negligent about our current and future income and expenses, we are totally unprepared to cope with a time when we will be too frail or ill to depend on only a paycheck to support ourselves. We mustn't believe that just because we've been good to others during most of our lives, we will forestall impending poverty. If we are married, we must ask ourselves, what will happen if he leaves? After all, divorce occurs in 50 percent of marriages. Or what if he dies? The odds are that we will outlast our spouses, and we are likely to have less to live on then than we do while they are alive.

RECLAIM RESPONSIBILITY

If you have yielded complete charge of the family finances to a partner, it may not be too late to adjust that. It is possible that he isn't especially competent at money management but projects an "I know" attitude because he was forced into a role he wasn't up to. Consider strategies about negotiating the money issue with your partner in a nonconfrontational, nonthreatening way:

- Raise the issue that you want to know more about the family's finances and have come to realize that it would be helpful to him if you got more involved.
- Explain that you appreciate that he has shouldered the entire burden of your finances and it's only fair that you share the responsibility with him as part of a team. And then be responsible!
- Don't express dismay if your assumptions about your current assets or where the money is invested are ill founded. That's why you are getting involved. Diplomatically work to revise them.
- Discuss all aspects of your joint and individual finances. Ask questions about how much money you have, what your expenses are, how discretionary spending decisions are made. This is a bridge to ongoing courteous discussions about priorities, ways to negotiate differences of opinion, and how to agree on a satisfactory plan.
- Agree to take on some responsibility for managing portions of your finances. For example, pay the everyday bills (if you don't already) so that you can have a better understanding of your expenses and how to cut back on them. Review credit card state-

ments each month for accuracy and for unexpected or excessive interest payments. Look at expenses that vary and consider how to control excessive fluctuations.

- Take part in all investment decisions. Suggest a time each month when you can review your investment statements together. If you have an investment adviser, participate in all strategy discussions.
- Discuss your long-term goals and visions with each other. Do they include putting more money aside for your daughter or son's college fund or your grandchildren's nursery school? Do you want to invest in a second home or sell off your current home for one with a smaller footprint and cost?
- Discuss how much money is being saved. Should it be more? Should it be invested differently?
- If you don't have a financial adviser, hire one to evaluate your current investment strategy and make recommendations about how to improve it.
- If your partner responds with "Trust me" or the equivalent of "Oh, don't worry your pretty little head about it," treat that like an alarm bell bonging loudly, telling you to take control before you find out he's pissed all the money away and your retirement is in jeopardy.

Although money management is a rational activity, some of us remain in denial about it because we are intimidated and embarrassed by our ignorance. Or even if we do understand our financial situation intellectually, we simply don't act on it in a consistent and useful way. We spoke to psychotherapist Susan Zigouras, who conducts programs and focus groups about the emotional aspects of money. She says talking to other women can help us recognize the emotions that govern our attitudes and how they developed. Zigouras finds that women in particular dissociate themselves from the subject to the point where they don't even realize they are not talking about it. She believes that as we start to discuss the subject and share stories, we begin to make connections between our actions and our feelings. If we are ashamed about not looking at a stock report because we don't think we'll understand it, admitting that and telling someone about it can start us thinking and help us get our minds back. It allows us to look in from the outside, which we cannot do if we don't realize we're not inside to begin with. Only then will we understand that managing money is about managing needs. If we find that thinking about money is humiliating or mind-numbing, we must do whatever it takes to get over it. If we don't, then the straits of transition will be unnecessarily difficult to navigate.

Punching Our Way Out

Mary is a preboomer whose Depression-era parents were the antithesis of good role models. Her father relied on hot market tips and not surprisingly lost huge chunks of money, which the family could ill afford. And her mother never wrote a check until her husband died. Discussions about money were taboo. Until her late thirties, Mary spent money lavishly, pulling funds from retirement accounts to pay for travel and clothes as she moved to different jobs. Her aha moment hit when she received ten thousand dollars from a real-estate investment made on a lark. The next years were spent trying to find her financial grounding, moving from broker to broker, reading books, and joining an investment club. But, despite her accumulated knowledge, her emotional response to money (including distrust of professionals like those that had misled her father and intimidation at the responsibility of managing her own money) prevented her from making informed and systematic investments. Instead, her investments were episodic and largely impulsive. Her answer ultimately was to hire a financial planner to assess her financial state. Because, as she claims, she is too cheap to pay the 1 percent fee of

> *Thinking about my net worth as the amount of money I walk away with when I no longer have a salary keeps me focused on saving for the future.*
>
> **—voice from a peer group**

a money manager, she is following the financial planner's advice and sees him twice a year for consultations. Together they choose a combination of stock-and-bond mutual funds under an asset-allocation formula that balances equities and bonds. While she is not making as much money as she would like, the growth of her portfolio is steady and she can forget about money for most of the time. Most important, she is no longer plagued with the sense of failure regarding her financial state.

Jean's story is an example of someone who grew up with immigrant parents who worked in the trades and supported the labor movement. Everyone they knew was poor and no one had investments. She was fortunate to attend an academically demanding public school, go on to a tuition-free college, and get a job where she earned good money. Years later Jean needed to develop her knowledge about money and investing. She joined an investment club, which awakened her interest in the stock market. That led to her developing a trusting relationship with the broker that was handling the club's trades. Contrary to the reputation of most brokers, this broker advised her not to buy and not to sell, more often than not. That guidance, plus the fact that she was able to eliminate her mortgage, gave Jean control of her family's finances. Her husband proudly supports her role as the money manager. She splits the family assets between broker-managed and self-managed accounts to make sure at least half is professionally managed, and happily pays the 1 percent fee. She has more money today than ever in her life and enjoys spending it astutely so that she will always have necessary funds available.

LEARN THE BASICS

Don't be discouraged about taking charge of your future. But before you make any decisions about how to manage your money, start by getting some financial basics. It's similar to learning a foreign language. You begin with key words and concepts, and as you become comfortable with such terms as "asset allocation," "equities," and "bonds," you will discover a fascinating, compelling new world. Here are some ways to get started:

- Treat learning about money the same as you would learning about any new subject.
- Watch business-news shows and read daily newspaper and mag-

azine business sections regularly to familiarize yourself with the issues being discussed and how they are expressed.

- Read one of the hundreds of books on the subject to help yourself get an overview of the topic and be able to define key words and expressions. (See the Resources section for several suggested titles.)
- Take advantage of one of the many free online resources that provide questionnaires to help you calculate your net worth, expenses, and savings requirements. (See the Resources section for more information.)
- Take the time to attend seminars sponsored by financial advisers or professional associations, or classes offered through local colleges. Solid introductory and midlevel courses are available widely. Most financial institutions give programs that show how expenditures and income play out when viewed against different longevity and health prospects and also in different inflation scenarios.
- Join a group, or form one yourself, to discuss finances and investments. Such groups run the gamut from investment clubs to informal discussions on a variety of topics, including mutual funds and asset allocations and how to work with an adviser.
- Meet with a financial adviser periodically to review your financial picture and get recommendations about how to improve your investment strategy moving forward. Financial advisers can be useful if you think of them as part of a backup strategy to help you make informed decisions and avoid serious mistakes.
- If you have enough net worth to justify hiring a financial adviser to manage your investments, invite several competing advisers to evaluate your portfolio and make recommendations. Advisers can be contacted through investment houses such as Fidelity, Merrill Lynch, and Goldman Sachs, to name just a few.

How Far Must My Money Stretch?

The life expectancy of women has increased to the point where the number of eighty-five-year-olds in the United States will double or even triple during the next forty years. Predicting an individual's life span is impossible, but studies show that one-third of us who are sixty-five today will live into our nineties. And, while the news is generally positive about the likelihood that we will grow older with vitality and good health, experts also think that we are in deep denial about the possibility that we will experience declining health and financial problems as we age.

It is certainly true that numerous obstacles have prevented us from being on the same financial footing as men. Most of us had lower salaries than men throughout our careers and thus have had less discretionary income for savings. In addition, many of us started our careers late or took time off to raise children. The result of this lost work time is that we had less time to save toward retirement and see our investments grow in significant ways. That translates into our having smaller pensions or other employee benefits to draw upon as we age. The Social Security Administration in 2000 reported that sixty-two-year-old women worked an average of thirty-two years, while men of the same age worked forty-four years. That twelve-year difference in overall income significantly impacts our retirement funds.

> *I worry about how long I can live this "dream" if I am going to live to be one hundred. If I knew how long I have (say, ten or fifteen years), I would not worry. It is the uncertainty of a long life. I'm not sure I want a long life if I can't live the way I am now.*
>
> **—Dawn**

And, no matter how much we save, we must consider that inflation will eat into our purchasing power and that health-care expenses will increase as we require more services. Not only that, if our partner becomes ill, it may force us to tap into our financial resources and may leave us with little money for our own costly medical care later. In addition, chances are high that eventually we will live alone as widows or divorcées and will be at risk of losing some of our late partner's or ex-partner's Social Security or pension benefits. On the other hand, if we live alone, we are likely to need a nursing home or assisted-living facility sooner than someone who has a family caregiver.

Laura dreaded the day she would retire because she feared she would not have enough for thirty or more years if high inflation were to devalue her money. A financial consultant analyzed her current and anticipated expenditures and assured her that her 401(k) and other savings could more than cover present and future expenses. She knew no one has a crystal ball to predict more than that. So she left her job and entered into the blissful, newly retired state of meeting friends for lunch, spending time with her husband, who is battling cancer, and finding her own rhythms and structure. Four months later, her fears about money reemerged, causing her to wake at night with anxiety about being ninety years old without money, means of support, or dignity. "I avoided the panic of 'What have I done?' and 'I've made a mistake!' by reminding myself that my retirement had been well thought out and was not a spur-of-the-minute decision. But I'm still extremely nervous that money comes from my investments and not from a paycheck or pension."

Her story is not unusual. After all, it is difficult to know exactly how much money is enough to see us into what may be a protracted future. There is no magic number that works for everyone. We all have different needs and expectations, and we use money to fuel them in various ways. Each of us has a standard of living to which we aspire and expenses that tax our comfort level. How we calculate the amount we need in retirement depends on many factors, not least where we live. If it is in San Francisco, then expenses will be much higher than if we settle in Tuscaloosa or Charleston. This and much more must be factored into our analysis.

A MAGIC NUMBER?

Most financial analysts claim you should figure on needing roughly 75 to 85 percent of your preretirement income to get by after you stop working. When you retire you will have fewer work-related expenses, such as commuting and needing to dress up. Generally, your taxes will be lower, you won't be making Social Security contributions, you probably won't be paying hefty college tuition bills or mortgage payments, and you will be able to cut down on other expenses as well. But if your dreams for retirement include such high-priced items as extensive travel or a second home, your expenses can increase significantly.

Matching Dream to Design

Say, for instance, that we want to work until age seventy and then sell our home and downsize to a less expensive one. If we are clear about what we want and it matches up with our financial picture, then all is well. But figuring out how to finance an unarticulated future is difficult because we have no idea what lies ahead. In order to get a handle on this, we must address some basic questions, starting with, When can I retire, and how can I finance the years ahead? How will I support myself if I no longer work? What kind of lifestyle is essential or desirable? And, last but not least, What dreams do I want to pursue and how do those dreams mesh with reality? No matter how extravagant or simple our goals for the future, we should have a reasonable idea about whether they are achievable and what it will take to make them happen.

This is where we begin to put our desires together with our resources to come up with a plan. Sally Hass at the *Fortune* 100 company Weyerhaeuser is among a small number of HR leaders who help employees cope with retirement issues. Hass has developed a series of programs to help her employees develop alternative plans—for what they want, and for what they will be able to do as they age. She urges everyone to make several plans: plan A is the current job; plans B, C, and D each consider various directions our lives might take, including the fulfillment of long-held dreams or our tackling something we hadn't thought of doing before. These plans might include continuing to work on a full-time or part-time basis, or maybe working pro bono, as a volunteer. Maybe they include buying a house in Ireland or Mexico. By making more than one plan, we can truly see how our finances fit into several kinds of scenarios and whether we must develop other options to fund our dreams.

Making a plan is the goal! This can't be stressed enough. A useful plan considers net worth and other projected income, such as Social Security, along with our desired retirement date and the amount we will need in retirement. Only then can we set an investment goal to get us to where we want to be. Without knowing this goal we travel blind. It is at this point that we can discover whether our goals add up or whether our retirement strategy requires compromise. We might need to revise the amount we expect to live on by looking at ways to downsize future expenses. Or we might have to give ourselves more time to save by adjusting our retirement date from sixty-three to sixty-seven or seventy. The plan might reveal that we must continue to earn money in our retirement through part-time work. A good plan lets us figure out the choices we can and must make. And every plan should have a best-case/worst-case scenario to allow us to understand how we will fare if we are subject to changes beyond our control.

DEVELOPING A PLAN

Your plans for retirement should answer these questions:

- What are your goals for and concerns about retiring?
- Are there others you need to think about (your spouse, parents, children), and are they likely to have money, health, or relocation issues that might affect your plans?
- Do you have outstanding debts from credit cards or a mortgage?
- What sources of income do you have (pensions, Social Security, annuities, inheritance)?
- What do you expect your future expenses to be?
- When do you plan to leave your job?
- How will you cope if you lose your job and are unable to work?
- Do you have a will?
- Do you have health insurance? Do you need long-term-care insurance?

When making a plan we also need to think about the amount of risk we want in our investment strategy. A plan can be devised that promises to reach all our goals in the shortest possible period of time, but that will usually depend on our taking big risks that assume the economy will boom or that we'll find that silver-bullet stock that will soar. Some of us are aggressive risk takers, whereas most of us want a balanced portfolio that includes some high-risk investments, and relatively secure ones to offset market dips or busts. And some of us don't want to risk losing any of the money we have and prefer to opt for conservative portfolios that won't grow much but are relatively secure—an option that isn't likely to get us to where we want to be. Assessing our level of risk depends on our personality and our current situation. Five years away from retirement, we may want to take less risk, because we cannot replace capital if the market takes a downturn. If we are about to retire and need to feel confident that our money won't be devastated by market swings (understanding, of course, that the market always entails risk), we may opt for a moderate or relatively conservative allocation of investments, including some with moderate growth and stable dividends.

HAVING MONEY ISN'T ESSENTIAL TO DREAMING

Some dreams may seem unattainable without money, but that isn't necessarily so if you look for creative ways to make them happen. For instance, if you yearn to travel abroad, consider joining the Peace Corps to pursue adventure while earning a small living stipend. Or stay in another city or country (Venice, Udaipur, or Morocco) by participating in a home-exchange program. Or contact a cruise-ship line and propose to teach a computer or art workshop in exchange for free passage. Or volunteer for a ballet company in exchange for opportunities to attend dress rehearsals for free. Finding no- or low-cost ways to fulfill your dreams simply requires innovation and flexibility.

Making Mistakes

We all make mistakes when thinking about money, which is usually understood best with hindsight. But we must try to avoid some common ones. Cameron watched the performance of her investments and was pleased to see that they hadn't gone down over the previous year. What she failed to take into account was that inflation ravaged the worth of her money, so that her "investments" actually took a loss even though the dollar amount in her account was unchanged from the previous year.

Joyce had put little aside during most of her career and had only recently saved a small nest egg, which she was frantic to grow so that she could quit work within two years. Deciding that the only way to get enough for retirement was to gamble on doubling or tripling her money, she invested only in high-growth, high-risk stocks recommended by a friend, which turned out to be a huge risk that lived up to its bad odds.

Zana owned several rental properties she got in the divorce from her first husband. She was so panic-stricken about managing them on her own, especially when they were not being rented, that she decided to sell them off. Now she realizes it was a very unwise thing for her to have done, because they would have guaranteed her income for the future. Her mistake was compounded when she invested the money from the sales in the stock market just before the market took a nosedive. Fortunately, she decided to go to a financial adviser, who encouraged her to hold on to her investments and wait until the market righted itself. She did and eventually was able to recoup her money.

Another mistake is to become diverted from our plan, especially because of greed or fear. If a solid stock or fund is not performing well, it is tempting to sell it because we fear it won't recover its value. On the other hand, it is also tempting to invest more money in a growth stock or fund that is going through the roof, even though chances are that when it drops we will incur a big loss that will be difficult to recover from.

The biggest mistake we can make is to not save for the future. Ideally, a retirement financial plan should be started many years before retirement, and at least five years before we should be saving aggressively. If we have a defined-contribution plan through our employers, then it is a no-brainer, especially if they match our savings, to invest the maximum amount possible in that account. Even if our employer matches only a portion of our savings or even none at all, a 401(k) is a good retirement-savings vehicle because the gains are tax deferred and the account is managed by professionals. We are usually offered options for allocating our assets among a variety of mutual funds and for investing in the company itself. All advisers tell us to diversify our investments, and Enron proved why it is that, even if our employer is hot, hot, with stock prices catapulting, or is a true-blue corporate institution, we should not invest more than a small fraction of our overall assets in any one stock. And if we don't have access to an employer-based retirement plan, there are tax-deferred IRAs for individuals and SEP-IRAs for the self-employed, both offered by all major financial institutions.

Financial Benefits to Working Longer

If we don't have much retirement savings, early retirement probably isn't in our cards. Just by continuing to work past sixty-two, we can make a big difference in our long-term financial picture. The advantages of staying at our jobs longer are enormous and far-reaching. First of all, if we continue to work, we can continue to stash money into a retirement plan and receive matching funds from employers when available. Just a few extra years of contributions to an investment plan can make a world of difference. Equally valuable, when we work longer we delay tapping into those savings, which allows them to continue to grow. In addition, by waiting to take Social Security until we are entitled to receive the maximum amount allowed, we improve our financial picture. Another plus to working longer is receiving health-insurance benefits provided by our employers rather than having to fund expensive policies ourselves. And, finally, working longer means that we have fewer years of retirement to finance.

Recent studies find that more than half of early boomers want to continue working past age sixty-two. This is a much higher rate than pre-boomers reported when they were the same age. Even more impressive is that nearly one-fourth of early boomers expect to work past sixty-five. And those of us who are self-employed and have flexible workplaces are also inclined to keep working. No one knows how these projections will play out and whether early boomers will actually do what they say they want to do, but there are several compelling reasons why they just might be true to their collective word. And improving their financial future is a major one.

RETIREMENT IS A NEW IDEA

Retirement wasn't always a part of the life cycle. Previously, people often worked until they dropped in their tracks. With industrialization, in the early part of the twentieth century, aging workers began to be seen as disposable and a threat to "progress," the great god of industry. This early form of ageism tossed such workers aside, to rely on their families for support or on charity for sustenance.

President Franklin Delano Roosevelt changed the face of retirement significantly in 1935, when he signed the Social Security Act, which was promoted in large part as a tactic to open up jobs for younger people. Retirement age was set at sixty-five to give workers a rest from their labors, but at the time a man's average life expectancy was sixty-three, so many people did not live long enough to collect benefits. As a result, the retirement age was later adjusted to sixty-two. Back then many people thought of collecting Social Security as degrading, just a step removed from being on the dole. That changed, and the story takes a different turn when sales and marketing minds set out to redefine the idea of retirement. In 1952, H. G. Kenagy, vice president of Mutual Life Insurance, wanted to sell more financial services and so tried to persuade workers to retire at fifty by promoting the idea that old age is about retired people blissfully fishing, playing golf, and sipping martinis. Shortly after, a real-estate developer with a clear profit motive took this idea even further. Del E. Webb conceived of a leisure community for retirees only, complete with a golf course and recreation centers. Packaged under Webb's catchphrase "the golden years," his first Sun City retirement community in Arizona was launched. The idea quickly caught on with a huge middle, "leisure" class that saw such communities as their reward for years of toil, and that could afford to live in them, thanks to their Social Security dollars and a booming real-estate market. By 1978 a curmudgeonly journalist writing in the *New Republic* about such retirees' being a drain on society and government labeled them "greedy geezers." More recently, long-term projections of a huge mass of aging baby boomers demanding payments and health services from Social Security provoked concerns that the Social Security system won't be able to support payouts to succeeding generations. Such dire warnings raised the specter of needy, elderly boomers turning America into a caretaker society. Despite the hyperbole, all of this is currently under debate, and new thinking about retirement and how we prepare to pay for it will affect much of this conversation. Stay tuned.

PART II

REDEFINING
RETIREMENT

CHAPTER
4

What Do I Get out of Work?

If money and health insurance are not keeping us in our jobs, then why are so many of us reluctant to stop working and leap into a life of retirement? After all, if we didn't work, we could be free to wake up and go to sleep whenever we chose. It would be our call as to what would be important and what we could ignore. We could set our own goals. We could be in complete charge of what to do and when to do it. We wouldn't be obliged to animate someone else's vision. Nor to repress our own inclinations, play office politics, or summon up enthusiasm for the project at hand. Full ownership of our energy, imagination, and time could be all ours.

Of course, many of us love everything about our work and thrive on being in an environment where grand visions and the challenge of worthy goals inspire us. We like to have accomplishments. It feels good to improve something. Even if we don't swoon with unmitigated delight about the work we do, we derive things from it that we cannot easily replicate or replace if we quit.

In their excellent book *Don't Retire, REWIRE!* Jeri Sedlar and Rick Miners urge us to "know what you'll be leaving behind when you retire, then figure out how to replace that in the future." Based on their research with retirees and pre-retirees, they identified eighty-five positive "drivers," the mostly intangible things that are important to us, that stimulate and excite us, that cause us to do what needs to be done and provide us with a sense of satisfaction and well-being. They are the things that make us feel that we belong somewhere, and they are the things that we crave, such as getting recognition from others and being part of a stimulating environment.

As we contemplate our "what's next" stage, we must think about those things that cause us to do what we do, especially, but not only, at work. We talked to women, in peer groups and individually, about the tangible and intangible things that make them get out of bed each morning. Most of us are motivated by positive goals, such as wanting to be a leader, or to become an expert on a particular subject, or to be of help to others. But we are also driven to do things to avoid a negative outcome. Think about the times we have done something in order to avoid feelings of boredom or isolation or embarrassment. Fear is a big negative motivator, although not necessarily a bad one. Think about when we voluntarily work long hours to avoid missing a deadline or to ensure the success of a high-profile project.

The point is that our positive and negative impulses are extremely personal and telling reflectors of who we are. They are what turn us on and off. And it is important for us to recognize what pushes us the most. Understanding that will bring us closer to figuring out why we feel good or dissatisfied, comfortable or stressed, at work. Certain things that motivate us have been constant throughout our lives, and those are likely to remain so. For instance, if we enjoy the process of brainstorming with others to come up with solutions to difficult problems, then that tells us that if we work in isolation, we're probably going to be disappointed.

Robin always gets a high from being productive and deeply involved. She expected retirement to be a joyous, guiltless period when she could finally do things she had postponed because of responsibilities to her family and her career as a family counselor. She launched into a life filled with theater, opera, lunches, bridge, golf, and exercise classes. It was "a pleasant routine to fill up the hours, but not adequate to protect me from the unwelcome, unfamiliar sense of feeling invisible." The problem was that before she had always stretched herself beyond her comfort zone. Not because she lacked a choice, but because that made her feel vital. Clearly, retirement without something to feed that need was a poor choice for her.

To figure out what truly gets us moving, it is useful for us to list as many positive and negative things as we can think of that motivate us. "Having a sense of identity" might head one person's list. "Connecting with others" might appear near the top for someone else. Or "Being of service to others" might eclipse everything else. How we rank the individual things that make us do what we do is an important clue to what we value most and will want to replace as we search for fresh opportunities or new careers.

Dorrie says that her office at the university provides her with a place to go where she is expected. Although other people, including her already-retired husband, suggest that she work part-time consulting from home, the idea puts her into a panic. One of her most powerful inducements for going to work is *not* staying home. She needs to get out of the house each day to go where other people wait for her. She is energized by being around others, especially her bright, motivated colleagues who enjoy their work. She fully understands that without that external framework to sustain her, she would spend too much time around the house doing things she doesn't feel are worthwhile and would fall into a pattern she calls "squirreliness."

Catherine loves her work as a teacher for the energy it demands from her. She must wake up every morning in a good mood to be "on" during the day, ready to face and solve problems on the spot. Teaching is full of action, and she thrives on it. She is proud of the fact that others respect and confirm her abilities. She enjoys being identified as Catherine, the teacher. She also needs her work for the structure it provides and as an outlet for all her energy. Summertime is when she refreshes and prepares for the next school year, but she also finds it difficult and wonders what summertime full-time would be like. "I think to myself, Okay, I've done two loads of wash, I've walked five miles, I've straightened the house and mowed the lawn, and it's eleven in the morning. I've always been pretty efficient, so I am puzzled about how to find things at home that will satisfy my need to accomplish a lot."

Putting on something better than jeans, and smiling and saying good morning to five people, whether they become big buddies or not, is important to me.

—Iris

What Eggs Us On?

The most important things that provoke us to action are a matter of our individual personalities and personal preferences. What follows are a few that regularly appear at the top of most women's list of things that make us do what we do and satisfy who we are.

Forging an identity at work is one of the most commonly cited things that motivate us. Our identity is often summarized by our title, which answers the question "And what do you do?" when we meet someone for the first time. Having a strong sense of identity can give us the confidence to enter a room with other professionals and know we are entitled to be there. It matters to us because it means that we have a place in the scheme of things that others accept and respect. For many of us our work identity also governs how we see and define ourselves outside of work. Like a pair of comfortable black slacks that always make us feel confident and well dressed, our work identity conveys to the world our expertise and status and gives us a sense of satisfaction about our place in life.

We also cite having structure as significant to us. It is why our alarm clocks blare each morning. It is why we dress carefully, apply some makeup, and know where to go on weekdays. It is structure that fills our calendars and causes us to create to-do lists that rule our time. We even build our personal lives around our workplace structure and decline to do those things that do not fit into it.

> *Because I'm needed for lots of meetings throughout the day and to help troubleshoot problems that arise, I rarely use up all my vacation. And partially it's also because I feel at loose ends when I'm home for more than three or four days.*
>
> —Yvette

Many of us enjoy the stimulation we get when we solve problems that stretch our brain cells and challenge our creativity, when we come up with fresh ideas at work, and when we deal on a peer level with other smart people. We like what it takes for us to stay informed and keep up with advances in our fields, and we especially enjoy feeling mentally active, alert, focused, and involved.

We say that seeing and spending time with coworkers on a regular basis is vitally important to us. Even if we do not consider workplace colleagues close friends, we associate with them regularly and feel part of a group or community. These are the people we rely on to hear our concerns, high-five our accomplishments, confirm our values, keep us on our edge, and offer sympathetic ears as we rant and vent. We also value humor at work for the way it spices up the mundane and connects us more closely with coworkers. When we are overly focused on what needs to be done, wit, laughter, and play are the things that help us release tension and even feed our creativity and inspire us to try something daringly different.

We also say we would find it hard to think of a life that is not productive. The idea that we have something to do is deeply ingrained in many of us. It is the motivation that spurs us to perform and rack up accomplishments. Most of us have learned to judge ourselves on how we use our time, on whether or not we produce something that has value. This is a message and measurement we've absorbed through work, and we use it to gauge who we are.

Those of us who have gone into government or service jobs are motivated by the idea that we can make a positive contribution to individuals or to society. We who work as teachers, nurses, social workers, or civil or consumer advocates, to name just a few of those working in the helping professions, put up with low salaries and no perquisites because we feel that what we do has purpose.

We are also animated by the desire to stay vital as we age. All studies about remaining healthy tell us to pay attention to three areas of our lives. We must get exercise, stay mentally challenged, and connect with others. Few jobs actually keep us physically fit, but most do challenge us to learn new things, recall information, analyze situations, organize information, apply logical and creative thinking, and develop solutions or decide on actions. And, of course, we use our social skills whenever we collect information or manage a project, a classroom, or an organization.

Not surprisingly, earning money persuades many of us to keep working. Certainly, having an income means we can pay bills, save for the future, and allow ourselves some luxuries. But money does not head up everyone's list as a prime motivator for working. When it does, it is often because of the intangibles money provides. Many of us revel in the sense of independence, self-sufficiency, and control we feel when earning good money, because it validates our worth to ourselves and to others. We see it as a gold standard by which to judge and measure our success. And for some of us it also allows us to visibly demonstrate that we are highly valued.

Many of us thrive on praise and recognition and would miss them if they weren't in our lives. Just as we enjoy tallying our accomplishments—putting another notch in our belt of self-esteem—we also enjoy the recognition we get. It can be a subtle nod of appreciation from someone who understands the effort it took us to make a project succeed. Or it can be a memo from the boss publicly recognizing our good work. Maybe it's the applause that follows our speech or presentation. Or it's a celebration in our honor.

> *I love that when someone wants to know what I do, I can say, "Just Google me."*
>
> —Jill

The respect we get when we walk into a room where others eagerly wait to hear our ideas incites many of us to action. We seek it when we agree to make a presentation at a conference. We feel it as we are sought after for our opinions and insights. We know we've got it when our phone calls are quickly returned or when we are recognized and warmly greeted by a colleague, client, or patient. Once we have it, it's tough to give up.

And those who have it say that power is a turn-on. The degree of our power can be measured by the number of our direct reports. But many of us say we seek authority for what we can achieve, not simply for its own sake, and prefer to handle power as a valuable precision tool that marshals people around a goal or gets a project through. Power can help us get promotions and cushy assignments. It can also help us achieve a broader good; for example, we might encourage our employer to side with socially responsible activities. Instead of thinking of power as a

WHAT ARE YOUR PERSONAL TURN-ONS
(AND TURN-OFFS)?

How do you sort out those things that are truly important—that make you tick—from those things you learned to consider important only because you got approval and rewards for them? One way to get a handle on this is to list what drives you to action. Then consider whether each factor makes the list because it genuinely reflects something you like about yourself or simply because you have been rewarded for it. For instance, is the fact that you are a good trouble-shooter going to give you long-term satisfaction? This exercise is a valuable first step toward helping you understand where you're coming from before you begin to make decisions about what to do next.

The following motivators were mentioned most frequently by the women we talked to. This is not a comprehensive list, so feel free to add other factors that motivate you or would drive you crazy if they were no longer part of your life. Use the chart that follows to note each factor that is important to you now (be selective), and then review the list again with an eye toward the factors you can imagine will or will not be important to you five years from now.

Have an identity
Work autonomously
Be part of a group or team
Feel productive
Be an expert
Be of service to others
Have an impact on something
Be valuable
Use high energy
Avoid isolation
Troubleshoot and problem-solve
Negotiate with others
Have new accomplishments
Be connected to an organization
Have external structure

Be intellectually stimulated
Be well compensated
Have purpose
Avoid boredom
Have influence
Organize complex projects
Be a leader
Be challenged
Learn new information
Meet new people
Get praise and recognition
Be physically and emotionally vital
Get respect
Have power
Mentor others
Manage others
Be creative
Feel confident
Take risks
Have direction
Have specific goals

IMPORTANT TO ME NOW	WILL BE IMPORTANT IN FIVE YEARS	WON'T BE IMPORTANT IN FIVE YEARS

gauge of our status, many of us see it as a measure of our visibility—of having a voice that others want to hear. However we use power, it matters when we have it, and it can be a shock when we lose it.

These are just some of the things that the women we've talked to have identified as the crucial rewards they get out of work. There are many, many such intangibles—mentoring others and working autonomously are just two more—that affect the way we see ourselves and, in particular, make us think about how we are likely to respond if we are unable to satisfy our need for our most important ones.

Now and in the Future

Knowing which intangible benefits are important to us now is one thing. We've also got to figure out which ones will, or will not, be important to us in the future. This can be tricky because what has spurred us on and seems so essential to who we are now can fade or take a 180-degree turn as we go through our transitions. Trying to figure out what works for us now and what will, or will not, work in the future is part of the dilemma addressed throughout this book: how to know before we retire which things will please and satisfy us after we retire. For some of us the answers come easily. For most of us there are few certain answers, and the truth is that it often takes several years before our real leanings become apparent. But that doesn't mean that we shouldn't actively try to guide ourselves through the process of discovering what will continue to turn us on.

One way to start to understand this is to ask ourselves which things we can't do without and which motivators we want to be rid of. Understanding this helps answer such questions as: If I have an opportunity to get meaningful work in a new field, is a hefty salary essential? Will my self-confidence dwindle if no one is there to clap for me? If I am no longer stressed or challenged each day, will my brain ossify or my energy wane? Will I feel inadequate without a job title from a well-known organization? Can I stand the idea that my phone calls won't be returned quickly? What will stimulate me to jump out of bed each morning?

Suzie, a former business consultant, is proud of her abilities to think broadly and strategically, worry only about things she can do something about, bring energy and passion to a task, and build relationships of trust. These qualities remain as important to her now that she is no longer working full-time as they did before. But she has added another characteristic to the mix—her ability to give and get the most out of every moment, every encounter, and every conversation.

During Laura's years heading up IT development for an international financial institution, the things she valued most in herself were her integrity, her commitment to accuracy, and her desire to strive for the best solutions. They are still important to her. But now she has added her ability to challenge herself and step outside her field of comfort. This change goes along with how she now measures success. Before, it was a corporate title at an investment bank; now, Laura says, it's "can I be the best person I am able to be? Will I do what I am supposed to do before I die, or even figure out what that is? It's about seeing myself from God's eyes, not the view from the public arena."

HOW TO DECIPHER WHICH THINGS MATTER TO YOU

Being able to identify satisfying past achievements will help you anticipate what is likely to satisfy you in your next stage. Start by making a list of your accomplishments. It might include winning a tennis match against a stronger player, throwing a party that everyone fondly remembers, or successfully advocating for new computers for your child's school. Maybe you anticipated and effectively warned your boss about a potential disaster. Or you made an important presentation, led a team to victory, taught a child to ride a bike, or traveled alone on an exotic vacation.

Look at each accomplishment and note what personal need it fulfilled. Did the accomplishment satisfy your competitive urge? Did you receive kudos? Was it meaningful? Were you an effective troubleshooter, a strong leader, a mentor, or an adventurous risk taker? Think about the accomplishments that gave you the most satisfaction and analyze the knowledge, skills, and strengths that you needed for success.

Many of us have a need to perform outstandingly, not just adequately. We will put in long hours and extraordinary effort so that our accomplishments will stand up to self-criticism. Fear of failure often goads us during our career-building years. What is interesting is that many of us report that it is one of the first motivators to go as we become older and wiser.

"Failure, who cares," says Lynn. At sixty-five she is no longer harangued by the voice of her inner overachiever. Recently, she took up pottery, and describes her first (and only) creation as the saddest, most lopsided, most weirdly glazed object anyone ever saw. In earlier days, her ego would have been wounded by her spectacular lack of achievement, but the need to succeed at everything she does is just not a major concern for her anymore.

Diana had a "dream job" as a senior editor at a national magazine in New York City, where she was responsible for developing feature articles and hanging out with celebrities and fashionistas. After the early thrill, she found the job emotionally and spiritually exhausting. The people depicted in *The Devil Wears Prada* were part of her world. Seventh Avenue, New York's fashion center—notorious for being heartless and narcissistic—wore her down. She felt under pressure to look great, sound great, appear excessively clever, and be seen at the latest club. She was judged by which parties she was invited to, who came to her parties, and which private schools her child attended. Even though she loved the creative work of sparking fresh ideas and overseeing photo shoots, competition was everywhere and unavoidable.

When Diana hit her late forties, she was demoralized by having to create superficial pulp features with titles that might as well have read "50 Ways to Suck Your Thumb" or "100 Tutus Under $30." She couldn't imagine herself in the role of an old editor in a young person's field, feeling like an aging chaperone on shoots with models and stylists. The job was preventing her from realizing the things that were most important to her, which were to grow intellectually and creatively. So with a huge sense of relief she left her job to go for a master's degree in psychology. She characterizes herself as anything but a natural academic and recalls developing an incredible case of hives, her body's way of showing her anxiety over her need to be an exceptional student. Competition was still driving her, but now she welcomed it as an impetus to do well rather than as a weapon to be used against others.

Eventually, Diana reinvented her life. She also realized how much being in a competitive mode had prevented her from saying what she thought and felt. It had caused her to appear as something more or different than she really was. Now Diana is happily part of a group teaching program at a New York hospital. She sees private patients and regularly meets and trains psychiatric residents and social workers. Liberated from her need to be competitive, she likes herself a whole lot better and feels far more confident than she did when she was a hot editor with a monthly byline.

> *I don't care where I am. I need to be productive and satisfied—involved. I live life in my head. I live life with my friends. I live life with my work.*
>
> —**Robin**

Newly Important Motivators

One value that seems to take on additional weight after we reach fifty is our desire for autonomy. Many of us place great emphasis on our ability to function independently, without close supervision. If we feel that our ability to set goals, manage our time effectively, and use creative solutions for problems that arise is being jeopardized, many of us say we'll head out the door pronto.

At fifty-nine, Betty has a solid reputation backed by several top awards for her work as a music consultant on documentary films. She has no intention of retiring, but she does want to be increasingly more selective about the projects she chooses to work on. She now accepts only those that offer her a chance to be more creative and that don't come front loaded with lots of depleting administrative responsibilities or micromanaging film editors who want to question and second-guess her expert decisions.

In the Driver's Seat

Shana, at sixty-four, knows what motivates her. So when she wanted out of her job as the head of the volunteer program at a major museum, she thought creatively about how to accomplish three personal goals. She wanted to continue receiving all the satisfactions she got from work. She wanted to eliminate political and bureaucratic obstacles that had made work tedious. And she wanted the flexibility to do other things that were also important to her.

The satisfactions she got from work were many. She loved being autonomous and feeling capable of running a smooth-sailing ship. She thrived on the volunteers' appreciation for the attention and care she gave them, and she enjoyed recognition within the museum world for her accomplishments. She also recognized that she is "freaky" about having structure in her life and would miss that terribly if she left her job without having another structure in place. And she knew she needed to exercise more control over her life, and travel to exotic places.

With ears alert to opportunities within her field, she settled on an unusual plan. A museum was in the process of moving to a new location and would need someone to direct its volunteers. Shana contacted the head of education there and was offered a job on a full-time basis to work for half her former salary and do "really boring things." In response, Shana made a proposal to them. She would design and run a volunteer program for the new incarnation of the museum. And she would do it for free. But she had conditions. They were that she would work only two days a week and in addition receive the title director of volunteer services, an office, a budget, recognition as a full member of the staff, and paid parking expenses. She made this counteroffer with some trepidation and needed to convince the museum directors that she was willing and able to work as an absolutely reliable volunteer. They "hired" her.

Her new job gives her the freedom to travel at least three times a year, with room to maneuver her two workdays around for shorter trips, as long as she is available for important activities. And it feeds all the things that motivate her. She feels she belongs. She is valuable, and that adds to her self-esteem. She also has a work identity, can lead and mentor the volunteers, and receives prestige, recognition, and structure. It works beautifully for her.

DO YOU NEED A LIFE COACH?

Life coaches basically help you make the most of your personal and professional potential. Most life coaches specialize in working with a particular population, such as women over fifty. You might go to a life coach for several reasons. You want to achieve certain goals—"I need to get back on track after my divorce." You want to move your life in new directions—"I'm facing retirement and don't know what I want to do next." Or you want to improve your performance—"I want to build a strong base for my work project."

Life coaching is not therapy. You are, and are thought of as, a functional and capable woman who just needs someone to provide a little support and validation to help you get "unstuck." According to Deirdre Aherne, a certified life coach, a relationship with a life coach is usually three to nine months long rather than a one-time conversation or a long-term process. It is the life coach's responsibility to keep you focused on your agenda and to hold you accountable for doing the things you commit to do. This accountability is a critical part of why life coaching is so effective. The American Society for Training and Development reports that the likelihood of your doing something you have agreed to do rises from 40 to 95 percent when you have someone to report back to. So a big part of the secret to life-coaching success rests in the question a coach will put to you: Who can function as an "accountability buddy" and hold you to taking action on things you truly want to accomplish?

CHAPTER

5

Suppose I Don't Want to (or Can't) Stop Working?

For most of us our best retirement strategy is to keep working. We say we don't intend to retire until we're seventy, if then. In many instances we plan to keep working because we are without retirement savings, pensions, or fairy godmothers, which means if we intend to pay the electric bills, we have only one option—to work.

Yet even when we are in good enough financial shape to retire, more than 70 percent of us say we don't want to. We wish to keep working because we reject outright the notion that our work life should end at some arbitrary number or date. But the main reason we wish to continue working is that, well, there are many things about work that we enjoy. It makes us feel strong, capable, and in control of our lives, and we don't want to lose that. And, as we saw in the preceding chapter, many things about work are important to us. Even if our current job isn't all we want it to be, the thought of life without work for the next twenty or thirty years pales in comparison with the unanswered question of what we will do all day, every day, to stay mentally alert, physically strong, and socially connected—the "big three" needed to age well. And, in fact, those over fifty-five make up the fastest-growing segment of the white-collar workforce.

Nearly all researchers agree that we will live longer and remain physically and mentally healthier if we are active. Of course, we can find ways to be active without working for pay, and this is discussed in later chapters. But the truth is that we have fewer opportunities to be active, engaged, and stimulated as we age, so if our work is neither backbreaking nor exceptionally stressful, we may be better off than we know.

And we seem to have figured this out for ourselves, since we say that work becomes more enjoyable and less worrisome as we age. In a major study that compared workers over seventy with workers in their early sixties, the over-seventy-year-olds said they enjoyed going to work more, had jobs with less stress, and did not plan to stop working until their health failed. Not only that, the number of women over sixty-five who choose to work full-time has more than doubled in the last twenty years, and the percentage is expected to increase dramatically as more of us reach that age. So just when others are telling us it's time to stop working, we realize that work is becoming more fun.

What Does It Take to Keep Our Work Stimulating and Appealing?

Sixty-year-old Irene feels she is on a trajectory opposite that of others her age who are thinking about retirement. Getting what she wants from her work depends entirely on her staying relevant. As a senior policy adviser at a government environmental-protection agency, she has reached a point where she has the independence to plan her own projects and find the funding necessary to pursue her goals. It wasn't always that way. Aware that she can't trade on past knowledge alone, she regularly takes after-work courses to improve her skills. She does not see work as an issue of just having a job and hanging on. For her the important thing about work is to be involved in something that reaches beyond her to the community and the world in general. She admits she's changed her perspective from an earlier time, when she administered eight hundred employees and a large budget. Now it's more important to her to work on substantive environmental issues, through which she can make a contribution and keep her brain healthy.

Along the way she discovered that her passion for being relevant produced an unexpected payoff she can only describe as Tom Sawyer–esque. Her project—targeting women of childbearing age who jeopardize the development of their fetuses by eating fish with high mercury levels—

became her whitewash fence and lured several bright young interns to work with her. Thrilled to have their energy on her team, Irene happily reciprocates by sharing with them her experiences and insights into policy. She is well aware that if she had worked only on projects for which she already had all the answers, she would have been bored and unable to attract the interest of others who would help make her work more stimulating.

When some of us think about our work, the topic of hanging on until we can retire often upstages the more pertinent issue, What does it take to keep our work stimulating and appealing? If we are in the game just to stay put and collect pay, we can easily become bored, and boring, as our enthusiasm and energy wane and our brains stagnate. This is when we become overly concerned with needing flexibility at work—by which we usually mean time off to pursue outside interests.

The good news is that we have the power to prevent this slide into ennui. It begins when we realize that by having worked for a long period of time, we really know things. We have a core knowledge in a technical, professional, or service field. And knowing how things work, in tandem with our life experiences, is a *huge* strength to draw upon as we search for ways to contribute to and enjoy work. Whether we are in our current job, tackling a new job, or striking out on our own, enjoying work requires that we look beyond day-to-day activities to the kinds of extras that will invigorate us, or at least keep us up-to-date.

For Irene, that meant supplementing her master's degree in urban and regional planning and her extensive on-the-job experience with evening courses on fund raising and philanthropy. Now, having earned a professional certificate, she is able to write grants to fund projects that excite her. But she might also have taken courses in communications, for example, to help draw attention to her projects. The subject she chose wasn't as important as her using the neurons in her brain. She knows that life will inevitably change, whether she does something or not. Her idea of transition is growth. This means being open to possibilities and having the wisdom to know what to transition into and when the time is right. For now, she's doing her utmost not to fossilize in place.

For some of us transitioning may mean picking up our talents and skills and putting them down in a different environment. That new environment might be the result of our taking on a new assignment within the same organization we currently work for, or moving from a large company to a smaller one, or switching jobs from one industry to another. Such actions can change the texture of work and reinvigorate our lives.

STAYING RELEVANT AT WORK

Here are some suggestions to help you grow personally and increase your value on the job:

- Do you consider your job from a technical perspective? Find out about recent technology or computer software, in your field or related fields, that is having an impact on the way a job is done or how it is analyzed.
- Do you read industry publications from cover to cover and subscribe to online newsletters that discuss new developments in the field? Don't overlook sections that may not seem to relate to your job, such as those on technology or marketing. Often, new ideas come from unusual sources.
- Where can you find opportunities to learn? Participate in training programs offered by your company whenever possible. Seek out lectures, symposiums, and seminars offered through professional organizations or through your local college or university. If nothing appropriate is available, or you can't commit time to a course schedule, then take online courses.
- Do you like to teach? Try teaching what you know at a local college, university, or professional organization or at your own company. It forces you to think about your work in new ways, and teachers frequently say they get back as much as they give.
- Do you regularly meet with others in related fields? If they are located nearby, meet for regular informal conversations over lunch or drinks. If they are not in your area, use e-mail to stay in touch and forward information you think they will find of interest, and ask them to do the same for you.
- Do you follow news of new research and studies that indicate business or cultural trends and directions? When viewed along-

side your job, even seemingly unrelated social or cultural trends can offer you a fresh perspective or revelation.

- Are you totally focused on your goals? Don't allow rigid thinking or things like your distaste for office politics, petty rules, or difficult people derail you from what you are trying to achieve. If you run into such obstacles, use your skills at negotiation to bypass them. You know a lot, and you have life experience, so use it.

How Our Attitudes Affect Our Work

Growing older does not necessarily mean that we become rigid and inflexible, although this can happen if we don't guard against it. Rigidity may show up as our not wanting to put up with foolish rules or procedures, or not having patience to deal with people who are territorial, rude, obstructionist, or just plain difficult. And often we are right to say, "Why should we?"

But Fiona has a valuable perspective on that. Before she began a new career at age sixty-three as a museum curator, she led the book-and-magazine division for a large service-membership organization and was used to keeping her eye on her goals. Like most of us, she gets annoyed at people with difficult behaviors at work, but she refuses to allow them to derail her. Rather, she feels that when we let such people take over, it reflects our not knowing what it is we actually want. "When I want something badly enough," she says, "I will put up with fools and do whatever is necessary to accomplish the things I care about."

Like Fiona, we all have responsibilities and know how to negotiate and make compromises when necessary. Her point is, what are a few more compromises if they give us an end product we want? By saying that we're not going to "put up" with a difficult person or situation, we essentially admit that we won't make the effort to accomplish our goals. Usually it comes down to priorities. Either we take the satisfaction of blowing off the difficult person at the expense of getting a project under way, or we tell ourselves it's only a stupid person and focus on what it is going to take to get what we need. Accomplishing our goals is about using our mental and physical energy to feed the "fire in the belly" that makes us go for something, no matter what obstacles stand in the way.

> *The best thing I can do to stay young is to stay involved.*
>
> —Irene

What Do We Mean By "Success"?

How we define success for ourselves tends to change as we age. Often, we use measurements such as importance of job title, size of budget, amount of responsibility, and size of staff to appraise ourselves. Typically, such measures governed our ambitious, career-building years, but the same qualities may no longer seem as valid to us now. Mina, sixty-one, who manages operations for a manufacturing company based in Cleveland, is clear that as long as she is in the full-time workforce, success will be measured by salary and title and status. On the other hand, fifty-two-year-old Carlotta's attitude reflects workplace changes that also suit her personal goals to guide and help others. In her job in the aerospace and defense industry, she used to consider success to be making the numbers and winning the bid. Now her standards for success are focused on her ability to help people become more absorbed and in sync with the company's objectives and feel they are contributing to results, whatever their position.

Tess, a high school art teacher from Buffalo, used to think success could be measured in terms of how much she could accomplish in one day. That led to her being a teachers-union vice president and publications editor, the chair of her department, a district art coordinator, a teacher, and an artist, with her fingers in everything, everywhere. Now she has eliminated most of the extra activities and says she feels "at the top of my game." She loves that current students clamor to enroll in her classes, former students want to student-teach with her, and all levels of teachers and administrators seem to value her opinions.

When Morgan worked for a large academic institution, success was about promotions. But now that she is running her own coaching business, she sets specific goals and evaluates her personal success as part and parcel of her business success. If she gets lots of referrals from satisfied clients and makes enough to support herself, then she sees herself as flourishing.

For years, Madeleine thought of success in terms of building a firm of business consultants to provide management strategies for large international corporate clients. Several years ago she thought of success as having fought and survived a particularly aggressive cancer. She judged her progress in terms of being able to do meaningful volunteer work and slowly grow an independent consulting business. Back to work full-time, she finds that she again measures her success by how much business she can bring in, although she admits that "sometimes that bothers me because it doesn't exactly feel right."

> *I used to measure success by how far up the corporate chain I could go. Today my feeling is that I've been there and done that, and don't feel the need to prove myself in that arena anymore.*
>
> **—Carol**

Each of us uses specific criteria to define what we mean by "professional success" and "personal success." As we transition away from the goals of our primary careers, other standards of success can orchestrate our plans and actions. One issue that the women we've talked to mention over and over again is the desire to have work that is meaningful. Exactly what that means is rarely defined but seems to be intuitively understood.

Samatha is an example of a woman who was determined to recalibrate the standards of success dictated by her work. Passionate about rural medicine and her practice as a solo family physician in a small predominantly white village in the northeastern part of the United States, Samatha, an African-American woman, built a base of loyal patients, was active in community work, advocated for family physicians, and served on her state's advisory board for rural and minority health issues, such as obesity. She admits that having been on her own, with complete autonomy in terms of time and job satisfaction, was as good as it gets. But it also meant she had little time off for kayaking or for giving more time to public-health issues she felt were important. In addition, reduced medical reimbursements made it increasingly difficult for her to earn a decent living, and the only options down the road were to see more patients or add other services, such as giving Botox injections, which didn't interest her and would eat into her time even more.

Just before her fifty-fourth year, Samatha was conscious of two things. The first was that she needed to control the stress that triggered early-stage symptoms of her muscular dystrophy. The other was that she felt less competitive and ambitious than she had earlier in her career. Then, she had put all her time and effort into career building, networking, having people recognize her, and "other ego-gratifying stuff," and suspects that she did it because she was both a woman and a minority who had not been allowed into the club: "If you tell me I can't do it, then I'll be much more inspired to go for it." Now she recognizes that despite her ambitious nature she is not really a political person who wants power for power's sake. But to do something important with power, yes, that's a different story.

Samatha chalks up this change to maturity: "You kind of see things come around and cycle through and you start to look at them differently." She decided to consider what her life might look like ten years later. It was clear that practicing at the same or greater intensity wasn't what she wanted to do. Older female "docs" were not an inspiration for her, since they seemed to become really tired and depressed by the isolation of working in rural medicine. But Samatha's idea wasn't about retiring.

She put out feelers for something else and an offer came to join the faculty of a medical school where she could teach first-year students about clinical medicine and the needs of special populations in rural areas. Actually, the offer surprised her. She knew that most medical schools have the reputation of being terrible about hiring women and minorities, so she had assumed that world was closed to her. But, with regard to her long-term goals about how to make a difference for the future, education and teaching have always seemed to be the way to go. She believes women's power is in their knowledge and wisdom. She is also inspired to help minority students coming into the field avoid stumbling over obstacles and prejudices similar to those she encountered as a medical student. She intends to use the authority of her new position so that her students will say with awe, "This is my professor." She especially wants them to know that it isn't necessary to be pompous, male, or white to be powerful, smart, and dedicated.

WHAT DO YOU MOST LIKE AND MOST HATE ABOUT YOUR WORK?

Women we talked to identified things they love and hate about their jobs. To take stock of where you are today, review the following list, add your own items, and then fill in the chart that follows the list. After you've completed your selections, consider the questions at the end.

Having a regular paycheck
Location
Flexibility at work
Long hours
Telecommuting
Some travel
Frequent travel
Major projects
Short-term tasks
Relocation
Troubleshooting
Stress
Friendship with colleagues
Developing new products
Title
Structure
Stimulating, energizing work
Being in charge
Office politics
Being recognized as an expert
In-depth relationships
Being a key team player
Being surrounded by high achievers

Vacation and personal time off
Putting out fires
Status
Exposure to new ideas
Respect
Meaningful goals
Autonomy
Contentment
Learning new skills
Networking
New technology
Being a boss
Being an initiator
Routine office work
Special access
Using organizational skills
Promotions
Recognition
Political environment
Seeing an idea through to the end
Time with family
Being an expert
Personal time
Mentoring others
Intellectual challenge
Being creative
Special perks
Expense account

IMPORTANT TO ME	NEUTRAL	REALLY HATE	MUST CHANGE

IMPORTANT TO ME	NEUTRAL	REALLY HATE	MUST CHANGE

How do you feel about your choices?

Did anything in the sorting process surprise you?

What actions do you need to take to adjust those items you've listed as "must change"?

Do the negatives outweigh the positives, forcing you to spend much of your time dealing with things that are perpetually stressful for you?

Can you remedy your concerns about your current job?

Is it time to look for new work opportunities elsewhere?

Serial Careerists

Just because we have a career in one specialty doesn't mean that we must continue in the same one for the next thirty years. Many of us say we want to continue to work, but at something where we can "find meaning and purpose." However, we are not talking about volunteering. Rather, we seek full-time work for pay that will engage and enrich us. Marc Freedman, founder of Civic Ventures and author of *Encore: Finding Work That Matters in the Second Half of Life*, discusses the desire many of us have to find work that is personally fulfilling and makes a difference in the world. Freedman is a visionary who believes that we older workers are on the verge of becoming the very backbone of society as we take on much-needed jobs in areas where there is a dearth of educated, skilled people, particularly in the health-care, nonprofit, and government sectors. He calls these "encore careers," which we take as part of an entirely new stage of life and work. He is referring in particular to the jobs we seek when we are in a position to reconsider our definition of success. When we do, we often find that our desire to earn a big salary doesn't equal our desire to have meaning—that our need to be practical can't counterbalance our need to find purpose, and our desire to pursue present goals doesn't hold up against our desire to pursue our vision of who we want to be and how we can make a difference.

What this leads to for many of us is a compelling desire to take our considerable skills and abilities, honed working toward commercial goals, and use them instead to work for something we believe will benefit others or solve societal problems. This impetus is strong. It is one of the reasons many of us who have worked for corporations and businesses gleefully accept the opportunity to take an early "retirement package" and use it to launch our next career, and accept the likelihood that we will earn considerably less than we did in the for-profit world. It's really about choice. This possibility may not have been uppermost in our plans as we saved for our retirement over the years, but perhaps what we have really been saving for is the chance to buy ourselves the freedom of choice. And that choice might be to work at something that feeds our souls. This motivates some of us as we are at last freed from big expenses such as children's college tuitions and pricey homes. This is what drives us to collect our pensions or retirement savings, accept buyouts or severance offers, take our Social Security benefits, and accept a job we deeply care about, even if it is for one-half or one-third the pay we were used to getting.

Gray Matters in the Workplace

Because a decline in educated, skilled workers is anticipated in the years ahead, many organizations mouth concerns about the hordes of employees who seem poised to flee the workplace and take with them the company's DNA—the precious knowledge about how the organization works, where goals originated, what has been tried before, and why key or obscure decisions were made. Top management is aware that if their older employees actually do leave in the numbers projected, they will face serious workforce shortages and lost skills, which will translate into slower economic growth and loss of services. While they worry aloud in their trade media about how to stop our talent, expertise, and basic knowledge from exiting en masse, they are not doing much about it. And as they procrastinate, we feel more empowered than ever to strike out on our own—to start a business, go to school for a degree or certificate, or find a new career path. Although dire predictions of workforce shortages after the first wave of boomers reaches retirement age are exaggerated, we may nonetheless be on the cusp of a new trend, where older workers like us want to work and employers actually want us to keep working.

WHAT EMPLOYERS MUST DO TO KEEP US

Suddenly, certain older workers look very attractive. Employers can stop our attrition by paying attention to a few of the things we would like to have in the workplace. The list begins with having businesses and organizations send us clear messages that we are valuable and then be responsive to our needs, which include:

- To feel wanted and valued—we want our employers to actually be concerned about our well-being and treat us with respect and equality.
- To be given the same opportunities for career advancement as other employees.
- To get honest feedback and solid financial incentives based on our performance so we know we are not being priced out of our market just because of tenure.
- To have health care coverage and competitive retirement benefits.
- To get training and other opportunities for development so we don't become stranded on mental or career plateaus.
- To be connected to colleagues and not shunted off to a work Siberia.
- To have meaningful jobs essential to the organization's mission.
- To have more flexibility and greater autonomy.
- To get coaching support to help us plan our financial futures.

- To have clear career planning that may include some form of retirement or phased-down work schedule.

WHY EMPLOYERS LIKE US

What is it we have to offer employers? We queried women over fifty about the positive qualities they feel they bring to the workplace, and found their responses are substantiated by numerous surveys of employers. Those attributes most often cited include:

- Wisdom amassed from work and life experience.
- The ability to anticipate problems and take a long view.
- Concern for the community and other people.
- Social prowess.
- The work ethic to do a job responsibly.
- The ability to organize, set priorities, and manage time.
- The perspective and unflappability to deal with crisis.
- The social and mediation skills to bring people together.
- The creativity to come up with new solutions.
- The motivation and commitment to get a job done right.
- Loyalty and reliability.
- The ability to identify with and serve the boomer population.

The Ugly Face of Ageism at Work

Ageism was first articulated in the early twentieth century, by a physician named William Osler. He gave a speech at Johns Hopkins University about how men over forty are dispensable to progress and how men over sixty are "entirely useless" because their inelastic minds are a drain on society. That speech had an enormous impact at the time, and his thinking became accepted wisdom throughout the rest of the century.

We've all heard some version of ageist stereotypes: that age necessarily brings on illness and disease and loss of cognitive ability; that it causes us to be physically weak, susceptible to ailments and accidents, prone to loss of eyesight and hearing; and that, as older workers, we take excessive time off from work and lack energy and endurance. And it goes on: we're considered slow to understand new tasks; we're rigid thinkers that resent change; it's difficult for us to learn; our skills and knowledge are outdated; and we are less productive than younger workers. And then there is the ultimate coup de grâce: that we are computer-phobic.

> *Maturity, wisdom, having a track record of success, ability to listen well, organizational skills, unflappability, creativity, leadership, passion, and strong people skills are just a few of the things we offer employers.*
>
> **—voice from a peer group**

Today's cadre of women over fifty have been shown to be healthier, more active, and more engaged in a variety of useful activities than women in any previous generation. We may need corrective lenses for our vision and to turn the volume up on our iPods, but few such declining capabilities are disabling factors in our workplaces.

However, many employers continue to believe that older workers lack energy and up-to-date skills and generally don't perform as well as younger employees. It doesn't take surveys to confirm that such ageist stereotypes exist, because we see them with our own eyes. Witness, for example, job postings calling for candidates with "energy" and "enthusiasm," which send the clear message that the openings are for younger candidates and that "oldsters" can just forget about applying. Or think about training programs directed primarily at younger workers, to the exclusion of anyone over forty. Each example repeats the insistent themes that we are not up to learning new skills and are incapable of being energized about our work.

Our Brains Still Work

Actually, evidence does not support the idea that our job performance is affected by age-related declines. That is not to say that age-related failings don't exist. In our twenties we are at our best when it comes to break-the-mold conceptual thinking, often referred to as our "fluid intelligence." Think for example about a mathematician who works out a new theorem or about when we learn a foreign language. Although such abilities begin to decline in our thirties, that doesn't mean we have peaked. Rather, age seems to be a plus when it comes to our capabilities for experimental innovation, with some of our best work taking place later in our lives, as we draw on years of observation and wisdom gleaned from trial and error. It is not until we reach our forties and fifties that our "crystallized intelligence," which is the ability to use stored knowledge to perform activities, is strongest, generally. In our sixties, our long-term memory for such things as retrieving previously acquired information and knowing how to use a keyboard remains intact, but our cognitive abilities such as short-term memory—which includes our ability to remember new names and unfamiliar telephone numbers—our attention span, and certain types of reasoning show modest declines and then plateau before they diminish further, as we close in on our eighties.

It will come as no surprise to most of us to learn that, even though there is some decline in our mental abilities, we have efficient ways to compensate for the things at work and in life that we can no longer do quickly. For example, we are often better than younger workers when it comes to analyzing information and making effective decisions, because we rely heavily on the extensive experience and savvy we've amassed over the years. When work requires knowledge and experience more than lightning-fast cognitive ability, we turn out to be incredibly valuable assets in today's job market. This was observed in a study that considered whether the practical knowledge bank managers got from on-the-job experience offset documented slippage in their mental skills. Results indicated that older experts employed at the bank were frequently among the most highly rewarded employees because they used things they knew and could interact successfully with others.

Unfortunately, negative myths about aging hurt us in more ways than one. Certainly, they put us on the receiving end of prejudicial attitudes from employers, but it is also often too easy for us to internalize such attitudes and believe them to be true. That can be devastating because

AGEIST MYTHS AND STEREOTYPES

MYTH	TRUTH
We are not interested in learning new skills.	We want to learn and have as much curiosity and desire to learn as ever. The catch-22 is that opportunities for learning new skills are available to us less often.
We will probably retire shortly.	All recent surveys indicate that most of us intend to continue to work for many more years. Generally, we stay with our employers longer than do younger workers.
We have difficulty with problem solving and decision making in complex situations.	Rather than jump to snap solutions, we tend to use our wisdom to grasp the relative importance of information to make reliable decisions.
We don't benefit from technical training as much as younger workers.	Frequently we come into training programs less informed than younger adults. It isn't that we aren't learning as much as they are; it's just that we have to start further behind.

Age discrimination is against the law. It frequently shows up in decisions in the areas of recruitment, dismissal, promotion, and training. If you work for a company that turns a blind eye to ongoing policies that block you from training opportunities or pass you over for juicy assignments on the assumption that you will soon

retire, you have some recourse. In 1967 Congress enacted the federal Age Discrimination in Employment Act (ADEA), which pro-
hibits age discrimination against workers over forty years of age in
firms with twenty or more employees. Enforced by the U.S. Equal
Employment Opportunity Commission (EEOC), the law covers
most conditions of employment, including hiring, firing, layoffs,
and compensation.

it can cause our self-esteem to tank, along with our energy and passion.
Worst of all, it can jeopardize our belief that we are in control and can
leave us wondering, Why even bother? On the other hand, anticipating
ageism, especially when it isn't there, can work against us. It's important
that we avoid subverting our opportunities because of our own faulty
expectations. For instance, when we go on job interviews or are considered for promotions, our interviewers—or bosses—may not be thinking
about our age at all. But if we anticipate that they will zero in on how
old we are, everything about our body language and verbal responses will
inevitably reflect the very thing we fear. We will flag our age as an issue
and send out high-voltage signals that invite others to wonder whether
our age is of concern.

Displacing Retirement

We want to work, we need to work, but sometimes the choice isn't ours.
We know there are no job guarantees, that things can change at any
time. It turns out that a third of us leave our jobs involuntarily, for health
or family reasons or because we are laid off. Competition, an economic
downturn, a need to restructure, or new management directions are typ-
ical reasons given for why we are no longer needed or wanted.

As older workers, it can be hard for us to get another job quickly,
especially when the salaries we want are on the high end of the pay scale
and our health and pension benefits are more costly. It is not a pretty
picture. But this is the reality if we don't have the highly technical or
specialized knowledge an employer is willing to pay our price for. It's an
especially gloomy outlook if we lack recent training or if our skills are
not up-to-date. That's when our price factor looms large. In a Bureau of

Labor Statistics survey in 1998, "displaced workers" fifty-five and older were less likely to find new jobs than those in the thirty-five-to-fifty-four age group. And, in fact, many older workers were ultimately inclined to drop out of the job market and join the ranks of involuntary retirees. Despite that glum news, most of us find work if we are savvy about how to search for a job and hang in there.

After working for many years in HR and career development in the banking industry, Phyllis found herself job hunting at age fifty-two "at a time when it didn't seem young." Desperate to work, she approached her job search with a vengeance. She had several false starts, taking two jobs that were ill-advised and inappropriate. It took eighteen months for her to find a job that suited her. A major university offered her an interesting position with a lesser title and one-half the salary she had earned at the bank. Seven years later, she says she loves the work and the people, and her position and title have improved, but her earnings are still thirty thousand dollars less than they were when she worked at the bank. This drop in salary is especially common as increasing numbers of fifty-plus exiles from the corporate and financial worlds take jobs in the low-paying nonprofit sector.

Finding a Job

Looking for a job takes massive doses of time, dedication, and desire. In fact, it just may be the hardest work we ever do. We talked to Anita Lands, a New York–based career consultant who specializes in working with midlife adults. She says the job search "is like hand-to-hand combat—every step of the way requires focus, effort, strategy, impact!"

Those of us who haven't been in the job market for several years will be startled by the new techniques and skills needed to search for, and find, a job. Just a few of the things we need to know are how to write a competency-based résumé, how to find opportunities online, and how to research industries and specific organizations.

In any job search we start with intensive self-analysis, in order to uncover what we want for ourselves—something that is not always obvious at first—and to figure out which skills and positive qualities we ought to be highlighting. Next, we must learn to communicate who we are, what we want, and what we can do in the time it takes to ride an elevator from the ground level to the uppermost floor. It will help us to look for information in the numerous books and on the numerous Web sites devoted to job-search techniques (some of which are listed in the Resources section of this book) or to hook up with a career counselor, who can provide advice about what to bring to the job-search process.

It is important to note that nothing else we do during the job-search process works as well as networking. In fact, it is the single most critical part of the process. Everyone qualifies as part of our network, from the person sitting next to us on an airplane to former employers, employees, clients, suppliers, and students. The list should be endless because each person we talk to leads to another, who may know someone who has a position that's perfect for us. Anita cautions us never to say no to a networking possibility. That's because it's entirely possible that once we're in the door, a position that sounded mediocre at first can transform right before our eyes into our ideal job.

Switching Careers

For many of us, transitioning means moving from our primary careers toward completely new ones in fields, industries, or sectors that we often know little about. As discussed earlier, many of us are looking to change our lives in some meaningful way and take on something that we've dreamed about or that will provide us with new opportunities and perspectives. This is precisely what being in transition is all about.

> *I realized I couldn't go from a really demanding, high-energy, all-consuming job to nothing. I had to find something that would engage me. I don't necessarily want to work at this high speed. I don't want to wrestle with big budgets and personnel issues. I want to do something worthwhile and significant.*
>
> **—voice from a peer group**

We also think about making a change because we are dissatisfied with our current job or we are disgusted with the industry we are in but like the work we do. We visualize entering a new industry or sector where our skills will be appreciated and our talents valued; where we will not have to put up with constant strife, change, turmoil, inefficiencies, and tedium; where instead we will encounter challenge, opportunity, and respect. Anything is possible, of course. But we will not find a new niche simply by searching through job postings in unfamiliar fields. Like every important change we have made in our lives, it will require serious research, which starts with us. Even if we claim that we got into our previous careers serendipitously, in all likelihood we found our jobs because we had situated ourselves in the path of opportunity. Consciously switching to another field involves a realistic appraisal of what we want for ourselves. It begins when we identify the things that motivate us at work (see chapter 4) and the things that demoralize us. It depends on our asking and answering the questions What do I get from work that I can't do without? and Which things am I willing to sacrifice to get what I want? For instance, if we switch to a new field, should we expect to get the same as or more than our current earnings? Is having a title with commensurate authority and prestige crucial? Is working for a leading company or organization critical?

We must also identify the skills and abilities we have to offer and assess whether they are up-to-date before we consider how they will transfer to another field. This was the process Roberta had to face. For ten years she honed her marketing skills working for a company in the food-products industry. Her talents included being able to excite and retain an outstanding staff, develop new strategies to increase sales, and deliver solid results. She thrived in her high-energy office and enjoyed the respect of her staff and her bosses. And, although she sometimes felt stifled by a work culture that seemed to deter people from taking creative risks, she enjoyed her relative autonomy to make key decisions and formulate strategies. That is, until the company was bought by an international conglomerate with a very different work culture. New executives were charged to integrate her company into the bigger one, and she found herself reporting to a big-ego type who knew little about the industry but insisted on micromanaging her work and second-guessing her decisions. It seemed to Roberta that it was time to think about tallying up her strengths and abilities and looking for a new job in another field. After all, she reasoned, marketing is marketing. Right?

If, like Roberta, we want to apply our current skills in a different industry, we must analyze what it is we really want and then develop several well-thought-out strategies for getting there. Impromptu decisions about a career that at first sounds exciting or promising can turn out to be a disastrous waste of time, money, and energy. Making an effective and satisfying switch requires research, and lots of it. (How to go about this is the topic of many excellent books and Web sites, several of which are listed in the Resources section, and we recommend you look to them for specific advice.)

Anita Lands says she urges anyone who wants to learn about a new career, industry, or sector to enroll in courses in a certificate program. Usually these are offered through colleges and universities as well as professional associations and business institutions. Certificate programs teach a wide variety of courses, including marketing, fund-raising, art appraisal, real estate, therapy, and baking. Taking classes is an excellent way to bridge careers because the courses generally provide an overview of a specific field in a relatively short period of time. And an added bonus is that the people who teach the programs are usually key players and top practitioners in their field, which can provide a leg up on the networking process. They are also valuable resources for gleaning what is happening in their field, especially whether the field is shrinking or growing or has certain niches that are overcrowded or underserved. The other big plus to completing a certificate program is that when included on our résumé, it loudly broadcasts to potential employers that we are serious about making a move.

Many professionals have discovered that volunteer projects can unexpectedly take on a life of their own and point them in directions they hadn't planned for. Educated as a lawyer, Gabriela spent eighteen years working at various jobs in a major financial institution, and during that time got involved with a women's network within her company and with a national nonprofit organization, where she served first as a board member and then as president. Both endeavors made her aware of her passion for people-oriented activities and prompted her to think about a future career path that would allow her to work closely with others. At first she thought to apply for an HR position within her organization, but quickly realized that HR was a shrinking area full of highly qualified people clinging to their jobs. So she took on a short-term commitment within her company while considering her options. Forty-eight and aware that the cultural environment in her organization was changing, she found the idea of a career in the nonprofit sector that served people more and more enticing. So she actively began to educate herself about the nonprofit world by talking to friends and contacts, learning to create a nonprofit résumé, attending seminars and courses on the topic, and subscribing to the leading journal for nonprofits, the *Chronicle of Philanthropy*. As her short-term commitment wound down, Gabriela faced facts, thinking, "You're turning fifty, and if you're going to make a change, do it now. Don't just take the same kind of job and endure it for a few years. Take the plunge and get out there and make something happen." As she was eligible for a substantial severance buyout package that she realized might not be available in the future, she and her husband agreed that having to take a cut in salary should not deter her from moving into the nonprofit world. Almost immediately, a job description for a position as the executive director of a new, national organization for women was forwarded to her by one of the people in her network. She says there was a little bit of luck involved because it arrived just when she had real time and the mental energy to pay attention: "If it had come three months earlier, I probably wouldn't have considered it." Gabriela took that position and has successfully helped transform the fledgling organization into a full-blown powerhouse.

The idea of searching for a new occupation is seductive, especially when we are disillusioned with our current work situation. If we want to make a longed-for career change to something dramatically different—for example, from being an economist to working as a clinical therapist—then we know that we must return to school for an advanced degree. If it has been several years since we attended a college, we may not be aware of the wide range of career-specific master's degrees that are available. Pursuing an advanced degree requires a significant investment of time and money, so it is essential to research the employment opportunities in the chosen field beforehand. Once again, the support of a career counselor can be a valuable asset.

> *I could try and brainstorm alone, but if I sit down with two or three others, at the end of the evening I've got five ideas and not just one.*
> —Moira

No matter which direction we want our next job to take, a successful search for the right fit will depend on our tenacity and our ability to keep our spirits and self-confidence buoyant. There is no better way to do that than by joining a peer or support group with others who are in the midst of, or have recently gone through, similar experiences. Talking, sharing stories, discussing possible leads, and giving and getting feedback get us through this trying time. At a meeting of about fifty women from the San Francisco Bay area who gathered to discuss careers and job hunting, a career consultant led a discussion about the importance of networking. To prove the point that anyone, anywhere, can be a potential lead, a woman in the group was invited to describe the kind of job she was seeking, and then those present were asked if they could help her in her job search. Another woman in the room responded that she worked in a related field and knew about a wonderful job opportunity with a good company. She happily gave the job seeker a name and contact information, along with permission to use her name as an introduction. Sometimes it can be that easy.

THE OLDER JOB HUNTER

Here are some guidelines for you to consider:

- Do not think, assume, or imply that age is an issue when interviewing. Most of the time you are the only one thinking about it. If your résumé does not include telltale dates (and it shouldn't), then interviewers probably won't guess your age. Referencing your age only serves to put the idea on the table when it might not have been there before.
- On your résumé, keep descriptions of past job experiences concise and show a clear connection between them and the job under discussion. It is tempting to list your full employment history, but this is a long story that can use up valuable interview time. Omit long-ago experiences unless they are relevant.
- Revamp your résumé in order to emphasize things that are important in today's work world. Get friends to help you critique it to make sure it's on target.

- Create a competency-based résumé, which emphasizes what you know and what you've accomplished rather than where you've worked. Omit dates from jobs and degrees.
- Rehearse for interviews and, in particular, practice answering "difficult" questions.
- When interviewing, address concerns that the interviewer may have about whether your knowledge of technology is up-to-date by mentioning how you recently completed a course on a new software program (if, of course, you have actually done that!). This will speak volumes about your interest in and ability to absorb new information.
- Tell interviewers anecdotes that illustrate your enthusiasm for working with people of all ages and interests. Simply saying "I work well with others" doesn't communicate it.
- Tell interviewers stories that illustrate your flexibility and interest in learning about new ideas and procedures. Mention courses you've taken, no matter what the topics. Just saying "I'm flexible and like to learn" doesn't have the same power.
- Know what it is that you are selling (this is also known as marketing yourself). Be aware of the positive qualities and attributes you have to offer and focus on developing stories that exhibit your valuable experience and ability to see the big picture.
- Be proactive and use your imagination. Think of a job or project that is needed and then submit a proposal to a potential employer that explains the need and how you can fill it.
- When interviewing, do not refer to the good old days when things were better or imply that new techniques are unnecessary. Instead, indicate your awareness of and interest in new management and technical trends—which you've learned about by reading trade and professional journals.
- Project an awareness of new developments in your field, gleaned from reading professional publications, talking to others, and getting daily updates from influential Web sites and bloggers.
- Offer to work pro bono on a project. This can help you hone your skills, get you back in the action, give you an identity, add to your self-confidence, legitimize your contacting others in the

field for information, get you in on the job buzz, and open doors that you might not otherwise have known about.

- Network, network, network. Contact everyone you know for informational meetings.
- Follow up, follow up, follow up. Just because your fifth call and eighth e-mail message haven't gotten a response, don't assume there is no interest. Be pleasantly persistent.

Self-Employment

"Self-employed" is not a euphemism for "job hunting" or "retired." Nor should the term be used to give ourselves a self-protective identity suggesting that we are busy, busy, busy as the CEO of Me, Inc., even if we have occasional clients to justify our claims. Many of us are in a good position to set up a full-time consulting business that draws on the things we know and do well and have it succeed through our already solid network of contacts. Or, backed by corporate buyouts, severance packages, stock options, inheritances, and savings, we can start up our own business in a different area. Well-seasoned by long careers, we often make good entrepreneurs because we're savvy and sophisticated, have strong reputations, and know how to negotiate and organize, and whom to call. Women became entrepreneurs in record numbers over the last thirty years, so we also have many excellent role models and supportive agencies that can help us make things happen. Being your own boss, setting your own agenda, organizing your own schedule, and knowing that you can claim credit for success can be exhilarating. Although the idea of running a start-up business is appealing, it requires time, money, a multitude of skills that go beyond creating the service or product being offered, and a personality suited to the task. For example, you may be good at designing jewelry, but turning this skill into a business requires knowing how to develop a strategic business plan, organize systems and processes, sell, market, write, handle accounting and technology, and manage people and operations. It's pretty heady stuff. Just ask a newly self-employed woman how she feels, and she will often say she is euphoric and depressed, overwhelmed and on top of it. And that's in a span of just three minutes!

ARE YOU CUT OUT TO BE AN ENTREPRENEUR?

Ask yourself the following questions before you set off on a new business venture:

- Are you someone who can gamble and feel comfortable with risks?
- Can you tolerate setbacks and stay focused when things go awry?
- Will you know when to bail out or change course?
- Are you able to jump in fast when the timing is right?
- Can you bob, weave, take a punch, bounce back, and not take it personally when blows come?
- Do you have lots of self-confidence and initiative, and an iron will that isn't threatened by economic dips and black holes?
- Are you prepared to work as long as it takes to get the job done?
- Are you good at planning ahead, staying organized, thinking creatively, and making decisions, even when complete information isn't available?
- Are you a leader who can get along with others, including people who are difficult?

Rachel has always been an entrepreneur and was restless to find something new where she could use her creative abilities and organizational skills. She realized she had found the right fit the instant she heard about a career as a professional organizer, because it was an extension of her earlier work showcasing houses for sale. She also knew that every profession has its professional association, so she researched the professional organizers' association and joined. "I knew what I was doing—just biding my time, talking to people, going to meetings, sticking with it." Since professional organizing is a new growth industry, the association was eager to publicize the profession, and Rachel was happy to work on its behalf. Invited to join the board shortly after, her new position gave her a wonderful opportunity to contact others in the field and introduce herself in her capacity as a volunteer director–member. "I used the opening to pump them for information about how they get publicity or overcome client resistance. Most people don't want to give up their professional secrets, but if you volunteer your time for the organization that is working on their behalf, they'll tell you anything." Rachel eventually became more visible to the members when she served as the association's program director, and that led to many more referrals. Now she is considered one of the leaders in the field and has as much business as she can handle.

FIND YOUR SELF-EMPLOYMENT NICHE

Being self-employed is about selling a product or service. What you sell depends on your interests and previous work experiences. Here are some questions to ask yourself about what you have to offer and how to proceed:

- What specific knowledge did you gain from previous work? For example, if you have skills and experience in an area such as bookkeeping, training, sales, programming, writing, wine making, engineering, therapy, dog grooming, or lobbying, try to market this knowledge to other businesses, companies, organizations, and individuals.
- How can you narrow your skill sets? Don't try to be a jack-of-all-trades. Instead, focus on a particular aspect of your background to pitch yourself as an expert.
- What kinds of products are needed? Based on your experience in and observations of an industry you know well, consider certain products or processes that are lacking and could be provided by a small company (yours) rather than handled within an organization.
- Who will be your audience or end user? Learn about their needs as well as the limitations and obstacles they encounter at work or at home. Find products or services that will address their specific needs.
- Do your peers in the huge boomer demographic suggest opportunities for new products or services? Talk to your boomer

friends, collect their thoughts and opinions, and, in particular, pay attention to their gripes. They are a valuable resource for generating new ideas.

- Has recent legislation or regulations created opportunities for new products and services? For instance, if your field is social work, develop expertise in completing complicated health-care forms and offer that service to hospitals and other health-care organizations.
- What are the trends and new directions within your field? Be creative about finding products and services that may be needed as changes take place. For instance, learn to use a new technology and then provide training to organizations and individuals.
- What skills and services can you sell within your community? Can you teach or tutor children, start a catering business, offer gardening and landscape advice, teach painting or tennis, or be a pet sitter?
- What products and services do you need at this point in your life? Chances are they will also be needed by others and the demand will grow as later boomers approach the over-fifty mark. You may be first on board with something that turns out to be a huge success.
- Who can you turn to for advice and support? Create your own board of directors and include professionals such as an accountant and a lawyer, as well as others who have been in business and can help you anticipate and avoid pitfalls.
- What knowledge are you missing? Take some business courses to fill in missing knowledge in areas like marketing, technology, sales, and writing a business plan.
- Who is your competition? Research who your competitors are and what kind of products and services they offer. Start your search on the Internet, since just about every kind of business has a Web presence.
- Where can you get practical advice? There are many nonprofit organizations that provide advice for entrepreneurs, and it is often offered by retirees on a voluntary basis.
- Is buying a franchise the best option for you? Check out established franchises; they are usually more successful than start-ups because they are built on a tried and tested idea.

CHAPTER
6

How Can I Scale Back on Work
and Find Some Balance?

As in the Peggy Lee song "Is That All There Is?" certain things that were so important to us yesterday disappoint us today and make us eager to open the doors onto fresh experiences. Long-dormant dreams from childhood—maybe to work with animals, serve as a nurse, perform on stage, or save the world—come to the surface and elbow current priorities aside. Exhausted by years of schedules and obligations set by others, we suddenly feel the need to ask, "What about me?" Although none of us looks forward to thirty years of idle leisure and the decline that seems to promise, neither do we want to continue to work at the same pace and intensity as we have for the last thirty. Somewhere, we can find a better balance, one that will let us keep the things we enjoy at work and at the same time give us leave to smell those proverbial roses.

If we are not quite there yet, we can expect such thoughts to infect us after we reach our midsixties, which is what many of us report happens. Even when income and health insurance are not decisive issues, we realize that, while we don't want to work as hard, neither do we want to give up working altogether. We have heard by now that if we fail to replace the positive things we get from work, our mental health may decline (by 11 percent), our risk of illness may increase (by 8 percent), and our ability to perform daily tasks may decrease (by 23 percent). Plus, there is the emotional consequence of shutting ourselves off from work-related friends and activities.

Lightening the Load

Few of us are prepared financially or emotionally to shut off work completely, but many of us would like to lighten our workload. Just before the age of fifty, Sofia was working incredibly hard at her growing ceramic-tile business and was dealing with a difficult, ruthless new business partner, which she describes as a trial by fire that ultimately toughened her. During this period she remarried and almost immediately afterward lost her husband to cancer. All of this shifted Sofia's focus about the business: "I came in, put my head on the desk, and said, 'I don't want to be here, but I don't want to give it up completely'"—especially the good parts, like working with architect, designer, and artist clients. She wanted to have more freedom. And be able to manage her earnings. And stay in touch with the people she liked and the things she knew best. So she became a consultant and sales agent for public-art projects around the country and is appreciated by clients for her passion about art and the technical knowledge about tiles she had developed over years and years of running her business. She says that it took a while for her to get comfortable in her new role and with facing a risky period with no income. But she is a self-confident woman who says one of her best skills is being a problem solver. "I've learned not to get scared, and I've learned that when things are not going exactly right, just to focus forward, not look back, and do what needs to be done."

Some of us, unlike Sofia, make the mistake of junking the things we know from our primary careers and searching for something entirely different. But that's like throwing the baby out with the bathwater. It's important to keep up our confidence in who we are and what we know in order to navigate any transition successfully. That isn't to say we shouldn't come up with new ideas and move in other directions that will intersect with opportunities. But if those new ideas have some basis in things we already know about and enjoy, then they are more likely to be effective and gratifying.

Finding a New Balance

Lots of us want more personal time yet find it difficult to imagine life without work and the structure it gives us. We still feel the pull of the workplace even as other things tug us away—a new grandchild, an ill parent, an exotic vacation, painting classes, or a health problem of our own. How can we manage all of it on our terms? Those of us who have tried to rebalance our lives know that active retirement can involve any combination of work, consulting, and volunteering, with time left for new adventures, caretaking, and leisure. It all comes down to reordering our priorities and finding the flexibility to live according to them.

> *At sixty-nine, I was flunking retirement, so I started looking for a job.*
>
> **—Robin**

So, how can we get some flexibility in our lives and still work? Cecelia hasn't had trouble finding jobs, although she admits that it helps that she doesn't need to be well paid. When she lost a high-profile job in broadcasting at the age of fifty-seven, she was unclear at first about how to keep some sort of a structured work life. It took a while before she could think about work in terms of something other than one specific job. Initially, it was by default that she chose to combine several paid and unpaid jobs that kept her active and challenged. These included teaching at a local college, performing narratives for documentaries, serving on nonprofit boards, and lending her expertise and credibility to several women's political causes. Basically, Cecelia took slivers of things that she liked to do and created a portfolio of jobs that offers a rich variety that draws on the many aspects of who she is and that allows her to be involved and visible in the professional community she values. But it took time, as she is the first to admit, before she was able to fashion such a satisfying portfolio.

> *Retirement is like a work in progress.*
>
> **—Sherry**

Searching for something other than full-time or traditional work isn't always easy. After all, the work world is built around full-time employment, and when some of us lobbied businesses during our child-raising years for flexible work schedules, we failed to make across-the-board gains. When we did negotiate some flexibility, it frequently came with strings attached, in the form of lower pay and few opportunities for career advancement. So why, we ask, might employers consider giving us flexibility now, as we approach retirement age? The answer, of course, has to do with our numbers. The fact that in increasing numbers we are reaching retirement age is threatening to organizations that see a pending shortage of knowledgeable, skilled replacements. Although that scenario may not take place, the possibility that organizations will not have enough competent people is beginning to change the employment landscape and inspire employers to do whatever they can to keep us around for a while longer—and even encourage us to come back after we retire.

Taking a Break, but Not Breaking Loose

Workaholic Jill occasionally needed to take a deep breath and unbind herself from a fully booked calendar and daily phone calls and e-mails. Mostly, she longed to take a sabbatical, to have time to reflect on what she was doing and where she was headed. But that didn't seem possible at the midsized design firm where she worked, so she decided to leave her job. Traditionally, sabbaticals are offered to tenured professors and professionals in academic and nonprofit settings as paid time off. Usually it is to help them refresh their thinking, complete a book or a study, or come up with new ideas. Sabbaticals in profit-driven workplaces are rare, although possible. Yvette works in New York City for a Europe-based multinational corporation that regularly offers sabbaticals to longtime employees based on their years of service. When she had the chance to take five weeks as paid time off, it was an offer she couldn't refuse. It was especially appealing considering that her longest vacation in her twenty-nine years with the company had lasted a mere two weeks. The sabbatical was meant to give her time to become reenergized, and she says she returned to her office feeling "like all cylinders were firing." Perhaps a similar break might have changed Jill's mind about leaving her job.

Take a Gap Year

Many students just graduating from high school take a "gap year" before they go off to college. The year is seen as an opportunity for them to find themselves through nonacademic experiences in which they can learn and grow without risk to their long-term goals. Why can't we do the same? After all, we are also in an intense kind of transitional phase, similar to adolescents that are giving up the life they knew for something entirely different. We need to breathe and just let go of all the stress and demands that rule our time. We need a free period in which to test out ideas and expose ourselves to new options.

As it turns out, many of us use retirement as the equivalent of a sabbatical or gap year, although we may not think of it in quite that way. Some of us plan it, using a break from our work to leapfrog into part-time gigs or a return to full-time work. Sometimes our retirement ends up being just a break by happenstance. At least, that's what happened to Frieda, who taught community organization in a school of social welfare at a California university. Under pressure from her husband to share his retirement, she had a "grand retirement party" when she was sixty-four. She then traveled with him by motor home through the northern and southwestern regions of the United States. When she returned home, Frieda established a pattern of meeting friends for lunch, playing with her grandchildren, and puttering around, but she soon decided that when play is unstructured all the time, it is no longer as much fun. So when her former employer asked her to stand in part-time for someone on leave, she jumped at the chance to get back into the social-welfare enterprise that had given purpose and meaning to her life.

The trend in which we stop work, even retire, and then jump back in is on the increase and bears labels such as "the working retired" and "the unretired" (suggesting that vampires have claimed our souls), although it mirrors in part our earlier winding, U-turn career paths and fits neatly within a future likely to be filled with more twists and turns.

Retirement Jobs

Many of us plan to continue to work in our present career or find some kind of retirement work. Flexible alternatives to full-time jobs come in many sizes and shapes, although the reality is that there are still too few opportunities out there to meet the growing demand, and what is readily available tends to be small in scale. Not-quite-retirement jobs, or flex jobs, take many different shapes and are called by many names. There is job sharing, telecommuting, the compressed workweek, part-time or seasonal work, the snowbird job, and the bridge job. We can work under a phased retirement plan, join a resource pool, or become contract workers, consultants, retiree casuals, or lifelong contributors. These are just a few of the options and some of the ever-changing lingo circulating among HR experts.

When it comes to negotiating flexible alternatives with employers, we are often in strong positions, although we may not always recognize it. That came as a surprise to Katie, who worked for twenty-two years with a large communications company as the director of information technology. One day Katie was told that the IT system was being changed and her area would eventually be phased out. Her supervisor made it clear, however, that the company didn't want her to leave. Instead, it wanted her to change her focus to a different field while continuing to handle her current projects. In other words, she was being assigned more work and loaded with more pressure to function in an area that didn't interest her. Katie was unclear about what to do and discussed her options at her monthly peer group meeting. This group of women who gathered for discussion, friendship, and support helped her realize that, rather than being in a crisis, she was actually in a very strong position. They could see that the company needed Katie's unique expertise to keep its existing system functioning and would be open to negotiating ways to keep Katie on board.

This perspective encouraged Katie to imagine the possibilities. She realized that if she didn't take on the new responsibilities, then she could handle her old system working just three days a week. Before making the case to her supervisor, she rehearsed her presentation to her peer group. The final arrangement with her employer actually exceeded her hopes. Because her company's policies exclude part-time work at her level, she was invited instead to retire with a pension based on her age and number of years of work, and become a three-day-a-week consultant. Under this arrangement, she earns the same amount for three days of work that she had for five. And she continues to get most of her health benefits, although she is no longer eligible for stock options or 401(k) contributions, nor is she in charge of or involved in some decision making.

Like Katie, many of us would have been rattled by the initial demands her company made of her. It helped Katie that others were there to help her see that she had the leverage to write her own job description. Her story is a terrific example of how our ability and experience give us power to manage our retirement work.

Our best chances to line up alternative work arrangements are, most often, with our current employer. If we have credibility and are recognized as accomplished, successful workers, then we stand a good chance of negotiating something for ourselves. Often, this requires us to separate our work into various parts and then consider which parts we want to keep and how those jibe with our particular strengths. It also means being able to grasp the organization's needs and then think about our own needs within that context. It's more useful to construct a new role for ourselves within our current jobs than it is to define a new job altogether. We also need to realize that going from a full-time to a part-time role involves trade-offs that require that we adjust our thinking about things such as our degree of involvement in leadership and our level of impact, as well as our earnings, benefits, and status.

HOW TO CREATE AND NEGOTIATE ALTERNATIVE JOBS

Here are a few suggestions to help spark your thinking about ways to reshape or restructure your work:

- Start with your current employer and build a case from your track record and credibility. Or approach previous employers that know your capabilities and work.
- Regardless of your organization's stated HR policy, consider that every deal is individual. You can often negotiate something special if you have credibility and are a known quantity. Often such

deals are kept quiet and only official policy is visible in the company. Finding out what others have negotiated is difficult; the best way is to know a couple of moles within the organization.

- The good old law of supply and demand kicks in during any negotiation. If you have skills that are valuable, everyone will get creative, especially in places where there is a shortage of good people.

- Keep an eye on trends in your workplace and in your industry. Even in places where there is downsizing, there is always some hot area of activity where resources, money, and people are building up.

- Concretize your ideas by making a proposal that outlines what you want to do. Include tangible ideas—essentially, talking points—that your employer can respond to. Your ideas don't need to be outlined down to the last detail; just putting them on paper will give them import.

- Propose how you will benefit the organization, even though the hidden—or not-so-hidden—agenda is how to benefit yourself.

- Be clear with yourself about trade-offs you may have to make, especially in order to get the kind of reduced role you will find comfortable.

- When negotiating a salary for a part-time-work arrangement, one approach is to prorate your full-time salary according to the number of days you continue to work. But be open to other options. Some companies have a policy that if you work twenty hours a week, then you'll be eligible for some benefits. If you won't get benefits, then simply prorating your salary is not sufficient.

Think of the Possibilities

There are a slew of different kinds of work arrangements turning up in companies and organizations throughout the country. Large corporations usually are the least flexible when it comes to part-time employment because they are bound by complex pension and insurance-benefit rules and regulations. That is why we often find small and midsized businesses and nonprofit organizations more flexible when it comes to hiring highly qualified people looking to work fewer hours and willing to work for commensurately lower pay. We spoke with Chicago-based business consultant David Hofrichter about this. He says that big companies are waking up to the idea that they need to make alternative deals with valuable employees considering retirement and that they need to become an active participant in the retirement process. Hofrichter is referring to ahead-of-the-curve companies that offer their longtime employees information about retirement planning as it relates to their pensions and 401(k)s, and, in addition, are willing to discuss possibilities for continued career opportunities. "A company may say, 'You can stay engaged with us in a number of ways and even move between various options.' Their incentive is the potential loss of critical knowledge, and recognition that the learning curve for replacement people is just too steep."

Here are a few of the different kinds of work options that are currently out there:

Part-time employment. This term traditionally refers to work of less than thirty-five hours a week. Most large corporations that don't use part-time workers as part of their ongoing strategy try to avoid having them because of legal and workplace-culture complexities. Instead, such corporations will organize different types of arrangements, such as retiring or giving buyouts to select employees and then rehiring them as consultants. A few businesses and organizations have developed creative new options for organizing part-time work, including setting up partial workweeks, seasonal months off, and compressed scheduling, all entailing fewer hours worked.

Job sharing. This is a flexible arrangement where two people—perhaps two older workers or an older worker and a mother with young children—work at the same job in part-time shifts. This idea has been around for many years. It is most often found to work for small businesses and nonprofit organizations.

Telecommuting. This refers to working from home or anywhere outside of the office. It may or may not be part-time, but the advantages to telecommuting over working in an office full-time are that we usually have greater autonomy over when and how work gets done and we can eliminate long commutes. The danger is that it can make us feel isolated from the work community.

Temping, or cycling. This can be part-time, project based, or seasonal, with an emphasis on the short term. Many organizations rent high-level people such as accountants, engineers, lawyers, marketing specialists, teachers, and even CFOs and CIOs to take on project management, prepare documents, and serve as replacement staff for open positions. Some 20 percent of temporary employees are professionals or managers, and the practice of hiring them as temps is growing rapidly. Temping, or cycling between jobs, offers us an excellent opportunity to control how we use our time, especially in order to travel and take seasonal breaks. And if we are looking for more permanent employment, temping gives us a chance to explore work in new fields, scout out desirable companies, and show off our abilities to potential employers.

Phased retirement. Like the sabbatical, phased retirement is a concept traditional in academia but not in business. However, this too is changing as more organizations become willing to negotiate reduced hours on a case-by-case basis for managers in highly skilled white-collar positions. Such arrangements allow us to either get ready for retirement or find out that we would rather extend our careers indefinitely. Joanne, who teaches at a rural college, says she felt some panic when she thought the guillotine was about to come down on her teaching career. The opportunity to phase out of her job allowed her to continue teaching one course on a subject she loved without having to attend departmental meetings or get involved in office politics. She describes it as "having my finger in the pie with lots of time to relax and explore other things."

Downshifting. This is another way we can reduce our work hours or move to a less stressful job. Many downshifters move from large-scale managerial initiatives with responsibility for budgets and teams of people, to a special project or a narrow area within a specific field. When Corinne was let go at age fifty-seven from her job as the executive director of marketing at a major media company, a savvy competitor offered her a three-day-a-week job handling a small, distinct segment of its overall marketing campaign. They also gave her full autonomy to develop it as she saw fit. She loves the work and also loves both the freedom to have a midmorning manicure and having time to volunteer for an organization that works with homeless men and women. She has been in this retirement job for more than ten years and doesn't expect to leave any time soon.

Bridge jobs. These can help blur the boundary between work and retirement. A bridge job may be a part-time or full-time position on a specific project for our employer, or it may be a different job for another employer. Organizations often see bridge jobs as a way for experienced workers to train and pass along valuable knowledge and skills to the next generation. A few companies take a slightly different approach to bridge jobs. IBM, for example, pays tuition and interim salaries to employees seeking new careers as science and math teachers.

> *My life is my investment portfolio. I put some of my resources in part-time work, some in volunteer work, and apportion the rest between travel, attending concerts, visiting friends, and being with my beautiful granddaughter. And if at any particular point the balance isn't right, I adjust it.*
>
> **—Mandy**

Going It on Your Own

If you've had it working for someone else, or, despite your searching, a salaried job hasn't materialized, it might be time to get inventive and make your own way. There are several kinds of independent-work options that offer you the freedom to decide how and how much you want to work.

Freelancer is a catch-all term for those of us who work independently to provide a wide variety of specialized services. A freelancer can be very similar to a consultant, although freelancers tend to handle more specialized tasks, and our pay is usually calculated on an hourly basis. Dentists, lawyers, trainers, coaches, babysitters and pet sitters, gardeners, electricians, and programmers are all technically freelancers, responsible for covering their own Social Security and IRS withholdings and insurance.

Consultants basically sell specific expertise and services to one or many clients. We may work on a single project or provide a range of services, in areas such as payroll, marketing, and training. Work is generally charged on a fee basis billed hourly or as a monthly or annual retainer. We usually don't receive benefits, such as 401(k) contributions or health care. On the plus side, we can choose the kinds of work we do and manage our personal time. On the other hand, it's either feast (too much work and no personal time) or famine (no money coming in and lots of time to spare). When we set ourselves up as consultants, it is important for us to have a clear idea of the specific services we are offering and to know how to explain what they are. Too often we oversell our skills and risk being seen as a jack-of-all-trades, not a useful label when clients are looking for an expert to fill a particular niche.

A *retiree casual* is neither retired nor casual. In a retiree-casual arrangement, we might return to work for our employer as early as the day after our "retirement" kicks in. This kind of setup requires that we work less than one thousand hours a year for our employer so that we qualify as a consultant with the IRS, a legality designed to protect full-time workers from being replaced by part-timers. As retiree-casual consultants we may work two days a week, or four hours a day, or full-time for less than six months. Hannah works two and a half days a week for the insurance company where she has been employed for the last twelve years. When she turned sixty-eight, she decided to work on a part-time basis. Although she continues doing much the same kind of work as before, she is not officially on staff but rather is considered a consultant on special projects who helps when things get hectic. About the transition, Hannah says, "I thought it would be difficult to give up control, but it hasn't been because I still feel connected to the work and the people." Organizations tend to like a retiree-casual arrangement because it helps them to retain knowledge we absorbed during our years of working for them. It also gives them a good source to draw on for job sharing, dealing with cyclical business patterns, and filling the position of someone on leave. We like it because it offers us time to explore other options.

Resource pools are a useful way for organizations to get access to our high-level managerial and technical knowledge after we retire. What they offer us is a way to stay connected with them in much the same way universities stay connected with alumni. Effectively, we are consultants readily available to be tapped to attend a brainstorming meeting, be part of a focus group to discuss strategies and ideas, share our expertise with others, work on specific problems, or mentor others. And we have a lot to offer as part of a pool of retired workers who know our former organization's culture and work styles, are already trained, have organizational skills and knowledge, and cost nothing to recruit.

Contingency workers, also known as contract workers, are independents usually in fields such as accounting, finance, law, information technology, sales and marketing, and human resources. As contract workers, we provide professional services for companies on an as-needed, generally short-term-project basis. Often this arrangement entails working very hard for short periods of time and then having time off with no work at all. Like most self-employed contractors, we receive few traditional workplace benefits, such as job security, health and retirement benefits, and paid vacations.

Through *seasonal jobs*, some companies have developed creative ways to manage employees who migrate south during the winter months and vice versa. Home Depot and Borders are just two companies that have created "snowbird" jobs so that some of their workers can continue working, wherever they are. Generally, these are for low-paying, low-skilled jobs, but with some creativity, perhaps we can change that.

ARE YOU PSYCHED FOR A RETIREMENT CAREER?

Many of us don't know what our next stage will be like, and the truth is, we don't have to get it right from the start. After all, this is a process that will take us in many directions, with false starts, things tried and discarded, and expectations adjusted. Here are a few items to consider before you leave your full-time job for "something else":

- Do you know what your financial situation is? Assess your net worth and expected earnings from various sources and know how they stack up against projected expenses, including the cost of paying for things that benefits used to cover. Calculate exactly how having less income will affect your retirement savings. If the answer is not encouraging, stop here and go back to chapters 3 and 5.
- What are your attitudes, values, and limitations? Identify the things that make you tick and examine which ones are likely to

be as important to you and which are likely to be less so in your next stage. Is the urge to get ahead, compete for promotions, or manage large initiatives appealing? Will you be comfortable with less responsibility and control? Is it difficult to summon the energy to be "onstage" each and every day?

- Can you visualize your ideal retirement job? Think about the amount of time you want to work and how you would like to organize your time. How important are location and commuting distance to you? Will you be happy if you no longer have a leadership role?
- Have you talked to others? Peer groups are fabulous for gaining feedback and emotional support as you sort through issues, clarify your options, and make your decisions.
- Have you done your research? Read newspapers and magazines for information about new trends in retirement work. Go online and learn what certain companies are offering, especially those in your industry.
- Have you talked over your ideas with prospective employers? Explore the kinds of salaried and self-employment options that may be available in the short- and long-term futures.
- Have you spoken with current and former employers? Let them know you are interested in exploring retirement-work options.
- Have you explored enrolling in retirement career–development programs or courses? Many are available online. Most charge a fee to guide you through the introspection process and help you figure out if you are ready—emotionally and financially—to retire. They then offer exercises to help you identify what will satisfy you and help you communicate who you are and what you want, and they show you how to develop an action plan. (See the Resources section for more information.)
- Is signing up with a life coach a useful option? Life coaches are trained to help you think clearly about your goals and values and develop strategies for getting yourself to where you want to go. (See pages 73–74 and the Resources section for more information on life coaches.)

PART

III

RECLAIMING
RETIREMENT

CHAPTER
7

I've Always Wanted to . . .

Barb is a Washington-based securities attorney who dreams about a little-studied Revolutionary War hero. It's not because she's horny. It's just that history is her passion. Over the years she has volunteered at a museum of American history and at other local historical sites. When she retires she wants to get a master's degree in history, which will give her a platform from which to pursue the object of her interest. Then she wants to go on for a doctorate and make a contribution to the field. She has a plan for and vision of how to make it happen.

Michele thought about moving from Boston to the California coast to try out retirement life. As an activist, however, she found it very hard to feel alive in a West Coast community that she describes as a Lake Wobegon look-alike where even the garbage dump is so gorgeous that visitors go there to admire it. Worst of all, she says, no one gets upset about anything. And that upset her. So she moved back to the East Coast, "to a less perfect place," to be with friends who lust to read and "know what's going on." There she feels comfortable, around people who share her anger, distress, outrage, and commitment to change the world, or at least to make it a little better. She knows what makes her happy.

> *I need groups of people in my life so I can absorb their vitality. They make me feel I can move along.*
>
> —Michele

This is our time, when freedom and opportunity coincide. It is when we can dream of really having it all. If we are in good health and have enough saved, anything seems possible. (Mostly) everything is doable. We have the capability and the freedom to take on big dreams and big goals. This is an exhilarating idea.

It can also be a confusing time. With so many options in front of us, how can we decide what is the right choice? Our dreams are as individual and as contradictory as we are. We say we want to travel widely. We also want a house in the country that we never leave. We look to move, downsize, and buy all-new furniture. We also prize familiar objects and people. We need to serve others and give back. We like to pamper ourselves. We hold back aging with surgical nips and tucks. We also tell our age to others and show off our gray hairs. We crave an action-packed life filled with new people and adventures. We also appreciate local activities with people we know well. We long to try things we have never done before. We feel comfortable building on what we know and love. We're ready to get going. We're paralyzed by old fears.

What Is Stopping Us?

It is difficult for Louise to focus on what will make her happy. Her dream was to write poetry, and she has written volumes, but admits that she's "never had the courage to submit them for publication." Fantasies about travel to exotic places are subdued because "it costs money." She also thought that she'd like to paint, something she had tried in art school, when she was a girl, but she would need to take a course "to get my 'eye' back." When she reflects on her career, she knows that her success had a lot to do with her energy and drive. Today she thinks those qualities are not relevant and therefore wonders, "Why bother?"

It is easy for us to feel that things aren't worth doing unless there are extrinsic rewards similar to the ones we got from work. The problem is that this can prevent us from embracing life, even while we seek pleasurable activities. And whining about why we can't do something just adds to our sense that we lack control over our lives and prevents us from reaching for what we want. It keeps us from taking chances. And when we risk nothing—we risk everything.

> *Sometimes it is easier to accept a bad known than to think about the unknown. Some people who can't or won't make choices will just stay on a bad treadmill and become more miserable each day. I think it's about getting in motion.*
>
> **—voice from a peer group**

When we come off a long career involving intense time commitments, new demands on our energy and time can push us into a self-preservation mode. Once removed from the work scene that defined us, we may sense danger in relinquishing our body and soul to something new. We may even become "commitment-phobic," afraid and reluctant to invest in something that will monopolize our time, energy, and passion once again. Although this attitude is understandable, it unfortunately blocks our inclination to make decisions, take up the new challenges that will excite us, and grab opportunities when they appear.

> *I had several ideas float through my consciousness but have not as yet followed up on them. I suspect this is reluctance on my part to be in a situation that is as all-consuming as my last job.*
>
> **—Marsha**

Part of the problem could be that we really don't know what we want. After Patricia retired from her job as an administrator at a large city hospital several years ago, she was comfortable as long as she knew each morning how her day would unfold. But this didn't entirely alleviate feelings that she was without direction and needed something more. It's not that she was bored on a daily basis; it's just that she thought of her life as tedious.

Too often we spend a great deal of energy trying to protect ourselves from boredom, as if it were an affliction to be avoided at any cost. That kind of thinking served us well when the only way we could effectively cope with all of our obligations was to plan out each minute with precision. And it may be comfortable for many of us to continue to function this way, since it is what we know best. But we also need to give ourselves permission to be without a plan, or even to become bored. In her excellent book *Inventing the Rest of Our Lives,* Suzanne Braun Levine wisely says, "It takes time to break free." It begins, she emphasizes, when we enter a fertile void where the things we have done before no longer apply, yet we haven't figured out how to replace them. Entering this void as ambitious, competitive, agenda-driven women, we must learn, she says, to take the "long, slow, deep breath—the gathering of strength"—that will lead us to a place where our priorities and goals "are less rigidly managed and perhaps more deeply felt."

LETTING GO

It takes a while to learn how to shake off the feelings of obligations and "should dos" that drive you ever forward. To help give yourself the mental and emotional space for a true you to emerge, consider doing some of the following:

- Go on a yoga or meditation retreat, immerse yourself in gardening, play with a child, take long walks, watch an ocean wave—engage in nonintellectual, noncompetitive experiences that allow you to suspend previous definitions of who you are and what you do.
- Think about those things that genuinely attract you when you read or watch TV. If you are no longer obligated to obtain certain kinds of information, observe what draws you in other directions. Are you a news junkie? Do you watch cooking shows? Do you clip articles about hospice volunteers? Do you yearn to weave fabrics, compete in the Iditarod, or go for your Ph.D.?
- Seek to experience something totally new. For instance, if you are a type-A personality, leave blocks of unscheduled time in your calendar for just daydreaming or doing whatever pops into your mind, and avoid making plans in advance to fill that time.
- Discard dreaded obligations. Decline to serve yet another term on your condo board. Excuse yourself from the next charity ben-

efit that doesn't interest you. Learn to say no to things that use up your time but are unsatisfying.

- Be open-minded and expect inspiration to arrive from unexpected sources. A visit to a local zoo may rekindle your desire to advocate for wildlife education. A newspaper article about house sales may inspire you to create a service business offering advice about feng shui.
- Say yes to new experiences. Join a friend on a spelunking expedition. Learn how to perform a Japanese tea ceremony.

What Makes Us Happy?

We are at a point in our lives where we have more time than ever before to think about what genuinely makes us happy. It is not a question we could easily have asked ourselves at an earlier time, when we were focused on meeting obligations and commitments. Most people think that wealth is a key source of pleasure and that it will free us from anxiety, but money turns out to be only relatively important as long as our basic needs are met. Work can be a source of happiness, but our positive feelings about it may wane as we age, and this is often exacerbated by changes in rules, standards, and people. Having many friends is also considered vital to finding happiness, but that is not always sufficient. Much as it is with noise and smell and pain, the intensity of happiness we experience and how we remember this feeling is different for every one of us. Not only that, it's difficult to self-monitor the quality and quantity of our happiness because our feelings can fluctuate minute to minute and day to day.

Many experts suggest that life is as good as it is going to get when several things come together for us: we become fully engaged, we chal-

> *This is the first time in my life I've ever spent so much time with people my own age. It makes me realize how important just doing what I want to do in life is.*
>
> **—voice from a peer group**

lenge ourselves, and we do something that has meaning. It is a simple yet profound equation. Certainly, pursuit of enjoyment and pleasure contributes to our happiness, but it is not as essential as being challenged and engaged in a meaningful activity.

Engagement is the first important component. When we become engaged, we form a deeply intense connection with something or someone. It can happen with our work or when we sketch a landscape. It can happen when we spend an afternoon with our grandchildren or when we are learning about something. It can happen when we sing or when we pray. The important thing is how *intently* we do something, rather than *what* we do. Athletes talk about being in "flow"—a term coined by psychologist Mihaly Csikszentmihalyi—when they are completely at one with their activity. So do musicians, painters, mathematicians, gardeners, and mystics. On some level, conversing with friends, solving challenging puzzles, or being in love can put us in flow. For centuries, those who have practiced Eastern spiritual traditions such as Buddhism, or military arts such as tae kwon do, or creative arts such as ikebana, the Japanese art of flower arrangement, have reported experiencing this sense of total involvement and commitment. When we are immersed in something, nothing else seems to matter. And the enjoyment we get from such engagement can remain with us and motivate us to experience the feeling again and again.

The exhilaration we get from being fully engaged is not, however, in and of itself, enough to make us happy. We also need to be both capable and challenged. For example, if we play tennis but our hand-eye coordination isn't up to the task of placing the ball in our opponent's court, we will not enjoy the experience, no matter how hard we focus or feel tested. And if we play against someone like that and we are a good player, then we'll feel frustrated, not happy. But if we have the skills to play a game against a challenging opponent, and we focus on doing it well, then it is possible to experience flow. Alternatively, suppose that we have a talent for meeting and talking to people. If that is the case, then we will feel excited and engaged serving as a spokeswoman or an advocate for a cause or working as a docent at a museum.

But there's still one more component that needs to be added to round out the equation. Sustainable happiness requires more than just our being engaged and using our abilities for something we find challenging.

We also must do something that we find meaningful and reflects our values. Meaningful activities and experiences are all around us. We find meaning when we tutor a child or help build a school. Some of us find meaning when we raise money for a charity, or lobby for a new training program to improve literacy. We can experience meaning by driving someone to a doctor appointment, baking a cake, or caring for a loved one.

Felicia's ninety-four-year-old mother lives in France and had been in good health until a recent illness. Now she needs assistance, so Felicia went to help transfer her into a retirement home. She feels that nothing else is as important to her at this time as devoting herself to her mother's care. This may seem a curious example of happiness. But Felicia's life at this moment is about engagement (she is focused entirely on her mother's comfort and care), using her skills (she is an excellent organizer), challenge (she has to learn about resources available in France), and doing something that has meaning (helping a loved one).

> *To be absorbed in projects makes the day work, whether it is rainy or sunny, hot or cold.*
>
> —Robin

Pursuing this happiness equation doesn't mean we should abandon our search for enjoyment and pleasure on a daily basis, because both are also extremely important to the quality of our lives. Enjoyment and pleasure are great goals, just as long as they are not primary goals. We feel joy when we accomplish something that is beyond our expectations: a Pilates class at the gym is even more pleasurable when we discover that we can do most of the exercises; we feel a sense of joy when we express thoughtful ideas we didn't know we had during a discussion with others. And seeking pleasure requires neither full engagement nor even accomplishment. We readily find pleasure as we shop, go to the movies, eat good food, laugh, dance, play with a dog, or spend time with others. During the last century, enjoyment and pleasure were considered the ultimate goals of retirement. They were to be sought through leisure activities such as golf and cards, collecting porcelain figures, drinking alcohol, or just relaxing by taking a passive pose and holding it for as long as possible. Now we understand that, although there is nothing wrong with any of those pursuits, the search for enjoyment and pleasure alone is not enough to make us happy.

Where Is the Passion?

We get the advice "Follow your passion" from nearly everyone, but what does this mean? We can be passionate about music, art, and politics. We can be passionately against brutality and homelessness. We can experience passion when having sex. We can be passionate about investing in stocks or skiing. Most of all we can be passionate about our grandchildren. Whatever it is that turns us on, when we have a particular passion, we know it.

Kristin played the cello as an undergraduate, but then she studied psychology and built her career as a psychologist, married, and raised two children. Making music was not a part of her adult life. She retired at sixty-three with the dream of playing the cello again, and of playing nearly as well as she had some forty years earlier. Eight and sometimes ten hours a day of practice did not come easily at first, but eventually she recaptured her lost skills and the rapture of making music. She found excellent teachers to study with at a nearby college and began to hold "salons" in her house so that fellow musicians could perform and experiment outside of an academic setting. Her passion for music defined her retirement totally, and eventually led to an invitation to play her cello with a city symphony orchestra.

But what if we don't have an all-consuming, or even a particular, passion? In a group of women talking about what they would do in retirement, a few spoke with enthusiastic certainty about their specific passions. One wanted to open a garden-nursery business; another, to become a full-time painter; and a third, to teach ballroom dancing. Their energy filled the room. That is, until a fourth speaker meekly admitted that she didn't have a passion and didn't know what she wanted to do. Her comment opened a floodgate of similar concerns among the rest of the women. All of them had done many different things during their lives. But most of them agreed that they had no interest in returning to those earlier interests and activities. They had no single passion to reclaim.

Catherine, a teacher, sees having a passion as an opportunity and feels it's important to act on it. The idea of missing an opportunity horrifies her. Her problem is that she doesn't know what her passion will be when it's time for her to retire. She says she isn't a "craftsy" person and cannot see herself making pottery or weaving baskets, as if those are somehow standards she should be targeting. She knows she'll be a wonderful grandmother when the time comes, and her friends tell her that will be her passion. But she also wants to "do something worthwhile, and have fun!" She describes her commitment to wellness as a passion and manages to exercise every day, eat healthy foods, and still enjoy a cocktail. She also knows that won't be enough. So she is searching outside of herself for the right cause to do battle for.

> *I did not have one particular passion I wanted to pursue. I simply wanted the time to find out who I am. Now that I've retired, I'm looking deep inside myself to ask what things really matter and what I want to do about them.*
>
> **—Carol**

Not all of us have one overriding passion or interest. Interests and enthusiasms come in all sizes and shapes, and many of us want to enjoy a number of them concurrently. When Linda turned sixty-two, she was no longer stimulated by her work for an art-book publisher, and she hated the commute. She dreamed of spending more time pursuing her love for working with horses—specifically, in order to train a young Iberian mare in dressage. In addition, she wanted to use her early experience in museum management to help her local historical society improve its nautical museum, which, she saw, was a unique gem in need of support and the kind of fresh energy she could bring to it. And as her interest in the community deepened, she became active in causes that included the civic association's effort to improve quality of life through a downzoning project to prevent overdevelopment, and she also regularly contributed stories for the local newspaper. As someone who had been a multitasker when she worked full-time, volunteered at school, and raised her son as a single parent, she saw no reason to limit her focus to one particular direction just because she was retired. Linda is happiest when she is involved in several meaningful projects and tasks that challenge her.

FINDING PASSION

The word "passion" may be problematic because it suggests an intensity of focus and concern that you might not feel about any one thing. So let's talk instead about yearnings, interests, and enthusiasms—the kinds of things that motivate you to get involved and take action. One way to find things that will tempt you in retirement is to answer these questions:

- What did you dream about doing when you were a child? Did you yearn to see the heavens or become a rock singer, a veterinarian, or a dancer before you moved on to more practical pursuits? Recall and listen to those yearnings, because they are a part of you. Then look for ways to rekindle them: take a course in astronomy and meet with other stargazers to discuss new findings; find a rock group to join through a music school or online bulletin board; take dance classes; or volunteer at an animal shelter.
- Where are your childhood friends? Often you can reconnect with your earlier, prework self and interests through the people you were once close to. Use your family network or the Internet to track down old friends, and rekindle friendships in person or over the Internet, away from your family and pressing obligations.
- What were your youthful activities? Search through attics and long-stored-away boxes for your childhood diary and other mementos. Gaze at family photographs to recall places and activities that made you happy. Look for clues in the kinds of clothes you wore and objects around you. Did you design and sew your clothes? Were you an avid tennis player? Did you collect canned foods to help feed poor children? Don't laugh off these enterprises. They were real and they were yours, so consider that you might find them compelling again.
- What were your favorite subjects in school? Long before you

were required to major in a particular subject or focus on a career, what excited your imagination? Was it an art class or a chemistry lab? Did you join your high school or college theater group? Write poetry? Were you part of an a cappella group?

- What hobbies attracted you? Did you collect dolls, pennies, or adventures? Did you carry a sketch pad wherever you went? Did you read long novels? Did you enjoy decorating your dollhouse or first apartment? Recall those interests and consider exploring new versions of those activities.

- What are you naturally drawn to when reading, watching TV, or Googling? Do politics or the arts fascinate you? Do you avidly read about other cultures? Do you clip recipes?

- What motivates you at work? Skip back to pages 67–68 to review the things about work that stimulate you. Pare the list to a small, manageable size and think about ways to keep those motivating factors in your life. For instance, if you enjoy networking with clients and coworkers, think about how to use this skill in a new way.

- What things have always been a part of your life, even when you had no personal time to pursue them? Do you enjoy collecting antique advertising signs, or bonnets? Do you follow local politics and try to support specific causes? Would you like to know more about them? Now may be the time to vigorously pursue such interests.

- What regrets do you have about who you might have been or what you might have done in your life? Of course, you can't change the past, but you can follow up on something you have always wanted to do. Do you regret never having had a bat mitzvah, getting a degree, seeing Machu Picchu at dusk, finding distant relatives? Think about your regrets and how you might alter them.

- What would you do if you lived elsewhere? Did you settle in an area because of family, or work that no longer excites you? Are your grandchildren in another state? Is your home now too big? Is the climate inhospitable? Do you want easy access to museum exhibitions, concerts, and theater? Do you want to be able to take long walks on the beach each day? Where do you want to go?

Figuring Out What You Want

Many of us say that once we leave the workplace, we have absolutely no desire to return. We take pleasure in rediscovering that person we may have glimpsed back in our college days or before a time when work and family responsibilities subdued our unproductive impulses. For many of us the simple act of freeing up time in our calendars is a heady experience. Friends can suddenly be enjoyed at leisure and not in increments measured by lunchtime meetings. Time spent creating a family photo album for our grandchildren is measured in loving hours rather than productive minutes. Not since we were young adults have our options been as varied—constricted now solely by our lack of imagination. Some of us jump in with abandon, but some of us find that such freedom can be paralyzing and must be taken one step at a time.

> *I spent my life responding to externally imposed schedules. Now I'm in charge!*
>
> —Laura

When Fran retired from her position as the director of development for a national nonprofit organization at age sixty-six, she felt she was on vacation. Actually, that wasn't an especially good thing, because she constantly thought about whether a particular grant had come through or if the office had made a follow-up call on a pending proposal. Four weeks later an opportunity to travel for a wedding gave her a physical break in her schedule that helped ease her adjustment. Since then she has been building her own structure, but she feels the chaos of not being fully organized. For example, she thinks she has gotten sloppy and can't always find things. While she doesn't feel awful about it, Fran admits to not feeling at the top of her game, as she had when she worked full-time. She tries to develop her own patterns by volunteering this day and maybe that day, exercising on other days, and then occasionally consulting and attending meetings for her part-time work. She observes that "there's not that external pull to set certain time frames or certain ways of organizing things." Her monthly peer group helps her sort through this issue and has inspired her to be a little more creative and dare to worry less about structure.

> *The principal change in my life is that I have choices about how I spend my time. I could do nothing at all if I want. I can stay in bed, read the newspaper all morning, or I can get up and go to exercise class. I have choices I've never had before.*
>
> **—Mandy**

Lois has a successful career as a professor, a business consultant, and an author. One would expect her to have carefully planned ahead for each phase of her life. Yet she describes herself as one of those people who wait to see what turns up and how it plays out. Structure doesn't seem to be important to her, which she thinks has probably kept her from having as much work-related anxiety as other people. She considers herself lucky because as each phase of her life has wound down, something else has always happened. It's not as if she expects someone to hand her a fabulous opportunity. Yet she will be quick to respond when something appealing seems right. As simple as that sounds, she knows well enough that luck is about putting yourself in the right place so that when an opportunity arises, you are there to take advantage of it.

When Suzie was in her midfifties, she planned to retire in three years. Everyone who knew her, especially her husband, thought she would become bored and incapable of adjusting to a less hectic pace. But she felt it was the right thing, as long as she could make a plan. She identified three things that she wanted to achieve: she wanted to become physically fit, do more volunteer work, and learn how to enjoy the now. Suzie describes herself as a woman who wants to give to and get the most out of every moment, every encounter, and every conversation. So she was concerned about how she would fill her day. Her retirement involved moving from England, where she had been a partner in a consulting firm, back to San Francisco, where she had lived previously. While the furniture slowly made its way there, she and her husband traveled throughout Europe. She refers to this as a "transition aid" that helped occupy her first three months of retirement and allow her to line up things that fit with her objectives. Three years later she had met her fitness goal through going to yoga classes twice a week and working out at a gym four times a week. She also felt fortunate that her church community welcomed her back with invitations to help with ushering and bringing gifts to the altar. Being able to reengage with the church and be part of that embracing community helped her find purpose. Now she happily does many different things for them, and, in addition, she also helps two nonprofit organizations with such things as performance management (a skill from her consulting days) as well as finance- and audit-committee membership and meeting facilitation. Regarding her third goal, to slow down and enjoy the now, she says that one really tested her patience, a quality she doesn't have in abundance. To accomplish it, she tried hard to focus on this goal and take additional time to build relationships. It's an ongoing commitment. "I think I had a fairly good idea of what I wanted my retirement to look like, and I've been able to realize that 'picture' fairly well. What is interesting to me now is how my retirement life will change in the future." That's because she knows full well that transitions never stop, and she intends to keep planning ahead.

Marsha is thrilled to not be driven by another's agenda for the first time in her life. When she figures out what she wants to do, it will be her own thing. It may be little else than concentrating on being a grandmother. She says that if someone comes after her to serve on a board or committee, she will run the opposite way. After years of administrating a nongovernmental organization, she doesn't want to be in charge of anything again. She finds that being a grandmother is "the best." It feels different from when she had her own children. She's not sure why, except that she thinks she approaches child rearing with more wisdom and more perspective, and she has much more time, so she can just sit and watch her grandson learn and react. She admits that she missed this while raising her son. "I've got lots to learn about being a grandmother, and that's another learning curve. I ask myself what I can do to be better at it. Those are the things I have my antennae out for right now. I don't think of myself as an especially creative person, so I've got to think of ways to reach the child. It's an amazing journey, more amazing and compelling to me right now than any work I could do."

Marsha was caught by surprise at the intensity of her feelings for her grandchild and her desire to devote much of her attention to him. Certainly, it was not something she had planned for before she decided to retire. Surprise can be a big factor for us, and it is valuable to give ourselves permission and time for it to spring forth. At this point in our lives, we have an opportunity to try out something that we may not have considered before. It's not about risk; it's about giving ourselves a chance to explore, test, and try out different directions and to open up space in order to find new experiences. The wonderful part of all this is that if we decide that our new course isn't right, we can swing off in another direction.

WHAT IS YOUR DREAM?

Do any of these dreams inspire you? Add your personal dreams to this list.

Start my own business
Travel with my family and grandchildren
Write my memoirs
Go back to school
Get religious training
Build a dream home
Become an artist
Have adventures in foreign cultures
Become an antiques dealer
Take ballet lessons and dance
Join an a cappella group
Sit on nonprofit boards
Become a hospice volunteer
Hike all the mountain peaks in the Adirondacks
Take cooking lessons in China
Become a yoga instructor
Design a line of clothing
Sail the Turquoise Coast
Teach English as a second language
Go on an archaeological dig
Own and run a B and B

Become a master gardener
Volunteer at an opera house
Act on stage
Advocate for better schools
Read great books
Learn more about technology
Compete in a tennis tournament
Become an interior decorator
Run a marathon
Learn to scuba dive
Train and work as an EMT
Advocate for clean food and water
Teach others about great art
See an unfilled need and fill it

Once you identify your dreams ask yourself:

What must I do to realize them?
How can I research information?
Will I need special training, and where can I find it?
How much of my time will it consume?
Whom do I know who will share his or her experiences with me?
Am I prepared to take on the challenges necessary to reach my
   goal?
Will following my dream require life changes? If so, what are they?
What will I need to sacrifice to attain my goals?
Will I have fun?
Will my current finances allow me to realize my dreams?
What can I do to fund my dreams?
Do I want someone to come along with me?
Will my partner invest in my dream?
When can I start?

Expectations Versus Reality

Having expectations about what we will do when we retire is valuable, if
for no other reason than that it helps to get us moving. However, once

we get started our adventures may take us down unanticipated paths. The idea of what to expect next overwhelmed Gail. Although she no longer enjoyed the work at her publishing-communications agency, it was an important part of her life, and the idea of retiring and being at home cleaning closets sent her into a funk. Her husband, an artist, had his work, but she felt she would be at loose ends without her own. When she joined a TTN peer group, she was relieved to discover a label for her situation—"clueless"—and to be with others who felt the same. The group encouraged her to explore what she would risk if she no longer had her office. Of course, it started with a list of things she liked and disliked about her work. On the Like side was *Having freedom to decide what needs to be done and how to do it without reporting to someone else* (autonomy). Next were *Exposure to new ideas, Being sought after and respected by clients I respect, Being able to stretch intellectually and creatively with colleagues who are also friends*, and *Being able to rely on someone who can deal with computer glitches and office problems*. At the top of the Dislike side of the list were *Repeating things I have done before, Having sole responsibility for the office rent and payroll*, and *Keeping my staff working at full capacity*. Then she made a list of the things she was good at, which included being entrepreneurial, perceptive about others' goals and agendas, confident about tackling something new, and able to communicate clearly and challenge traditional assumptions. Next, the peer group urged her to list her goals for the future. At the top of that list was her goal to become a better horseback rider and do things she had never done before, such as raise and train a foal. In addition, she wanted to get involved in furthering women's issues; visit museums; exercise more; travel to exotic locales; read to kids; take classes on public policy, cooking, and bridge; and continue to consult part-time on specific work projects that interested her. Her idea was to launch this plan within two years, to coincide with the end of her office lease and her sixty-first birthday. Although she told her employees well in advance, she avoided officially announcing her retirement, ostensibly out of concern about future client referrals, but in truth this reflected her lack of confidence about letting go. So when the time came she left without much fanfare, which seemed a bit anticlimactic after forty years of working in a tight-knit industry.

During the next few months, Gail tested what it was like to be without an office, staff, or structure and found that it wasn't an especially joyous period. Sometimes she was downright bored and spent too many hours playing solitaire on the computer, which she knew indicated a degree of depression. But she expected something would bubble up, because, above all else, she hated feeling bored and lazy and knew that would motivate her to action. So she treaded water and remained open to new ideas and opportunities.

Three years later Gail compared her earlier lists with her current situation. Several items at the top of her wish list had been nonstarters. Her horsemanship had improved, but no more so than if she had ridden on weekends and vacations, as before. And the foal she had wanted to raise and train never materialized. Both goals seemed less compelling once she had unlimited time to spend on them. Going to museums and taking exotic vacations were also not the major attractions she had anticipated. She hadn't signed up for classes. At first she had taken on several clients, but, no longer eager to keep on top of the information needed to do an outstanding job, she had turned down further opportunities.

What did she do? She became even more involved in an organization that focuses on women's issues. She volunteered at a local zoo, where she spoke to visitors about animals and wildlife conservation. She became an advocate for a primary school in East Africa, where she spent several weeks organizing a library for students who had previously had access to textbooks only. She also tackled something that had not appeared on her wish list, although, in truth, it had been in the back of her mind for many years. The idea that sparked her enthusiasm was to write a book to encourage women to question and redefine traditional expectations for retirement. For Gail, it was a creative concept that was hers to develop; it was intellectually stimulating; it took her throughout the country to listen to and brainstorm with extraordinary women who were finding new, resourceful ways to reinvent themselves; it fulfilled her need to be involved with something that has meaning; and it allowed her to give something of value to an organization—The Transition Network—that she respected. And it taught her that making a transition is an evolving process that requires time, patience, and an open mind.

The Search for Meaning

We need to express spirituality in our lives, and that becomes more apparent to us as we grow older. Spirituality and religion are sometimes thought of as one and the same, but, while we may have a spiritual side, we might not be religious. If we belong to or as we seek to return to a house of worship, we connect with religious beliefs and the rituals that are a part of them. Such actions affirm those things that have meaning for all of us, whether we worship in a formal setting or not at all. What we share are concerns about our relationships with our family and our friends, our relationships with others and ourselves, and our relationship with the universe, all built on love, compassion, and respect for life.

Getting in touch with our spirituality can happen at odd times and in odd places. Arriving at the top of a mountain and gasping at a magnificent view is just one example of connecting with our spiritual side. Listening to a beautiful piece of music can do it. So can contemplating a poem or learning to meditate. We can feel it happen when we see a child's smile as we enter a room or when we glimpse a beautiful bird on a walk through the woods.

Linda says that her friends "started going to church later in life because they saw the pearly gates looming up ahead and wanted to be sure they could get in." There is something to that. It is a kind of coming to terms with our lives and viewing our accomplishments in light of what is truly valuable. And there's also the fear of going to hell!

After her retirement from a publishing company, Camille became a lay minister at her church. "I like that best because in the Catholic faith we believe you are offering the body and blood of Christ." When she offers the Communion wafer, she looks people in the face while giving them the body of Christ. "That's the most rewarding thing I can do."

Sometimes the strength and stability of our spirituality may be compromised by events we commonly encounter as we age. Major change can rock our beliefs. Loss of a loved one and the loss of our own independence are big factors. Sometimes change is forced upon us by such things as retirement, having to move from our home, and getting a divorce. These things can fill us with anger as well as self-doubt and guilt, leading toward depression. Connecting with and holding on to our spirituality are important to recovering from such changes and finding our way. How we deal with them and reclaim hope can usually be anticipated by how we dealt with other potentially devastating events during our lives. If we normally see the positive side of things, then we can expect our natural optimism to help us get through a crisis. If we tend to expect the worst, then we may need help from others to navigate a change.

> *Spiritual renewal means asking myself, Who am I, what are my values, and how should I live these values? When I have my "exit interview" with God, I don't want to say, "Oh, I meant to do that, but everyday life sort of took up too much time."*
>
> **—Laura**

Creativity

A close association exists between spirituality, creativity, and nature. Each involves our being able to step beyond our analytical selves into another realm. Creativity draws on our innermost emotions and our imagination. In the act of creating, we often feel the kind of flow described earlier. And that experience can be as, or more, important than any product or activity it leads to. It can even help us recover from negative experiences or loss. We needn't be an artist or a poet to qualify as a creative person. Philosopher Rollo May describes creativity as "the process of bringing something new into being." And that can mean coming up with a way to raise funds for a charity, or the act of starting up a discussion group. The point is that we needn't have something to hang in a gallery or get published in order to be creative.

> *I love the idea of quiet contemplation, of Zen and yoga, which have left me calm, recharged, and committed to going on relaxed and positive.*
>
> **—Kari**

Like spirituality, the act of being creative gives us a sense of balance, control, and integrity in our lives. There are a handful of well-known woman artists who either first discovered their creativity late in life or continued to be enormously productive well into their eighties and nineties. Primitive artist Grandma Moses first comes to mind. So does sculptor Louise Nevelson, who believed that "when you put together things that other people have thrown out, you're really bringing them to life—a spiritual life that surpasses the life for which they were originally created."

Actress Ruth Gordon, a fifty-year show-business veteran, accepted her first Oscar at age seventy-two, saying, "I can't tell you how encouraging a thing like this is for a young actress like myself." There will be more of us added to lists of older achievers as we age and enthusiastically take on creative endeavors. But not all creative achievements will or should blaze in neon lights. There is the kind of creativity that changes the world: think of Mother Teresa or Madame Curie. And there is the kind that allows us to express ourselves in ways that are meaningful to us and perhaps a few others. Think about someone who makes a gorgeous birthday cake or starts a book drive for a library. Most of us are imaginative and inventive on a small scale. The level of our creativity is not important. What is important is the process of being creative, which originates from our individual capabilities and allows us to shape an idea that hadn't existed before. Some of us create by thinking analytically or spatially. Others are able to move expressively. And some of us have intuitive visions of how to improve our lives and the lives of others.

> *I will produce art. I think I will create large, welded sculptures, maybe work in neon . . . The sky's the limit.*
>
> **—Emily**

Theresa, formerly an attorney with a government agency, now studies modern dance about three times a week because it gives her an opportunity to change her direction totally, from analytical work to art. She thinks her desire to create reflects a human need all of us have. "When we were young kids in school, we loved to draw, sing, paint, and dance, but then we had to make a living. And since few of us could do it in the arts, we went off to other things and lost touch with the creative side of our personality. I want to get that side of me back."

> *Imagination is the highest kite one can fly.*
> —Lauren Bacall

As we age we seem to need art in our lives more than ever before. Even if we personally are not artistic, we seek out the creativity of others as we join garden tours, volunteer to be docents at museums, or visit local artists' studios. Evelyn suggests a reason why this is true. A year into her retirement, she thought about taking up the piano again after a very long absence. The idea rattled around in her brain but went nowhere for months. Once or twice she took out her old sheet music and just laughed at how impossible it looked. She couldn't remember the notes or the time value of the symbols, and, she says, "I had begun to develop arthritis in my thumbs, and, of course, I would have to cut my nails, which had been very long and glamorous for at least twenty-five years." Despite that, she managed to find two courses—Piano Basics, Level 1.2, and Music Theory—and found someone she describes as a really wonderful piano teacher. Why has this been worth it to her? She knows she doesn't play as well as she did when she was young and that the virtuosity will never come back. But her teacher articulated one beautiful reason: "We aren't doing this so you can play in Carnegie Hall, although some pieces you will do beautifully. We are doing this so you can *touch the genius.*"

NURTURING CREATIVITY

Conditions must be right in order for creativity to blossom. To start, you need some time alone with periods of inactivity so that you can connect with yourself and focus without distractions. Until you do this, you cannot go on to the next steps, giving yourself over to daydreams and letting your mind wander in new directions. And once that happens, you have to be ready to grasp where your imagination leads you and be open to exploring and accepting what emerges without self-derision or cynicism. And, finally, you need the discipline to apply the techniques, thought processes, and trial-and-error repetition that will bring your creative endeavors to fruition.

Taking New Paths

Going off on a completely new path is a theme that runs through many of our stories about transitions. Janice Taylor is an illustration of someone who was determined to take a new direction. When she left her job at age forty-eight, she decided to turn her fifty-five-pound weight loss into an art project about her personal transformation and reinvention. Her goals were easily articulated: "I'm going to get famous first, and then I'll get a book deal." She admits she had little to base those goals upon, but that didn't stop her from walking out on a well-paying job in spite of the fact that everyone she knew was telling her she was crazy. Her rationale was that "if I continue working, I won't have time for what I really want to do." With little more than conviction supported by her unique vision, a terrific visual talent, and a seat-of-the-pants marketing savvy, she created the *Our Lady of Weight Loss* newsletter and a corresponding Web site, which together attracted a wide following and served as the basis for her successful book of the same title. "I listened to my inner voice and not to the naysayers," Janice says.

When Jacqueline Atkins was fifty-eight, she decided to go for a doctoral degree to pursue her longtime interest in textiles and her fascination with Japanese culture. For this former editor of several professional publications, it was a big step. "Taking my GREs was probably the most nerve-racking part of the whole process." In school she began to explore "propaganda" textiles created in Japan, the United States, and Great Britain around World War II. To her amazement the subject hadn't been explored much, which meant that she had an opportunity to make an important contribution to scholarship. Her research took her into private collections, textile designers' archives, and people's homes. More than once she remembers feeling awed when a Japanese elder brought out an unexpected treasure in the form of a Japanese kimono or wrapping cloth that had been in hidden storage for more than fifty years. "They had not even shown it to their children," she says. Six years later, Jacquie had her degree. She was also the curator of the touring museum exhibition Wearing Propaganda, which opened in New York City to prominent acclaim and scholarly praise, and she was editor of a book of the same title based on the exhibition.

> *I think you have to keep on challenging yourself: "Okay, what else is out there that I haven't tried and might like?"*
>
> —Jacquie

Many of us return to school, not necessarily to earn a degree, but for the pure pleasure of learning. Katie, who now works three days a week, likes to read college catalogs from cover to cover and choose lecture classes that appeal to her. The fact that learning staves off cognitive loss is a major reason why so many of us want to continue to learn and why adult education is directly linked with vital aging. Exposure to new ideas promotes our mental prowess and challenges our analytical skills. It also incites us to find our purpose and passions, challenges us to be self-aware, and increases our creative and spiritual capabilities. But perhaps the biggest single gain we get from attending classes is the opportunity to connect with others who share similar, or different, interests and enthusiasms.

LIFELONG LEARNING

Want to speak Italian, appreciate Picasso, learn about nutrition, or get online? Because more and more of us want to experience the joy of learning, there has been an enormous growth in all kinds of accredited and nonaccredited learning opportunities. Many are informal, community-based programs found through libraries, senior centers, public schools, museums, churches, clubs, and alumni organizations. The longest-running learning programs for people over fifty are the institutes for learning in retirement, known as ILRs. These programs and others like them have multiplied like lusty rabbits in small and large colleges and universities throughout the country. Some ILRs offer classes run by participants, who develop the curricula and teach the classes, while others are lecture format. Demand for lifelong-learning opportunities around the country has also prompted an increase in the number of classes and courses offered by community colleges. Most are fee based, but many American colleges and universities welcome older alumni to enroll tuition-free in classes. It seems that learning opportunities for seniors can be found almost everywhere: in shopping centers, through investment companies, labor organizations, hospitals, and banks, and online.

Jan Hively, founder of and senior adviser to the Vital Aging Network, based in Minneapolis, is a volunteer teacher at the Osher Lifelong Learning Institute at the University of Minnesota, one of many such programs available at colleges and universities around the country. People interested in this program usually pay a small fee each year that entitles them to take as many courses as they want. Jan notes that a lot of new retirees focus much of their lives around their courses, taking Spanish-language, bridge, and bicycling classes, participating in travel programs, and much more.

After Michele moved to New York from Boston, she interviewed for admission to the Institute for Retired Professionals at the New School, a program that offers peer-designed and peer-taught courses. This New School program was the first of its kind and is now widely replicated in many areas throughout the United States. The way it works, says Michele, is that first you apply and are interviewed by an admissions committee. Once you are accepted, she says, often two people decide on a course they want to teach together and develop a study guide for thirteen programmed sessions. "I find that generally about twenty people attend a class, with discussions occurring much like they do in book clubs." Michele enjoys the wide variety of good discussions and the people she meets. She says that most are interested in taking courses on topics such as *Ulysses,* or Gilbert and Sullivan, short stories, or international literature. But she says there is also a course on time, another on physics, and one on art. Since she is not eager to teach a class, her contribution is to serve on a committee or help develop programs.

> *I am challenging myself with my art classes. I'm not just painting. I'm learning. I'm studying. I'm going to exhibits, I'm reading, I'm pushing myself. I'm not doing just what I know.*
>
> —Zana

Risk Taking

Going back to school, starting up our own business, and acting in a play all involve taking risks. Often, risk arises when we take a chance on something we might never have considered before. Most of us say we are not risk takers, for we see risk as part of a very broad spectrum rather than as an either-or calculation. How do we think about the risk of investing in high-growth stocks? Does that risk compare with that taken by someone who gets on a raft to escape from Cuba? What is the risk of taking a new job or moving across the country? If a high-wire artist falls and there is a safety net, did she really take a risk? Most of the time we don't think about taking risks; we simply do what needs to be done because we have no other choice. Often we do something to avoid pain and discomfort—sometimes staying in place can be more painful than taking action.

One woman defines risk as putting herself in a position where she is not in control of her environment. Another says risk means doing everything other than what is expected. Still others feel that risk is trying new behaviors or leaving behind what we know well in order to attempt something that is foreign to us. But, looking at it from another perspective, others suggest that we risk our ability to be creative and playful when we are overly preoccupied with order and tradition.

For thirty-three years Alice and her husband lived in Atlanta. They hadn't intended to stay there all that time, but the work was interesting and life was good. They decided to retire, he from a professorship in art history, she, in her early sixties, from her psychotherapy practice. They were drawn to San Francisco, a city Alice thought of as "a candy box of opportunities." During a weekend visit to the Bay Area to see their daughter who lived there, they heard about a small architectural gem of a house. Alice calls it her soul place. They decided to make "an enormous leap." It meant leaving behind their other daughter, a new grandchild, and numerous friends in Atlanta. She describes the experience of starting life in San Francisco as akin to facing a blurry canvas, to which, she hoped, professional contacts and a lively art community would provide definition and texture. But she really didn't know whether people would be interested in what she had to offer. Not only that, they were moving from a reasonably priced area to one of the most expensive places in America. As a result, living their dream meant they had to downsize and leave behind the kind of space needed to install a dishwasher or put up family and friends. But Alice feels that she has moved back to a simpler way of doing things and that this has renewed her optimism and energy.

> *For me risk is traveling on new terrain with no familiar road signs and having to figure it out along the way.*
>
> *—Sherry*

Women are presumed to be risk averse in business, although it is well known that we control more than 50 percent of privately held companies, and more than half of us say we willingly take above-average financial risks. And woman executives in high-tech companies say that risk taking has been as important to their career development as having a broad knowledge base.

Because risk taking is thought to go hand in hand with being a successful leader, we spoke with executive-search expert Millicent McCoy about her interviews with candidates for top executive positions to learn more about the differences between the way men and the way women approach risk. She says that she would ask candidates to tell her about risks they had taken in their careers. "The men literally would puff out their chests and promptly tick off three or four different occasions when they had taken risks." However, when she asked women, she says, "they usually hesitated and said they didn't think they'd taken risks in their careers. But as the interview continued it would be apparent to me that they had taken enormous risks. They just didn't see it in those terms."

We all take various degrees of risk. Lois considers herself a gigantic chicken when it comes to physical risk and says you won't get her on a Jet Ski for anything. Financially, she is a moderate who seeks a balanced portfolio. Emotionally, she thinks she is a pretty big risk taker who prefers being "out there" to seeking safe ways to keep an emotionally level environment. She points as examples to her three marriages, her adoption of one husband's two young children, and her adoption of an infant. In her career, however, she feels she has been a very big risk taker who stood up and said things she felt needed to be said when no one else would, and she believes that that inclination continues in her retirement jobs.

Seeking Wider Adventures to Make a Difference

Many of us believe there is no adventure in playing it safe. We don't want *Here she lies and rests in peace* on our gravestones. We'd much rather have loved ones read, *Except that she died, she would have conquered the world.*

For Shirley, "adventure is international and means having another cultural sense, along with the expectation of meeting new people and learning how to navigate within a different culture." At sixty-four, after retiring from teaching college anthropology, Shirley contacted the Peace Corps and was chosen to teach teachers of English in Cape Verde. She lives there with basic comforts, although she says that going without normal American conveniences is not an issue for her, because, if necessary, she knows how to have a bath in a cup of water. She considers herself physically adventurous and loves connecting with another culture through meeting new people, and learning how to cook and care for herself in a different environment. " 'I want to learn more' is my mantra. I've always been interested in languages and linguistics, cooking, dancing and singing, and writing analytically in my journal."

While a two-year Peace Corps commitment is not for everyone, exotic travel appeals to many of us. Trekking in Uganda to see the mountain gorillas, hiking in Nepal, touring Vietnam, going on yoga retreats in India, and collecting crafts in Guatemala are just a few of the things we may never have thought about doing when we were younger. But now doing such things and traveling to such places seems not only desirable, but possible. Nelia, at sixty-eight, says she wants to do her difficult traveling now because she suspects that later on she won't be able to deal with some of the discomforts and difficulties she has encountered in her earlier visits to developing countries. Touring the easy, tourist-ready countries of Italy and France is on her agenda, but later.

When Felicia turned fifty she decided to do things she hadn't had the guts to do before. She decreed that every five years she would excite and challenge herself. At fifty she went on a twenty-three-day high-altitude hike across the Himalayas, at fifty-five she hiked the Andes in Peru, and at sixty she climbed to the top of Kilimanjaro. She says each trip "made me feel like a strong person." Sylvia is another intrepid traveler who hasn't let a divorce or back pain slow her down. At seventy she traveled to India for the first time and later that year booked herself on a cruise to the Antarctic because she had always wanted to see the penguins.

> *I was asked what surprised me most about my transition experience and realized it was how easy it had been.*
>
> —**Beverly**

How Many Transitions Does It Take to Find a Lightbulb?

Sometimes it takes several attempts before we find our particular adventure. Paola Gianturco is good friends with Dinah, an Ndebele bead worker in South Africa, with Rosa and the Shipibo potters in Peru, with Zofia and other flower painters in Poland, and with Mankorba and her group of mirror embroiderers in India. These women with world-altering dreams are "heroes," Paola says, who use money earned from selling their homemade traditional-style crafts to buy vegetables or maybe some meat, uniforms, shoes, and notebooks for their children. Paola's journey to meet these women occurred after she had gone through several transitions, each a result of her passions and untapped creativity.

Early in her primary career in marketing, she was fortunate to have worked for the country's first all-women advertising agency, and she describes the experience as "a rare eye-opener, to be around seventy-five women, deeply involved in communications to women, who had created a supportive workplace." There she met Toby Tuttle, who later was to share in some of her adventures. After several years at the agency, and by then divorced and with a son in tow, Paola moved to a San Francisco–based corporate advertising group that later became part of the international communications firm Saatchi & Saatchi, and she eventually became the executive vice president responsible for client service and business development. But then, in her early fifties, she found herself thinking about "something else," although she couldn't imagine how to begin again, much less what to do. For almost two years she pondered how to "start all over again at this late stage," and ultimately hit upon the idea of writing a book about the glass ceiling, drawn in part from her unique experience working at the women-only agency. Taking the perspective that the large amount of her untapped vacation was a gift it would be ludicrous to give up, she took the time off, in half-day increments, and created a patchwork quilt of courses at Stanford University to study women and organizations. Thus began transition number one: *becoming a student.*

As part of her research at the university, she developed a model to demonstrate why the glass ceiling exists, which led to an invitation to teach a course about women and leadership. This seemed to be a good opportunity to leave the advertising agency and divide her time between teaching and running her own communications business advising major corporations about women and the glass ceiling, a hot topic in the mid-1990s. This was transition number two: *becoming a teacher and business consultant.*

But again the question What am I doing? nagged at her. Neither consulting nor teaching seemed right for the rest of her life. At that point two things occurred that affected her deeply. Her beloved physician father, who had been wildly productive in his retirement career and the dominant role model for her, died. It was shortly before Paola's fifty-sixth birthday, and she was engulfed by a sense that it was her turn to make a contribution to society. Serendipitously, she read an article in the *Economist* about the 1995 United Nations Fourth World Conference on Women, in Beijing, which focused on women in the global South who were able to send their children to school with money they earned through microindustries. For Paola, it was an incredibly provocative story—her personal lightbulb of recognition. She already knew a lot about women in large organizations and felt compelled to know more about women in microorganizations, one person at a time. She asked herself, "What if for one year I do only what I love best and not the things I get paid to do and am good at but don't love?" That was how the idea to write and illustrate a book about women in developing countries who run businesses in their own homes began. This was transition number three: *becoming a world traveler and researcher.*

The exciting thing about this idea was that it involved something Paola had never done before. Up to this point in her life, her work had been supportive of writers and artistic people. She was the one "responsible for putting gas in the engine and keeping the business going." But it didn't allow her to tap her own creativity. With her new idea, she would be able to put in one basket those things she loved most—travel and photography; what she knew best—women and business; what she wanted to learn about next—women in small businesses; and what she enjoyed doing—appreciating folk art. Suddenly everything coalesced. There was no risk. She had no commitments. Her son was self-sufficient. Her second husband had his own projects. She could do it!

Actually, Paola thought it was a big risk. She'd never done the kind of travel she was contemplating. She'd never been a professional photographer, although she had taken pictures since she was eight. She'd never written anything other than business correspondence and academic papers. What she proposed was profoundly ambitious. Finding a partner seemed like a good idea, so she asked her friend Toby to join her. It was only when the two were deep in Guatemala that they first wondered whether anyone would publish their book and sheepishly realized the idea simply had not occurred to them before. As Paola describes it, "I had jumped into the deep end of the pool without checking to see if there was any water."

It took almost three years for Paola and Toby to document the diverse lives and universal aspirations of ninety women in twelve countries and on four continents. The result is a book of sumptuous photographs and warm, informative text called *In Her Hands: Craftswomen Changing the World*, which was published in both hardcover and paperback editions. In addition, photographs from the book were exhibited at the Field Museum in Chicago, at the United Nations in New York, at the United States Senate, and as part of the Smithsonian Folklife Festival in Washington, DC. The book received rave reviews and Paola and Toby were invited to talk about it on the *Oprah Winfrey Show*. This was transition number four: *becoming an author, photographer, and public speaker.*

If asked to name one of her greatest satisfactions in life, Paola will point to the surprising ripple effects prompted by the book. She proudly tells how the director of the Girl Child Network, in Zimbabwe, was so inspired by a story in the book about women who made traditional crafts that she decided to teach the girls in her network to do the same. Many of these girls had been raped because of the myth in parts of Africa that if a man is HIV positive and has sex with a virgin, he will be cured. Unable to find husbands, they were being taught to make bedspreads and pillowcases to support themselves. Leafing through Paola and Toby's book, it occurred to these girls to sew underwear out of batik—to make and successfully sell "fancy pants." Never in Paola's wildest dreams could she have imagined that she would inspire young women in a distant part of the world to find a way to better their lives. This was transition number five: *becoming an inspiration to others less fortunate.*

Paola continues to travel and interview women throughout the world and has published three more books about women in developing countries. There is no doubt that Paola found her personal lightbulb.

Leaving a Legacy

As we age we begin to think about leaving a part of ourselves behind after we're gone. There are all types of legacies. We can leave behind money. We can do something that will have a beneficial impact on others while we are alive. We can create something concrete such as a work of art, a memoir, or a quilt. We can leave behind an endowment, or a house, or a genealogical map we've researched. Our legacy reveals the things we value most.

Family rules and rituals are part of our legacies. When Gwen misbehaved as a child, she was told to wait until her father came home to punish her. All meals and kitchen cleanup were her mother's responsibility. When Gwen raised her family, she discarded such rules, which reinforced hierarchy and rigid role assignments, but she imposed others: no television until schoolwork was finished, be home to walk and feed the dog, eat healthy snacks, respect others, and keep weekends for family time. Even if her son does not adopt the same specific rules when he raises his family, she hopes that he will pass on the valuing of education, responsibility, love of animals, healthy living, respect for others, and family they reflect.

Most families have traditions that revolve around holiday observances and celebrations, although we have many distinctive ways to acknowledge them. The rituals that are part of these observances are what adds spice and meaning to our lives, and we tend to savor them even more as we age. Family rituals often develop around the celebration of birthdays: Wilma didn't have to help with the dinner dishes when it was her birthday, a tradition she continued for her daughter. Or holidays: Betty had a dozen close friends over to her house for a formal dinner party each New Year's Eve. Or to welcome autumn: Gwen roasted a pig, pressed apples for fresh cider, and plotted complicated treasure hunts for the kids who attended her annual harvest party, an event that remains a potent memory among family and friends.

Giving Part of Ourselves

The idea of leaving a legacy segues naturally into the question of what it means to be a grandmother. Our grandchildren are our physical, genetic, and cultural legacies, and we have important roles to play as retainers of family histories, values, and beliefs. Marsha, a thoroughly modern grandmother, manages to connect with her distant young grandchildren through computer videophones, which allow them to play clap-hand games, sing songs, and have intimate conversations.

Zana's daughter Alex remembers her grandmother talking to her about what it was like to be a woman long ago, and Alex attributes her own self-confidence as an adult to those wonderful conversations. Zana is writing a legacy for Alex that will cover all the things she could not discuss earlier without frightening her about being in the world. She refers especially to the fear she felt at being a Jewish child growing up during the Holocaust and the profound effect it had on her life. Zana thinks it's important to express these feelings to her now-grown daughter, and empathizes with those who learned too late about their mothers' stories and felt bereft at not knowing about them while they were alive.

After her parents died, Cheryl decided to research her old Chicago neighborhood as part of her plan to write her memoirs. Although the area had changed totally during the forty years since she had last been there, suddenly "I had all these memory flashes of walking through the park with my mother, pushing my little brother's stroller, and shopping in the stores." She doesn't know if her curiosity and self-awareness have had more time to flourish because she is not working. In any case, she wants to leave something for her children and grandchildren. "You know, you don't always get to tell all your old stories, and, although they know Grandma, they don't know all of me."

STORIES TO TELL

There are many ways to tell a story. Numerous books as well as adult-education courses teach memoir writing, and technology can capture your tales on video or audio recorders. You can also participate in an oral-history project such as StoryCorps, a nationwide program sponsored by the Library of Congress, Sound Portraits Productions, and public radio stations that helps people record interviews with their family and friends. A small donation allows you to work with a facilitator to make broadcast-quality recordings and receive a copy of your interview on CD. Small recording studios, called StoryBooths, have been built in various public spaces around the country, and there are also studios on trailers that travel to small cities and towns. Go to www.storycorps.net for more information.

Wills Are More Than Legal Documents

By writing our wills, we leave legacies that point to the people and things we care about most, usually our children and grandchildren, nieces and nephews. Such legacies are commonly described in terms of assets and other things of monetary value we want to pass on to our families and to organizations with missions we believe in.

Rita, who is very much alive, has decided to leave nearly all she has to her children and grandchildren, but she also included several of her friends in her will as an expression of her love and appreciation for their friendship. To one friend she leaves a small sum with the directive that it be used for pleasure only—*Have a good meal on me.* In several instances she identifies her favorite objects and clothing items, with an invitation to her friends to take the ones they want to remember her by.

Giving money annually to various charities and organizations expresses our values, although there are many additional reasons we contribute. Even though we don't have Bill and Melinda Gates–level resources, our urge to give may reflect a desire to share our bounty, as well as show our empathy for others' plight. We give money for many reasons—to fulfill a sense of obligation, ensure the continuation of a tradition, get recognition, or memorialize a loved one. We donate so that we can meet others who share our beliefs. We do it for prestige and to have access to insider opportunities. And we donate to assuage our guilt over something from our past. Many of us feel compelled to leave our stamp on something. And we are not the first to feel this way. Think of the numerous eighteenth- and nineteenth-century needlepoint samplers that include the words *when you see this, remember me.*

GIVING TO A CHARITY OR A NONPROFIT ORGANIZATION

Before you decide which organization(s) to donate to, consider these recommendations:

- Take time to identify causes and match them with your values instead of simply reacting to solicitations.
- Think about what changes in society or other outcomes you'd like to support.
- Go online and check out an organization's Web site to under-

stand the specific causes it supports and how it measures its success.

- Look online for publications, such as the *Chronicle of Philanthropy,* that rate the organization you are considering.
- Eliminate the middleman wherever possible. Professional fund-raisers use a hefty chunk of the money they raise to support their fund-raising efforts. Send contributions directly to the charity or cause so that the money will bypass the fund-raising effort.
- Beware of impostors that use names similar to those of well-known charities. At best these are legitimate organizations, just not the ones you want, or they are scammers who intend to confuse you.
- Confirm the organization's tax-exempt status, especially if it sprang up in the aftermath of a disaster.
- Check out the charity's commitment to honor your privacy as a donor and not sell your name to others.
- Check into the financial health of the organization and, especially, how most of its money is allocated. If a large percentage is used for operating expenses, be cautious.
- Review the compensation given to the organization's top executives and check it against performance and such compensation at other, similar organizations.
- Aim to give to a few organizations rather than to many.
- Keep a small discretionary fund available for requests to support charities favored by friends and neighbors.
- Share your intention to make a long-term commitment to a designated charity or organization with that charity or organization. Let them know about your interest. They may offer special perks you will enjoy.

CHAPTER
8

How Can I Give Back and Enjoy It?

> *I'd like to put my skills to work for something that I would enjoy doing rather than what I need to do to earn my paycheck.*
> —**Rita**
>
> *Everybody wants to retire and become a teacher or go into a nonprofit. It's become so fucking popular; it's terrible.*
> —**voice from a peer group**

I want to give back." "I want to do something meaningful." "I want to help others." "I want to make the world a better place." Refrains like these pop up in nearly every conversation among women over fifty. They are well-meant mantras we can all *om* to. We genuinely want to be useful and have a positive impact on someone or something. We make life better when we fund-raise for cancer research, educate people about the arts, shop for a neighbor who is disabled, serve on the local planning board, lobby for better voting machines or women's rights, build a school in Tanzania, or join the Peace Corps. Many of us look for ways to volunteer. Sometimes we wait to be asked. A few of us see something that is needed, articulate it, and bring others together to help meet it.

However we end up volunteering, our instincts are good. But we must ask, Do these instincts jibe with reality? Is the world of volunteering and civic activism ready for us? Are we ready for it? Can we afford to volunteer? Can we afford not to?

Boomer numbers are expected to change the world of volunteering. We have already given ourselves over to multiple causes during our working years, and as we have more and more time and freedom to contribute, we are expected to have an enormous influence on what the world of volunteering looks like. And that also means we can have a major influence on how society's problems are tackled.

Our motives for volunteering spring from several sources. Generational influences such as the Great Depression, the political and social activism of the sixties, and the self-actualization movements of the eighties have made their marks on us. We are also affected by our different life experiences. If we hail from small communities where civic involvement was a natural part of our lives, or from places where strong ethnic or racial values demanded engagement and action, or where religious affiliations were powerful forces, we are strongly inclined to volunteer.

It has been observed that women seem to volunteer more frequently than men, for reasons that aren't entirely clear. Perhaps it has to do with our historically having more time for activities that focus primarily on our extended home turf of school, church, and neighborhood, as compared with men's tendency to use their time for broader civic involvement. Another reason may be that men prefer to volunteer for "purposeful activities" such as constructing homes for the poor and developing strategic plans, rather than for the kinds of things that require casual interactions and relationships with people they don't know.

And then there are the nonvolunteers, commitment-phobic men and women who hesitate to become engaged beyond the most limited volunteer experiences. This reluctance may be the result of practiced self-interest. Or it may be burn-out from the all-consuming sacrifices demanded by their jobs, or the fear that volunteering will jeopardize hard-earned personal freedom.

The Drive to Volunteer

Volunteering our time and services fulfills critical needs in our communities and helps better the world. These are no small things. Most of us volunteer because we believe we owe something for our good fortunes and the advantages our education and abilities have given us. Some of us want to help others because we have seen less-fortunate people suffer and we truly empathize with their hardship. We also volunteer because we have personally overcome obstacles not of our own making and want to stand by others facing similar roadblocks. Such motivations lead us to search for something that has meaning beyond ourselves.

Such a newly emerging desire to be of service may even catch us by surprise as we transition from our overcommitted forties into our caring fifties and sixties, a result of a powerful inner need to give of ourselves and leave an imprint on the future as we get older. Psychoanalyst Erik Erikson identified this as a key developmental impulse in the later stage of our lives, when contrasting inclinations toward what he labeled "generativity versus stagnation" take over. The conflict within ourselves implied by the "versus" is whether we choose to commit ourselves to being creative and productive, and to leave a legacy that benefits future generations, or whether, instead, we are driven by self-absorption, which leads us to vegetate. The way we choose to care for the future and make sense of our lives is expressed by our beliefs, the commitments we make, and the things we do, as well as the things we do not do.

When Rita was growing up in Newark, New Jersey, around the time when the Holocaust was fresh in people's minds, she vividly recalls a "very formidable rabbi who would get up on the pulpit and say 'six million Jews' in a big bellowing voice." It left a lasting impression on her. So when she was casting about for something to do after she retired from years of teaching, and heard about the Museum of Jewish Heritage, a living memorial to the Holocaust, she knew instantly that this was where she wanted to be. "I feel my mission is to teach others about the Holocaust and Jewish heritage and to fight anti-Semitism. Now, as a gallery educator there, I feel purposeful. I'm in this to make a difference."

But before we get all warm and fuzzy about the subject of volunteerism, let's put altruistic considerations aside and look at the personal perks we get from volunteering. After all, if our volunteering does not satisfy us beyond our desire to do good, we are unlikely to stay with it, no matter how noble the cause. So, what is it that energizes us to search for the right kind of volunteer work, decide how much of our time and energy we want to invest in it, commit to staying with it, and truly satisfy the unselfish urges that started us on this track to begin with?

The reasons are many. One of the most important is the opportunity to make our lives more satisfying. We look to volunteer to keep active and involved and have a chance to accomplish things we cannot do by ourselves—and to receive recognition for them. We like being able to apply things we know to areas that may be new to us. We volunteer for the opportunity to uncover our creativity and reconnect with our spiritual side on behalf of something that has purpose. We do it so that we can stretch ourselves and take risks as we try out things we haven't done before. We do it to expose ourselves to different ideas, new people, and new skills, and in return we seek to rekindle our enthusiasm and zest for life. We also volunteer to add structure and activities to our lives, two things we know we need to keep ourselves physically healthy and mentally alert. And, most important, we do it to be with others and make new friends so that we can stave off the much-dreaded demon *isolation*. Volunteering also satisfies our negative motivators, not the least of which is the search for redemption for past sins or guilt. It is also a way to offset our indulgences in leisure and self-gratification and counterbalance the "I deserve it" factor.

> *The feeling of accomplishment, that's the most important thing. The feeling of doing some good for this organization which you are very fond of or love . . . it's more of a reward for what you're doing and the sense of contributing.*
>
> —Suzie

Linda started the volunteering habit many years before she retired, working for the parent-teacher association at her son's school. She eventually got involved in her community newspaper, which was staffed by volunteers who had graduated from the PTA at the same time their children graduated from high school. Once she retired, her flexible schedule allowed her to attend meetings with politicians and hearings at city agencies and report back on them for the newspaper. Much of her volunteer work involves research on the Internet and working with digital photography, which she appreciates because it keeps her up-to-date with recent advances in computer technology. She says about her life now, "When I worked full-time, it used to be that I knew a few people in the community by name. But now I've really gotten to know many more terrific people who share my concerns for and pride in our town. I love being an informed and integral part of where I live."

Lorraine, sixty-two, had been in workforce development on a national level for both for-profit and nonprofit organizations before she realized that she no longer was career building or felt the need to prove herself. Her life became divided into five different areas important to her: family, coaching, painting, exercise, and working with the local community college, where she has served on the board for eight years, the last few as the chair. When she thinks about her involvement with the college, somehow "volunteer" doesn't describe it. "I mean, that's a job for me. What I do for the college is a job. I don't get paid for it." Instead, she says, she receives nonmonetary rewards. "I use every bit of my skills and I'm getting a tremendous education and opportunity to be out in the community as its representative and to advocate for educational issues that are important to me." Lorraine is particularly interested in keeping access open to young people coming out of high schools who otherwise can't afford college, and she advocates, on state and county levels and at national conferences, on their behalf. "When I started doing this I just thought it would be something interesting. I didn't think it was going to take over my life."

FINDING THE RIGHT FIT AS A VOLUNTEER

Uncovering the right volunteer experiences for you is not so different from thinking about the kind of job you would like to have. Similar principles apply. Before you consider what you want to do, you need to have a solid handle on the things that motivate and excite you, the skills you enjoy using, the amount of time you have available, and your impetus for wanting to volunteer. Here are some things to consider:

- Why do you want to volunteer? Analyze your reasons for giving of yourself to another organization, group, or cause. Perhaps, for example, you come from a background where civic involvement is an integral part of your family life, and you would feel remiss about not participating. Or perhaps you need a place to go and make new friends. Make sure your volunteering decisions fulfill your motivations.

- What specific things that you enjoy about work do you want to maintain in your life? Consider whether you are a people person who wants to connect with others, a person who enjoys having a leadership role with broad responsibilities, or someone who prefers working alone. Ask yourself if having a place to go where you're expected and recognized is important. Or whether you desire to stretch yourself in new, untested directions and rack up new accomplishments.

- What kind of environment would you like to be a part of? Consider whether you are interested in working for the arts, with civic leaders, with green groups, or advocating for someone less fortunate than you. Also, think about whether you want a micro-level, hands-on experience, such as working directly with individuals in need, or would rather make things happen on a macro level, such as through fund-raising, communications, or strategic development.

- How much time do you have? Just as with a paying job, when you volunteer you make commitments to show up at certain times and to do what you say you will do. Often, the amount of time you give as a volunteer increases in direct proportion to how much you like what you're doing. If you're not sure about making an extensive commitment to something, consider taking on a short-term activity, such as delivering food during the Thanksgiving and Christmas holidays to people who are shut-ins, or offering your services one day a month.

- Can you try it on first? If you think you may be interested in a particular volunteer program, ask to take on a project with an end date. This will give you a chance to become engaged with the volunteer organization, look at how it is managed, and determine whether or not you enjoy the people you meet. By moving cautiously, you can easily disengage yourself if it doesn't seem right for you or if you have other commitments.

- Will you be trained? Usually, larger nonprofit programs have a volunteer coordinator who oversees everything that has to do with volunteers, manages your comings and goings, coordinates projects with the paid staff, and makes sure you are trained for the job. This usually is a good sign, indicating that the organization has a plan to effectively train and use its volunteers, and suggests that there is a solid link between the organization's management and staff and its volunteers.

- Does the volunteer opportunity offer any appealing perks? For example, if you volunteer as a docent for a local opera company, find out if you can attend select dress rehearsals and special performances and get to know the performers.

- When should you say no to new commitments? Usually, there are so many opportunities to become involved within your family and community that you can quickly find yourself overbooked and overwhelmed. Give yourself a chance to evaluate the amount of time and energy you are being asked to give and to gauge your enthusiasm for the activity.

- Can you expect to do whatever you want? Start out prepared to do exactly what the organization wants you to and not what you think it should want. Once you are involved and have had a chance to understand the organization's priorities and how it functions, you may have some ideas about how to improve something. But be sensitive to the fact that the organization is probably short staffed and underfunded, is likely to be overwhelmed by the need to meet its mission, and has to deal with political issues that may not be immediately obvious. If you feel compelled to offer advice, prepare a proposal that spells out what you want to accomplish, how you will implement it, whether there are any costs involved, and how it can be managed without putting undue stress on the organization's already limited staff.

Is Society Ready for Us?

So, how will nonprofit and civic organizations use all the good energy, enthusiasm, and desire that's coming at them? And are they prepared to train and manage us and keep us engaged? We talked with Marc Freedman, a social entrepreneur and the founder of Civic Ventures, a think tank on volunteerism. Freedman sees us as a remarkable, educated re-source that is available to work in areas essential to the well-being of society. But he also sees a structural lag: "Society's outlook toward us is hopelessly behind the times," he says. And that's because most nonprofits and government institutions don't know how to use us. And we are wary too, concerned that our good intentions and abilities will be ignored, underused, or abused. That generally isn't the case at large service insti-tutions and organizations, which are usually savvy about recruiting us for what we know. Think about large museums, or organizations such as the American Red Cross, which have highly developed programs for train-ing and managing volunteers. The effective ones do a remarkable job of whipping volunteers into reliable and dedicated nonpaid "employees."

When we volunteer for an organization or institution that doesn't have a program or policies for managing and training us, dissatisfaction on both sides can be more the rule than the exception. In these situations we often can show up at will, and are frequently asked to do the simplest of tasks—"stuffing-envelopes syndrome"—because no one has thought through or planned how to use us effectively. And, to our credit, we are very willing to accept simple tasks, as long as we know that they will have value and contribute to the larger picture.

Since when we volunteer we work by choice rather than obligation, it is important to us that our efforts be appreciated and recognized. Too many of us are escapees from corporate or bureaucratic jobs and will be turned off by volunteer situations that we discover are characterized by office politics, cliques, hostile staff, misrepresentation of our roles, and abuse of our goodwill. Generally we want to work on concrete, finite projects that have a beginning, a middle, and an end and in which we have clear roles. This is true whether we develop a strategic plan or com-plete a financial analysis, establish a brand identity, help to fund-raise, work on communications, or do any other such thing. The list of what we can do is endless, particularly for the many, many nonprofits that don't have the resources to buy our talents but would benefit enormously from them.

An organization will begin to take us seriously when we take volun-teering seriously. When we approach a volunteer situation, many of us submit résumés along with applications, and use our professional know-how and experience to solicit interviews, create proposals, and exhibit what we can do. And we feel a commitment to do whatever we take on with the same degree of expertise and engagement that we brought to our paid careers. Victoria, retired from academic life, has six different projects going at one time. Three of them are paid through grants, and the other three are unpaid. "What I notice is that I treat the unpaid work the same as I do the paid work, even covering expenses out of my own pocket." For instance, when she launched a Web site for her college class, she paid the Web designer herself. As a result of the highly developed site, her class was able to connect with more people than they had before and to raise more money for the school. She was enormously appreciated for her efforts and is proud of her accomplishment.

Madeleine is a victim of good intentions gone sour. She volunteered for several breast-cancer organizations but left when she discovered that "they were more about competing with one another for contributions than fighting for the cause." She felt a few had even become "cults" that had lost sight of why people were giving their time and money. "That's just the sort of thing I am *not* looking for," she says.

> *Most organizations don't know how to use volunteers, and you end up just sitting around.*
>
> —Jered

On the other hand, Michele is elated by her volunteer experience with My Own Book, which was launched by a man who developed a small family fund that provides books to disadvantaged children in New York City schools. The program is managed by a fund at the board of education. TTN learned about the project and decided to take along a dozen of its members who wanted a hands-on, short-term volunteer experience. The program reaches third-graders from some thirty schools, most of whom do not own a single book. Even though—or perhaps because—it is a small program, it seems to work flawlessly. Volunteers are assigned to a school to meet with a class and its teacher. "When I go into the classroom, the kids are prepared for me and eager to talk about books," Michele says. The next time Michele sees her class and its teacher is when they meet up at a Barnes & Noble bookstore that the kids travel to by subway, since there is no bookstore near their neighborhood. "I help the kids find the books they want to own and tell them to write their name on the inside of the cover. You can't believe the excitement. Their enthusiasm and the serious purpose with which they select their prize is beautiful. The bookstore manager tells us that some of the kids come back with their parents. One of our volunteers had retired from working in book production for a publisher, and her face lit up when a child asked how a book is made. She had a wealth of information and a ready audience of eager listeners. It was an amazing afternoon." After the kids have owned their books for a while, Michele and the other volunteers return to the school to meet once again with "their" class to hear some children read from their books, or to listen to a book report, or to have a discussion. Michele says, "I go into *my* school and meet the principal and teachers, who look at me with great affection. I feel I belong there and am giving the kids hope because I want them to succeed and let them know that reading is the path to success."

Purpose Versus Pay

Because many of us are driven by our desire and need to continue to work, we are effectively displacing retirement with new combinations that involve work for pay and volunteering. Just as discussed in chapter 5, Marc Freedman sees us as taking "false retirements," which are effectively just sabbaticals from midlife overwork, as a chance to stop and catch our breath before we head into another phase of work. But he also sees that our need to find purpose is becoming as much or more important than compensation as we seek our next work phase. He believes this will lead us to seek a hybrid experience that builds on the benefits of work and the purpose of volunteering, a different kind of work, which will promise tangible benefits along with personal meaning. It might mean that we will do some work pro bono, or we will receive small stipends, salaries, fees, or valuable perks such as tuition reimbursement or health-care benefits.

Dawn is one example of this kind of hybrid worker. A retired academic, she admits to "not knowing how to watch the clock" at her paid, part-time advising job in a lifelong learning program for seniors, and so volunteers far more hours than expected for the low pay she receives. She says she would probably give the job her all whether she got paid or not but then immediately contradicts herself, saying that she wouldn't do it exclusively as a volunteer because she equates self-worth with paying jobs, even though the amount earned is unimportant.

Elise's story is an example of how volunteering can morph into something else. In her fifties Elise left a full-time job as a marketing vice president for an international corporation to begin a consulting career, but she found that lunching with clients didn't keep her from feeling lonely much of the time. She volunteered at a botanical garden, not because she had a particular knowledge of horticulture, but because she thought it was a pleasant place to spend time and meet people. At first she volunteered two or three days a week, eventually increasing the time as she and other volunteers had a "fabulous time" developing a greeter program at the garden entrances and working on a children's program. After several years of volunteering, Elise was offered a full-time job at the garden. This puzzled her at first, because she was neither a horticulturalist nor an educator, until she realized they wanted her marketing skills and wanted her to run the continuing-education program. That was something she could do, and she happily accepted the position. Eventually, her job grew as she assumed expanded responsibilities, and a few years later she was named vice president in charge of overseeing education programs for the eighty thousand schoolchildren who visit the gardens each year. "It never dawned on me that my volunteering would lead to a new career that I could feel passionate about."

VOLUNTEERING TO WORK

In our fifties and sixties, we begin to search for more meaningful work. For many of us, the desire to move from the for-profit to the nonprofit sector reflects this sensibility. However, making such a career change is not easy, which is why career counselors tout volunteering as an excellent way to get exposure to a particular career or organization—to effectively "try on" a different field or job to see if it fits. While volunteers can rarely expect to be paid for their contributions, there are potential opportunities for some combination of pro bono and paid work. Such a new approach to work will likely occur first in areas such as education, health care, social services, and government, where huge labor shortages are forecast and careers offer a spirit of volunteerism. It is also expected that when these sectors fully grasp the problem, the divide between the non-profit and for-profit sectors will narrow, with pay rising in the non-profit sector along with opportunities for much more flexibility.

Another area with potential work/volunteer opportunities is national service. There currently exist several programs for senior service, including the Retired and Senior Volunteer Program (RSVP), the Foster Grandparents program, and the Senior Companions program. Up to now, national-service programs have focused primarily on American youth, with interesting short-term civilian and military service programs that connect social involvement with educational opportunities. The Progressive Policy Institute has an interesting idea: it suggests that the government initiate a Boomer Corps, in which participants would volunteer for one year in grass-roots civic projects to provide at-home care for the needy, or tutor, or organize and coordinate community activities. Workers serving in such a program, the institute poses, might receive a tax-free monthly stipend along with a health-care voucher, an education award to be used by themselves or by their children or grandchildren, or other valuable perks. At the moment it's just a dream, but maybe someday.

Volunteer Opportunities

The truth is, if we are to find volunteer opportunities that suit us, we first need to open our eyes. Sometimes it's chance that gets us into the right place at the right time. More often it's a hunger that forces us to make things happen. Recovering from an illness, Monica was at a point where she was looking for something to engage her. Over breakfast at a favorite café in San Francisco, she watched a table of four women about her age who were obviously having a meeting, because they had yellow pads and were talking animatedly. She thought, "That's what I want! To be involved in something exciting." Surprised at her own nerve, she walked up to them and said, "I've been admiring your energy and enthusiasm. What organization are you with?" They gave her a folder explaining the organization and how it provided a whole range of services for homeless youth. When she told them about her background in social planning and program development, they asked for her résumé to take to their director. Almost immediately, she became immersed in the organization as a volunteer on its management board. Monica says she thought it was serendipity at first, and then said, "No, I really took the initiative to make that happen. I'm proud of that." Since then she has attended meetings to go over operations and details, helped to hire an executive director and caseworker who is partly funded by the city, represented the organization at city committee meetings that relate to homelessness and youth, and participated in joint planning with other organizations. "The work means a lot to me, and I adore the people I've met," she said.

> *The first half of life is about compulsion; the second half is about choice.*
>
> —Shoshana Zuboff

Finding the right volunteer opportunity may take more time for most of us than it did for Monica. Cheryl discovered that just because she wanted to volunteer at her nearby children's hospital, it did not mean that the hospital would simply open its arms wide to embrace her. She had to be persistent in order to get accepted, joining an orientation program, going through interviews, taking required inoculations, and accepting a variety of assignments. The first was in pediatric rehab, which she found fascinating, but she felt there wasn't a whole lot she could do. Another was to help hospitalized children with their schoolwork by reading to them and bringing them laptops to work with. Finally, after she had given the hospital more than one hundred hours, she was graduated to the work she most wanted, which was to care for the babies in the intensive-care nursery. Cheryl says, "I essentially hold and rock infants whose parents can't come until the evenings, or who will be going into foster care. At first I was somewhat nervous holding babies hooked up to monitors, but I learned how to deal with all that. The nurses are extremely grateful. And so am I."

> *It either works out or it doesn't. If it doesn't, you find somewhere else to volunteer, until you're in the right organization, where you enjoy the people and the work.*
>
> —Cheryl

Wendy, fifty-seven, describes how she walked into the office of a high-profile senatorial campaign during an election year and was floored to realize that everyone was in his or her twenties. After a while, and feeling ignored, she was approached by someone and asked about her work in previous campaigns. Since she did not have campaign experience, she was turned away. Such a discouraging moment is when we are likely to think ageist attitudes are at work against us. But the truth is that Wendy had no political-campaign experience to offer to that well-oiled campaign office.

What should she do about it? Rather than crawl away to grumble, she should go out and get experience by volunteering for local representatives or for other community-run organizations, which have smaller staffs and fewer volunteers than the more celebrated politicians. It's not ageism that was the problem; rather, it was her expectation that she could be helpful despite her lack of useful skills.

Mandy remembers her mother telling her never to do volunteer work. "Make sure you get paid for whatever you do because people will not respect you unless you are paid money." Mandy thinks that, although her mother volunteered for good organizations and did quite valuable work, she felt as though it didn't count. Fortunately, Mandy, who had been a highly paid business consultant, doesn't feel that way. She would like to be a hospice worker and remembers her long-ago dreams about going to medical or nursing school. So, after Hurricane Katrina struck and refugees were stacked up at the Houston Astrodome, Mandy felt compelled to travel from New Jersey to offer her services. She arrived to a chaotic scene; no one seemed to be in charge and people needed help. Since she is good at organizing things, she found ways to be useful, helping kids find clothes from the piles of items that had been donated and taking food to those who were unable to get it for themselves. She says she found it tremendously satisfying to do something that did not require a lot of the same kind of mental work she had done during her career.

GLOBE-TROTTING VOLUNTEERS

The Peace Corps is the best-recognized U.S. public-service organization for those who wish to volunteer abroad. Although it traditionally targets young people, it welcomes older volunteers through its 50+ initiative. A Peace Corps tour is normally two years, with the most popular service areas being general education, health education, and disease prevention. During a tour volunteers receive full medical and dental care, a monthly living allowance, and round-trip airfare. Housing is modest but comfortable, and the program provides language and cross-cultural skills and technical training.

One of several other service programs is Global Volunteers, a nonprofit organization that takes small groups of people of all ages abroad (or to select locations in the United States) to work for short periods—two, three, or four weeks at a time—on projects that help people in poor communities better their lives. Most of the volunteer work is centered around helping schoolchildren learn or working on construction projects determined by the community. As a volunteer you must pay a fee that covers such things as your living expenses and a donation to the community.

New Ways to Think About Volunteering

With all the volunteer talent we have to offer and the tremendous need for such talent, why is it frequently so difficult to find volunteer programs that get it right? It seems clear that new models for volunteering are desperately needed and that we are the ones to initiate such change. It will start as we encourage nonprofit and civic organizations to think differently about how to use our skills, and organize and coordinate what we have to offer.

Throughout the country many innovative programs have been developed to pair our energy and enthusiasm for being useful with community services and schools. One such program, Experience Corps, currently operating in some nineteen cities, puts people over fifty-five together with community-based programs in some two thousand public schools so that they can mentor disadvantaged students. Experience Corps is successfully bringing good management skills and leadership to local schools through the deployment of highly committed and rigorously trained members working in teams for maximum impact. The results are that the students learn, the schools improve, and the volunteers who participate in the program are happier and healthier for the experience.

> *Never doubt that a small group of thoughtful, committed citizens can change the world; indeed it's the only thing that ever has.*
> —Margaret Mead

Linda Sicher, a member of TTN and a volunteer, looks for opportunities in small organizations where a few people can make a big difference. Through her efforts, a team of TTN members became involved with Bottomless Closet, a local organization that provides professional clothing, career skills, and image coaching to help disadvantaged women negotiate job interviews with confidence and success. Previously, Bottomless Closet had seen clients three days a week, but with TTN members' input, clients now have access to the program four days a week—a 33 percent increase in services provided. As Linda explains it, "Our group goes in on Mondays to help the women select wardrobes for their job interviews. Normally, each woman arrives in jeans, and a volunteer helps put together outfits, pairing shoes, handbag, scarf, and jewelry for an appropriate presentation. Then we photograph her new look, give her a print, and hang another copy on the bulletin board. And all the while, we talk to her about what she needs, answer questions about what she can expect during a job interview, and offer tips on how to present herself well—the kind of soft skills one needs for interviews." Once she gets the job, she is encouraged to come back for more outfits and workshops that provide advice on such topics as managing finances, personal and professional development, and parenting skills. Says Linda, "I love drawing on my professional knowledge to help smooth the path for someone without such experience."

Valuable new volunteer efforts usually begin small and grow out of a desperate need within a community. One example is a nonprofit organization launched by a dozen residents of Boston's Beacon Hill to help others in the area continue to live at home even after they are no longer fully independent. Beacon Hill Village, now several hundred members strong, provides a range of household services, including computer-problem solving, transportation for members, assistance with weekly shopping, access to home-delivered meals, and concierge services such as mailing packages, hanging curtains, and picking up prescriptions. Residents over fifty years old may join for an annual fee, which is adjusted for those who cannot afford full freight.

The original Beacon Hill Village organizers are *social entrepreneurs,* a relatively new term used to describe unique individuals who see previously unnoticed needs in society and tackle those needs with daring, fresh solutions. Social entrepreneurs are visionaries who figure out how to make change happen, seize opportunities to improve existing systems, and invent new ways to get things done on a large scale. Above all, they are not ones to sit back to wait for the government or a business to come up with solutions.

CHAPTER
9

How Can I Stay Connected with Friends and Make New Ones?

Friends matter to us! They fill our lives with pleasure, companionship, stimulation, warmth, laughter, and affection, and they provide us with sympathy and concern when we need it. Friends are our lifeline, there to inform, advise, and support us, or just listen. They allow us to be ourselves—to be silly and frivolous, to expose our uncertainties, or to vent our anger and frustration. They incite and encourage us to be more than we think we can be and are ready to take us down a notch when we are trying to be something we're not. Friends are a crucial part of our lives, and without at least one person to call "friend," we feel an enormous lack.

In an early stage of The Transition Network's development, thirty-five women sat in a living room discussing the topic of friendship. It was clear that to a few of them, the word "friendship" could define only a relationship that had gone on for years and was so deep and rich that they couldn't use the word "friendship" in any other context. Puzzled by such a rigid interpretation, others in the room asked whether "friendship" might also be applied in relation to a friend at work, or someone they had lunch with occasionally, or a new friend whom they had known for only a year. But the absolutists strongly objected to the use of the word "friendship" in any casual way.

"How loaded this topic of friendship is," many of us who were there remember thinking.

The very notion of friendship is, indeed, a loaded topic. We have different definitions of and perspectives on friendship. Confronted with an unyielding definition such as the one given by a few of the women at the meeting, we can feel guilty or inadequate if our friendships don't come close to meeting such standards of what a friend should be.

How do we define friendship? How do our friendships at this stage of our lives differ from those we developed when we were younger? Why do some friendships stay constant and others fade? How do we make friends? And why are friends vital as we make the transition from midlife to our next stage of adulthood?

> *We shared our ideas like sweaters, with easy exchange and lack of ownership.*
> —**Ann Patchett writing about her best friend, Lucy Grealy,**
> *Truth & Beauty: A Friendship*

Who Is a Friend?

We claim a wide range of friendships with other women and, less frequently, with men. Some women become our new "best" friend. Others animate us with new thinking and interests. Some become frequent companions at lectures and concerts. A few are ever ready to play bridge or poker with us. Others, we greet at a party or local event and talk with about safe, impersonal topics.

We refer to people we know in many ways, but the language is imprecise. When we say "friend," we usually qualify it by tacking on an adjective that will explain something further about the kind of relationship we're talking about. Is she our good, close, or best friend? our longtime, new, or casual friend? our work, school, raised-our-kids-together, tennis-playing, met-while-on-vacation, or common-cause friend? Or is she an acquaintance from the neighborhood, work, church, gym, or dog run whom we speak with often but with little intimacy?

Many of us do not have friendships in which we share ourselves with total trust on a daily basis. In their book *I Know Just What You Mean*, Ellen Goodman and Patricia O'Brien write about their remarkable relationship, which began when they were in their thirties and remained constant, even while they lived in different cities and relied on the telephone to keep in touch through new jobs, first marriages, child raising, divorces, and new marriages. A peer group discussed the Goodman-O'Brien friendship and expressed envy over their relationship and sadness that none of them could claim one like that for themselves. Myra, age sixty-six, said she was jealous of the friendship described in the book and would love to have a relationship like that. "They would vent, they would *listen*, they would really take it in, and each would respond. I didn't have that. My friends tend to talk at each other or past each other, or they interrupt; they don't really listen."

In fact, few of us have a best friend, someone we speak with often about our intimate feelings, and we don't necessarily see that as a negative. Rather, many of us think such a relationship could be stifling and overly riddled with a kind of undesirable neediness. Instead of longing for a friend who fits the ideal of best friendship, many of us see other desirable patterns of friendship for women over fifty emerge.

> *Some people make me so envious about childhood friends and how absolutely irreplaceable they were in their lives, and my feeling is, "Huh? God, I don't have any of those."*
>
> **—Myra**

Linda is an example of someone with many different interests and a wide variety of friends who share those interests with her. Widowed since fifty and now sixty-six, she has numerous friends of both sexes, whom she enjoys individually. For example, during her regular exercise classes, she talks at length with her friend and trainer about their shared interests in movies and sports. Her conversation switches to gardening and questions about garbage disposal and house maintenance when she sees her immediate neighbors. Then she has the friends she sees at church most Sundays and at weekly meetings where she volunteers to help poor families in the community. She also volunteers to work in her local representative's office, where she connects with her politically passionate activist friends. In addition, Linda keeps up with longtime friends from college and people she met when she worked full-time. Then she has other friends who share her love of books, art, and travel and her general enthusiasm for life. No one or two friends could ever stand in for this wide array of people she enjoys and depends upon for social connection and support.

> *With my current friends, being "close" does not mean that we do everything together—I don't desire or need that.*
>
> **—Linda**

Male and Couple Friends

When we talk about friends, it is usually about woman friends exclusively. We were likely to have had male friends at some point in our lives, but marriage seems to change things. Often, having a partner creates discomfort over anticipated sexual issues, not because we are concerned that our friendship with a man might turn into a sexual relationship, but rather because we are sensitive to possible misunderstandings or hurt feelings developing in his spouse or ours. Fern, who runs her own software company, has been married since she was twenty-one. She regularly meets a male friend for lunch or for dinner during the week. But for reasons she doesn't clearly articulate, she draws the line at meeting him for dinner on weekends unless her husband is included.

Even when we are single, the potential of a sexual relationship becomes a wedge in our friendships with men. If our male friend is married, then his wife is part of the picture, even if she is not around. If our friends are a couple, then we feel like the odd woman out and find it difficult to fit into their lives easily or reciprocate appropriately. And if the man is single, there is a concern that one person wants the relationship to become more than "just friends." The exception is when our male friend is gay. In the absence of sexual concerns, we feel as comfortable with a gay friend as we do with our female friends, and he offers the additional benefit of being an acceptable escort at couple-centric parties.

The perception of sexual tensions also exists in couple friendships.

Yvonne and her husband, Walter, are close friends with Joan and Gary, and the four of them often get together. The friendship actually has a couple of permutations: good friends Yvonne and Joan connect separately, and Walter and Gary do the same. If Joan and Walter are unavailable, Yvonne and Gary will meet up to do something together, but they feel that if they do this too often and do not invite their spouses along, then a level of discomfort may arise and stress the friendship.

Youthful Friendships

Before we took on adult roles and responsibilities as wives, mothers, and/or careerists, most of us believed that our friends shared our every thought and experience. During our teens and early twenties, when we were in the process of loosening our emotional ties to our parents and discarding labels they assigned to us, such as "ditz" or "clotheshorse," we looked to our friends to appreciate us for what we knew we were, which was funny, spontaneous, or stylish. That was a time when we were shopping for our true selves by trying on different people and personas. If we felt like misfits who were out of sync with one group of friends, we searched for an identity that fit. Barb, a successful lawyer, remembers suffering from being labeled "brainy" by her fellow high school students in a Wisconsin farming community. In her first year at college she bonded with a group of honors students who had all felt like nerds in high school because they were the "smart" ones. During her last college year, she changed friends again when she joined a theater group and hung out with fellow actors—the green room crowd.

At a point in our lives we shift from using our friends to define us and start to look within ourselves for our own authority and insight. As we feel more capable and independent, we begin to seek out friends who speak to our intuition and inner voice. Such a shift usually kicks in during our late teens and early twenties. However, Sara says it was not until she was fifty-eight that she felt she was a more or less fully formed person who had been through enough and had tried out things in enough ways to know who she was. She believes that the reassuring feeling she now projects is the same thing younger people are responding to when they say about an older woman, "I like being with her; she's just so comfortable with herself."

Interestingly, we have fewer friends in our thirties and forties, when we are enveloped by obligations. For those of us who marry, work, and have children, the time and energy we devote to friendships is extremely limited. At the same time, old friends tend to move away or follow different paths, and we report letting them fade from our lives.

> *At every stage of my life experience, I've had good, bonding friendships (in grade school, high school, college, work)—except for the years during my marriage.*
>
> **—Mindy**

Work Friends

When we first start working and engage with others in a common endeavor, many of us make friends who remain close to us over the years, and we continue to form such friendships during our career. However, as we acquire more experience and responsibilities, many of us do not make new friends at our jobs or, if we do, find that the friendships are cemented only after we, or they, leave. This is understandable if we think of the workplace as a family. When we first start working, we are a bit like siblings in need of friends and allies. As we advance in our careers, our roles change and we become the bosses (parents) of those we supervise (our children). Such a hierarchical structure in the workplace can make it difficult to form or maintain lasting friendships with fellow workers.

Men tend to experience friendliness at work differently than we do. They engage in a form of camaraderie that allows them to joke and tease each other and "talk shop" about things at work or about sports and gadgets. Such friendliness is seen as a promise of reciprocity, with an invitation to play golf considered an opportunity to pitch new business ideas or further the progress of a promotion. For us the power of friendship at work usually lies in forming relationships based on mutual trust and affection. Because we see these relationships as personal rather than purely professional, an invitation to play golf can have complicated overtones.

Our shoptalk tends to be about our feelings and relationships. Although this is denigrated as gossip by some, columnist Liz Smith believes that gossip at work helps us relax and is vital for exchanging important information ("Jane thinks Jim won't have the report ready in time"). Such gossip can also help us build our status as an insider and contribute to our self-esteem as we affirm our people skills and ability to fit into the group.

Veronique, who, at sixty-three, is a senior account director for a large advertising agency, faces another kind of problem as the sole elder in a sea of youthful coworkers who have no idea how old she is. Most of Veronique's earlier workplace friends have left, and her ability to make new friends there has become complicated. "Hiding my age and squelching those stories that might reveal my age has become a part of my life. As long as I work—and I intend to keep working for many more years—I feel I can't expose my age to my coworkers or clients. If they had any idea about how old I am, I'm sure it would change the way they think about me as a colleague and friend and how they value my skills and creativity. I just don't want to risk that." But having to guard her words adds stress to her day-to-day interactions and threatens the workplace camaraderie she considers important.

Alicia too experienced a sense of being different, as the oldest person at the foundation she directed. In her early sixties at the time, she never thought about the difference between herself and the people in their thirties who worked for her. She recalls befriending a young woman who worked on a fellowship in the legal department. They went out to lunch a few times, and once Alicia invited her to a concert when she had an extra ticket. When the fellowship was ending, several of the young woman's coworkers organized a party, and nobody thought to invite Alicia. She says it was very clear that they didn't see her as one of them, even though she felt like one of them all the time she worked there. It made her see that there was a difference, and, she says, "it hurt, it really hurt."

Despite these obstacles, we want and need a community of friends at work. We may be part of a group glued together by nothing more than small talk, but small talk can become quite personal, whether it is concern for our parents' health or sympathy for our frustration over the time it takes to complete a kitchen renovation. What this work community offers is daily companionship and camaraderie, which give us pleasure and contribute to our sense of belonging. One of the reasons Fran gives for wanting to retire from her job at a national nonprofit organization is the lack of human interaction there. She describes the people as so incredibly busy that she had to use e-mail to reach them and schedule appointments, even when her office was right next to theirs. "There was no personal interaction, which made me wonder why I bothered to leave my home each morning."

Hannah, who now works part-time for her longtime employer, loves her work environment. "We're an idiosyncratic group of mixed ages and interests, who mostly talk about work-related issues. But there's always humor. We love to tease each other about our quirks. Mine is to buy bottled water to keep on my desk, and most days someone will mention the free water cooler close by. My colleagues mean a lot to me, and I think of them as good friends, even though we rarely see each other outside of work."

The truth is that once we leave the workplace, these friendships tend not to last. Despite good intentions on both sides to stay in touch and meet regularly for lunch, we may find it difficult to keep a former work relationship going. Gossip that fueled our earlier conversations quickly stagnates once we can no longer contribute to it, and unless we have other things in common, such as a mutual passion for art films or travel, the friendship tends to slip away, although it may linger through e-mail jokes and in holiday-card rituals.

Friendships Change

It is no surprise that the friendships we make now differ from those we made when we were in our twenties, thirties, and forties. Back then, our friends were confidantes to whom we opened our hearts and shared our fears and concerns, and loved for knowing the latest gossip; for being funny, attractive, or sexy; for their savvy about things we found unfamiliar or scary; and for being our counselors and cheerleaders. Those friendships were shaped by circumstances that no longer relate to our current situation. Susan Zigouras, a therapist who has led many women's discussion groups, thinks that at this stage we no longer need our friends to be reflections of us. It is not that we are actually changing or becoming different, she says. It's that as our earlier roles and obligations recede, we become more like the person we really are. Which may be a major reason why we don't feel the need to replace the water-cooler-gossip type of bonding we experienced earlier.

Yet we continue to want to forge relationships with others to replace the ones we formed through the workplace or through our child's school—except that without such centering places in our lives, it is difficult to find new people to bond with. The challenge thus becomes how to find ways to build relationships that feed our newly prioritized needs for such things as empathy, respect, stimulation, companionship, and fun, and how to de-emphasize the kinds of relationships that no longer energize us.

Certainly, we continue to value friends for providing emotional support, companionship, and intellectual stimulation, the thing we most fear missing when we leave our jobs. But a new element that our younger selves never gave much thought to enters into the friendship picture, to become increasingly important as we age. That element is our ability to rely on our friends to be there in the event that we need hands-on help.

We are often surprised to hear ourselves say at this point in our lives that we need more woman friends. Yet as we become older, our friendships tend to be less about sharing emotional moments and more about sharing the experience of aging, with friends being a vital part of our support system. In fact, this kind of friendship may well be a whole new relational pattern that doesn't yet have a name.

Marge was sixty-five when she retired from an executive position with a major health-insurance provider. She didn't know what she was hoping for when she retired and didn't try to make anything happen, figuring something would bubble up. Something did! She had always had trouble with her eyes, but eventually it became a real disability and not just an inconvenience. Although classified as legally blind, she is able to get around and enjoy movies and plays. Marge's sight problems make a difference in her friendships. She no longer feels she can call someone up and say, "Let's go to the movies," because that means, "Will you take me to the movies?" Having a disability means "just walking into a room changes the molecules." Because friendships are Marge's lifeline, she has given the subject of friendship a great deal of thought. "No relationship stays the same. They get negotiated and renegotiated every day. People's attitudes and priorities alter. I think good friendships can change greatly. Several of mine are better, some are not. Sometimes a door will close and you won't even hear it. You have to work at a friendship if you want it to continue. Each thing that happens to us as we grow older requires an adjustment."

Marge learned that she could not predict which of her friends would come through well and which ones just didn't know how to do it. She has several good friends, although as she cuts back on her activities, "the crew gets smaller." She knows she has to bring something to the party. She has a good sense of humor, and that goes a long way. And she is always available by telephone to friends who know she will be a dependable and discreet safety net when they have problems.

Friends Keep Us Healthier

It turns out that our desire to connect, laugh, and play with friends is not only enjoyable, it keeps us healthy and aids our recovery from illnesses and accidents. When we are socially isolated, without friends or family, we are at a relatively high risk of dying prematurely. People without friends succumb to heart disease and depression earlier than those of us who are socially connected. Loneliness is a chronically stressful situation, and our bodies respond by aging more rapidly. Having supportive social relationships has a direct impact on our health. Even the common cold can be worse if we are without social connections, while having them helps us fend off colds and infections.

Antiques-show junkies Tina and Jeanne, both in their late fifties, wander through the various exhibitors' booths at local fairs, ever watchful for the perfect "bad taste" object, which they then offer to buy for the other's home, saying "This is you!" They can't go to a show without playing this game, and each enjoys being the first to spot a seriously offensive object.

A peer group discussed the nature of fun, and all agreed that fun is being with others and sharing a physical activity from childhood. As the conversation and memories deepened, a few women recalled how they had loved to dance, and bemoaned the fact that they hadn't done it in years. One person knew of a place where they could take a dance lesson and then just go at it. So the group arranged an evening for all to show up to dance—to salsa, do the Lindy, tango, try a bit of everything. Talking about their experience afterward, they interrupted each other enthusiastically with "I had fun" and "It was really great." Would they do it again? "Absolutely!" They even had a bead on their next outing—to take singing lessons together—and started priming the adventure with competing claims about whose voice was worst.

A WOMAN'S BEST FRIEND

"My dog is my best friend." Those of us who are animal lovers know few limits to our commitment to feed and care for a pet, readily adjusting the way we live to accommodate it. The dog, cat, or bird that shares our home is an important part of our daily focus. Those of us who live with animals score high on tests of happiness and satisfaction, good health, mental alertness, and self-confidence more consistently than our non-pet-owning peers. Rather than seeing the responsibility of caring for and nurturing our pet as a burden, we take pleasure in focusing on this other being. As a result, pets give our days routine, a sense of purpose, and structure, and increase our amount of daily exercise. Dogs are also perfect for starting up conversations and friendships with others.

There are more than ninety million cats and nearly seventy-four million dogs in the United States. Over half of the dog owners say they are more attached to their pets than they are to another human being, and more than one-third of pet owners display a picture of their pet in their home. Dogs and cats are wonderful at helping us dispel feelings of loneliness and depression by encouraging us to release chemicals such as endorphins, the same chemicals that cause runner's high, and serotonin, the antidepressant neurotransmitter, as well as lowering our release of cortisol, the stress hormone. They also help us reduce our cholesterol and triglyceride levels. An oncologist at the Mayo Medical School even instructs his patients to get a pet to help themselves cope with cancer.

Loneliness: The Elephant in the Room

Some of us find ourselves anticipating or actually facing a degree of loneliness we have not experienced before. Such feelings can be triggered when our children no longer need our full attention, or when we lose old friends, or if we are uncomfortable with the free time retirement affords us.

Harriet lost her dear friend Pam several years ago to cancer. She does not think of her all the time, but there are moments when she says to herself, "Oh, Pam would have liked this." They often went shopping together for shoes and liked slightly eccentric styles in oddball colors. One day as Harriet passed a shoe store, she saw a pair that would have sucked Pam inside. "We would have gone in together. The idea of my trying them on without calling her first still seems strange. I do miss her."

Loneliness can loom over us like the impossible-to-ignore "elephant in the room." Single women are generally more comfortable with being alone than women who have lived with partners for a long time. That is because they have learned to enjoy quiet times without feeling lonely or maudlin. Yet, whether single or partnered, as we contemplate how retirement will remove us from activities that have informed our days, all of us must also think about how to replace our daily contacts with new relationships and how to strengthen existing ones. This requires making an active effort to expand the network of people around us. Ten or twenty years earlier, our urge to invest in new friendships was probably stifled by lack of time due to obligations and responsibilities at work and at home. Now that we are in our fifties and sixties, we want to, and must, connect anew, and we have the time to do it.

ON FINDING NEW FRIENDS

Without the earlier workplace or schoolyard "hooks" to draw in new friends, we need to actively look for new places to find communities of people. Below are some ideas for finding such communities—but the best advice is to follow your interests and see where they lead. Above all, recognize that it will take some effort. You must get out—and reach out—to make it work.

- Join book clubs. Ask your local librarian about book clubs in your area. Check the library bulletin board for notices, or post one yourself. Start a book club of your own by approaching friends and asking them to invite people they think will be interested.
- Check out churches and temples. They usually have many organized groups and activities, including book clubs, investment clubs, social clubs, travel groups, lectures, and more.
- Form a club to share information. For instance, if you like to manage your investments, invite like-minded friends and acquaintances to meet regularly to discuss investment possibilities. Also ask your accountant and friends for suggestions about others who might be interested in such a group.
- Take courses in whatever appeals to you—pottery making, music, drawing, history, politics, anthropology, physics—to find others who share your interests. Look at programs given by local colleges, museums, or other organizations.
- Join an existing peer group, or form your own around a specific topic. If you are interested in exploring issues around, say, unstructured time in retirement, let it be known to everyone you see that you'd like to explore this and other topics of intellectual interest. Usually, you'll find people who are interested.
- Volunteer. One of the best ways to meet new friends is to volunteer with a nonprofit organization. Opportunities for volunteering are everywhere. (Look in the Resources section under Volunteering for ideas.)
- Find an event you want to go to. Buy an extra ticket and invite someone you know, even if only slightly, to go with you. She or he will appreciate it and be likely to reciprocate in the future.
- Join a choir or choral group through a church or local college. It will give you a chance to befriend people of all ages who share your enthusiasm for music and singing.
- Talk to strangers on plane trips or at other times when you're thrown together with people you don't know and the opportunity is right. As you talk, you might find you share similar interests, which can lead to new opportunities for you. It works time and time again.

- Be open to new possibilities. Cast off any shyness that may have been part of your earlier self. Remember that others are probably as open to making new contacts as you are. Everyone has a story and will be eager to hear yours. Take the initiative. People are often flattered at being approached.
- Follow up with new people you've met. Invite them to join you in an activity you enjoy, or plan a dinner party (make it a pot-luck meal if you're not up to cooking everything yourself) and invite them.

Finding Friends from Long Ago

This is a time when many of us become more aware of longtime friends, especially those who have shared various stages of our lives. If they are part of our lives, we cherish them more and more as the years go by. Old friends and best friends hold a place in our hearts that no new friend can penetrate. The bonds that seal these relationships formed years ago, and we share a common history and memories of when we were there for each other, during crises and moments of bliss. Usually, full sentences are unnecessary in order for us to communicate with one another; a few unfinished phrases work miraculously.

> *A longtime friend is someone who knows everything about me, and I know everything about her. When we meet, it is like we met just yesterday. It's a bit like being sisters. We speak a shorthand because of our shared history.*
>
> **—Patty**

Some of our old friends are not everyday friends, in the sense that we live far apart and are not in regular contact with each other. But a strong connection based on nostalgia for the past, and our memories of good times together, exists nonetheless, and if an earlier friend has faded from our lives, we may search for her or be genuinely delighted when she finds us. Retired for five years, Keisha, age sixty-one, received a surprise call from her best friend from fifth grade, who was living in Pennsylvania. "I hadn't seen her in thirty, thirty-five, years. We met at a hotel, and as we walked down the long hallway toward each other, she screamed, 'You haven't changed a bit!' 'You haven't either!' I screamed back. It was so great; we remembered each other from when we were twelve. It's as if, no matter how old we are, we were still twelve. And there is something quite wonderful about that."

> *People's lives change. To keep all your old friends is like keeping all your old clothes—pretty soon your closet is so jammed and everything so crushed you can't find anything to wear. Help these friends when they need you; bless the years and happy times when you meant a lot to each other, but try not to have the guilts if new people mean more to you now.*
>
> **—Helen Gurley Brown**

The Internet has been a boon to those of us searching for long-lost friends. Googling names from our past may yield results, although it usually takes more serious searches to find someone whose name has changed since the time we knew them. But once a connection is made, e-mail is a remarkably easy way to maintain the friendship. Just sending a quick *Thought you'd be interested in seeing this*, along with a link, or forwarding a joke, serves as a reminder to our friend that we are thinking of her.

When Old Friendships No Longer Fit

It is during a transition that a friendship is most tested, and we become uncomfortable when old friendships no longer fit. Over the course of our lives, certain friends drift away, and we often make little or no effort to continue these relationships. Allison recalls that when she was in her thirties and forties, her family moved frequently between various American cities and Europe, finally settling in a suburban area in Ohio. She attributes her feeling of separation from friends to distance, busy schedules, and the fact that what they had in common isn't there anymore.

She also tells the story of a friend of hers who basically "cleaned house" and stopped seeing all the people in her life she thought were a negative influence. The friend reports that she's much happier now, adding that it must have been the right thing for her to do.

We cherish and value friends when they fit, but relationships can also become threadbare and cling uncomfortably, until we decide we just can't take it anymore. Sylvia and Martha's friendship goes way back to their school days together in Brussels. Both came to the United States at about the same time, and they remained friends over the years. Sylvia completed her doctorate and went on to teach at a well-known university; Martha went from one bizarre job choice to another, complaining all the while about her lack of success and luck. Finally, Sylvia realized the friendship was and had always been all about Martha and her troubles, which she increasingly cloaked herself in as she whined. Often, such a friendship does not end officially, with exchanged words, but simply trails off as we gradually withdraw and become less available.

> *I'm not happy with the state of my friendships. I could use more. How to get them is what concerns me.*
>
> **—Eva**

Sometimes circumstances change the way we react to each other. Sherry, a former high school teacher who lives in Los Angeles, has a dear friend with several serious disabilities. Where their friendship was once based on equality and interdependence, it has shifted to one of dependency and accommodation. Sherry says her friend is eternally grateful for whatever she can give her, but that only makes Sherry feel guilty for not giving more. She says she is very committed to the friendship, but it has changed in ways that make her sad.

Communities Without Walls

At this point we want to build a community of friends that will share a slice of our life—but not necessarily every aspect of it. We find ourselves reaching out to those who will complement us, or add something fresh and exciting, or challenge us in specific ways. We are eager to expand our network of friendships but also find that it is harder to make new friends now, even though we may have fewer family commitments and more free time. We used to meet people on common ground—first in school, then at work or at the PTA—but now we must search for new outlets. It takes effort, despite the fact that we are better able to express our thoughts and feelings in various kinds of friendships and have the social skills to reach out and connect with others.

> *At the very beginning we were a group of complete strangers. Which was good, because we couldn't fall back on "What are your kids doing?" kinds of conversations.*
>
> **—voice from a peer group**

When Michele and her husband moved from San Francisco to Boston, they were surprised to find that making new friends was a challenge, after years of working for a local university where they were surrounded by colleagues with similar interests. Recognizing the difficulty one can experience trying to make friends in a new situation, Michele sympathized with a woman who had recently moved to Winnetka, Illinois, and had been unable to make new friends. Since Michele's sister lived in Winnetka, she called and asked her to call the woman, adding the incentive: "You both play golf, so I figure you might have something in common." She still cringes when she thinks about her sister's response: "Since she's new, she can call me if she wants. I don't need any new friends." Because of her own experience trying to make new friends in Boston, Michele acknowledges that this is not an isolated sentiment and thinks that it is more difficult for someone to meet new friends in a small, well-established community than in large metropolitan areas such as New York, Chicago, and San Francisco, where people seem more open to making new connections.

We all have had communities of friends in our lives, each drawn from a specific area. When we get together with our college friends, it's just our college friends. When we meet with our work friends, it's just our work friends, and we segregate them even further, according to a particular job or a special project. As Janna was about to retire from a top position with a state-government agency, she wanted to be with others who were struggling with the same issues as she was and with whom she could share interests. Her solution took her along several paths: she volunteered at a nearby museum, where she met people who shared her passion for collecting pottery; she went to work for a political candidate and met people who had similar political values; she joined a book club; and she formed a peer group with other women who were interested in talking about stimulating topics.

When our parents' generation began to retire, they were sold the idea of finding the good life in the kind of "brick-and-mortar" gated communities built around golf courses or recreational centers. Nowadays, many of us don't want such focused, couple-centric, nondiverse communities. Instead, we want communities without walls, where we live independently among people of all ages, ethnicities, and occupations and can connect when we choose with others who are going through similar life experiences.

> *I've made friendships with others who are struggling with the same issues I am. These were people who would not have entered into my friendship circle at all. They are from different backgrounds, different professions, different fields, which is why it is such a rich, rewarding experience.*
>
> **—voice from a peer group**

The single biggest success story of The Transition Network is the establishment of groups of women who come together to discuss issues around transition. Initially organized around subjects such as renewing careers, preparing for retirement, launching new businesses, and pondering deep thoughts about the meaning of time, the groups eventually developed their unique styles. The conversations range from talking about books to discussing living singly or living with partners; from visiting ethnic restaurants to discussing foreign affairs. The point is not so much how the meetings are structured or where they take place; it's that everyone talks and listens.

> *At first, we didn't listen to each other that well. Everyone wanted to talk. But we started talking topically, rather than personally, and then relationships developed. Now we've jelled into a group of like minds. We feel we're in a safe environment to talk about issues that are really important, and that we are there for each other.*
>
> **—voice from a peer group**

Usually, the women who join a group will not know any of the others there. At the start of the first meeting, each one identifies her work background, retirement status, and goals and a brief reason why she is there. What is so extraordinary is that within the two hours of the first session, a powerful bond develops. Over and over again, groups come together as the women recognize that others have similar concerns about the future and also want to grab hold and make that future their own.

Delia joined the Next Chapter peer group shortly after she arrived in New York to start a life away from her newly "ex-ed" husband and their suburban Pennsylvania life. She says with obvious pride: "The women in my peer group are good new friends. Most of all, they inspire me to embrace the richness of New York's cultural life and to look forward to many other things I had not imagined for myself. It's like I have nine sisters who are there for me."

Having opportunities to meet and talk with others is enormously valuable for us at this stage. Peer discussion groups can mimic the communities of friends we had through school or work, but, in addition, they offer a ready-made set of common interests that address our aging and the transitions that are a part of it, and they nurture our need for intellectual stimulation and social contact.

At a December peer-group meeting, Bertha, now sixty-six and retired for two years, casually asked, "Anyone want to go to Puerto Vallarta?" Patty, also retired, spontaneously replied, "Oh, I do." Even though they had been in the peer group for only a short time, they felt they knew each other well enough to travel together. The trip lasted a month, and they considered it such a success that they are planning a cruise down the Danube together.

Our need for a community of others is powerful. A woman from Alaska inquired about joining a TTN chapter. She had grown up in Anchorage and was looking for a connection, but with a slightly different variation on the theme. She said that women in Anchorage normally leave the state when they retire, so the population of women over fifty is always low, and those who stay are thus part of a very small community. She didn't feel comfortable forming a peer group to talk about some of the challenges she was facing with women she had known since kindergarten and whose parents knew her parents. Instead, she wanted to find some kind of Internet chat room where people from remote communities—or those who wanted to be part of a remote community and not stuck in their own geography—could discuss issues in a convenient and discreet environment.

> *When I retired I found I missed the people I had socialized with at work. I think that's one of the reasons my peer group is so important to me—it's the connection to others that means so much.*
>
> —**Evelyn**

Such chat rooms currently exist on the Internet and will continue to grow according to need. TTN has virtual peer groups composed of women from different parts of the country who either cannot easily commute to existing peer groups or who wish to connect with women outside of their geographic areas. Each month, these peer groups "meet" by telephone- or Web-based conference call to discuss a predetermined topic and offer one another emotional support and friendship. In addition, there are Web-based discussion groups in which members of specific TTN chapters opine about important issues based on shared and personal experiences, in a secure online environment. These are just two examples of how technology can open up our lives to include others and create both nearby and far-flung communities without boundaries.

Women Lead the Way

Fifty-one percent of women in the United States are unmarried. Many live with a partner, but many live singly, having been divorced or widowed or having never been married. Psychotherapist Mary Beth Kelly says she believes that women living alone are defining the way the rest of us think about this point in our lives. We know the statistics show that we are likely to outlive our partners, and this expectation influences our thoughts about how we will sustain ourselves if and when we become single. As part of such forethought, some of us are beginning to consider living communally or in close proximity to friends. It's happening as we move into condos or other living situations to be among people we know and to reduce the burden of individual effort. Says Kelly, "It makes a lot of sense for us to invent ways to keep all the carefully cultivated connections we've made over the years from falling apart just when we need them most." It's a new direction for friendships to take, and we may see more such alternatives develop in the future.

CHAPTER
10

Why Is My Partner Driving Me Crazy?

Devotion and intimacy . . . commitment and caring . . . laughter . . . sharing and companionship . . . pleasure. Love. We give so much of ourselves in an intimate relationship and get so much in return. Since few of us live in a vacuum, we can't approach retirement without considering our life partners or, for that matter, our dependent children or aging parents. And such close bonds push and pull us in directions that can temporarily threaten our dreams and goals for the future, or set us on an unalterable course.

It is impossible, of course, to speak about any intimate relationship as a general experience, because every couple is unique. There's no question that retirement spotlights and reinforces what already is, with happy relationships likely to improve and unhappy ones to deteriorate. The stress of retirement on an already strained relationship can easily become the proverbial straw that causes it to collapse. In addition, marital stress seems to increase when one of us retires and the other does not, and even more so when the decision to retire is not within our control. But, although the rates of over-fifty divorce are beginning to rise, the fact is that many marriages stay intact in retirement, and marital satisfaction usually rebounds from previous lows, to reach new, higher levels.

Those of us who have satisfactory marriages and value the time we spend with our spouses often try to retire early and to do it at the same time they do, or at least within two years of them, although if our spouses are more than five years older than we are, they will tend to work longer in order to retire nearer to the time we do. In fact, newly retired men with wives who continue to work frequently claim to be dissatisfied with retirement. While we may aim to retire together, achieving that goal can be stymied by a partner's health problems or by an involuntary job loss. When such a thing happens, especially if it occurs before Social Security and other retirement benefits kick in, the other spouse will usually continue to work.

> *Negotiations about how much time to spend together become more of an issue because we have more time.*
>
> —Diana

How we respond to retirement as a couple depends on whether we are looking at the *event* of retirement or at what happens during the elongated *process* of retirement. Most of us find the event stressful and say that clashes increase during this stage. Two years after, we often realize that the process of retirement has increased harmony and improved the quality of our relationship.

The Assumptions Game

No matter whether our relationship has been a long- or short-term one, when something like a retirement transition forces us to reevaluate what we want, and to consider it in tune with our partners, we can discover astounding things—particularly that our assumptions about what our partners want to do, how they want to spend their time, and where they want to live are completely wrong. That's because retirement puts us in an entirely different environment.

Having retired from teaching, Mindy was waiting for her husband to leave his law practice so that they could "really travel." But when she finally mentioned her wish to him, he told her, "I don't expect our life will change much. We'll still travel some, but I won't be earning money, so we'll have to be very thoughtful about what we do." That really upset her: "I had this fantasy I thought we shared."

Faye thinks that when the topic of retirement comes up, we are prepared to think about and negotiate it, "whereas men don't notice that anything has changed except that it's a quarter past nine and we're still in our bathrobes instead of in the car commuting." For many men the issue of restructuring life together usually gets resolved in an ad hoc way. For example, when a man retires and wants to relax and enjoy himself, he may find that his wife doesn't want to sit still. Rather, she looks for projects. She wants to give back. She tells him, "Why don't you go out and be a mentor? Why don't you call up Steven and have lunch with him?" *Why don't you do this, why don't you do that?* And he says, "But now I'm retired!"

With each aspect of their lives that comes up, the world looks different. He asks, "Are we going to have a place in Florida? Will you take up golf again and join me? Will you want me to go to all those cultural things that I went to the office to avoid for all these years?" He may want to talk about long-term-care insurance and his will, but not about things that have to do with the relationship.

Ask us about our plans for retirement, and we'll tell you. Ask us what our partners think of those plans, and we'll admit that we haven't discussed it with them because our partners don't believe that retirement will ever happen or that anything will change. Ask us again why we haven't discussed our dreams with our partners, and we may admit concerns that they will shoot them down before they have a chance to take flight.

Kari and her husband planned to retire on the same day from their respective jobs for the federal government but had a rough time talking to each other about what they wanted to do. She saw herself working as a consultant and thought he would work part-time as well. He planned to stop working and thought she would do the same. After she mentioned the possibility of getting a good job in another city and he brought home literature about a cabin in what Kari describes as "the middle of nowhere, six hours from the nearest airport!" they realized they'd had a major communication glitch. In a panic, Kari told him, "We can't retire. We're not ready. We don't know where we're going, and if you just quit and start looking for a place to go and veg out, and I go in a different direction, it's just not going to work." Both had their own ways of spending time, mostly apart, and both realized how out of touch they had become. So they tried doing more things together. She worked with him around the yard. He took a part-time job. She agreed to work a bit less. And they moved to her family house in a small farm town so that he could have a rural environment while she could continue to work part-time and take day trips to the nearby city. In another bow to their renewed relationship, Kari also agreed to join him in an exercise plan. "It isn't a bad idea for us to walk and maybe play a little golf—anything to keep us connected." Now both are happily retired and determined to make their relationship work.

> *I am hoping retirement is romantic. We get along well and I can see us having many more wonderful times. It's like adventures with someone you want to hang out with.*
>
> —Catherine

Negotiations: Everything Is up for Discussion

Our relationships and patterns of behaviors become fixed over the years. Retirement tests them in every which way. Suddenly, or so it seems, everything is fair game for reappraisal.

It is critical to start to discuss retirement goals early. Two-thirds of couples over fifty presumably have communicated enough to say they have the same goals in retirement, but nearly a quarter of couples admit they haven't talked about it at all. Frequently there is a clash of expectations. Where will we live? Do we share interests? Do we want the same things? How shall we spend our money? And do we have a viable financial plan? All are important issues that may not have been discussed in depth since the beginnings of our relationships.

If we have paid attention over the years, we will have compatible values and goals. But retirement makes us look at major personal changes, as we grope with new identities and spend time together without the buffers of children or jobs to derail difficult conversations. Suddenly, our former communicative "sound bites"—quick hellos and good-byes—are no longer adequate. And previously established household roles are no longer comfortable. In addition, we must become better attuned to things we do that stress our partners, and vice versa. For instance, when we go out to be with our friends for social or community activities, we may threaten our partners' sense of togetherness. Sharing a happy retirement with our partners comes down to the obvious but difficult-to-implement notion that we must plan the future together by exchanging ideas with candor—and with a great deal of diplomacy, affection, and humor.

Gloria, age fifty-three, admits that during the last twenty-four years, conversations with her husband focused almost exclusively on the kids and then, when the kids went away, on what the kids were doing. She asks, "How do you have a conversation about where you want to live for the next twenty years, or whether you should take the retirement package being offered now, when the focus hasn't been on what's going to make the two of you happy?"

Differences Between Women and Men

Of course, not all men and women see the world from differing points of view or find themselves in a face-off over incompatible visions and goals. But stereotypes about gender patterns and behaviors in relationships are worth noting because they are often based on true observations. Let's look at a few.

Retirement is a time to relax, he says. She bristles at the word "relax," conjuring up images of a couch potato without goals or direction.

She wants to get out of the house, have new adventures, and maybe travel to exotic places. He likes to putter around the house making repairs, being with the family, and meeting a friend for a game of tennis or golf.

She wants to become absorbed in volunteer work for a worthy cause. He joins the board of a nonprofit organization to volunteer his management and professional expertise during monthly or quarterly meetings.

She engages in conversations primarily with other women, through book clubs and discussion groups that widen her circle of friends and acquaintances. He considers his spouse his best friend and gets together mostly with male friends for sports and camaraderie, preferring not to spend time with strangers.

She wants to discover new activities, and learn new skills and about new ideas, outside of the home. He enjoys unstructured time to watch television and allow his day to unravel at will.

She may become impatient with his being "underfoot" or dependent on her for organizing activities and social schedules. He is willing to "help" with chores as long as she identifies what they are and makes most of their social arrangements. And so on.

An example of different gender styles is apparent among a group of couples who spend free time in a rural upstate New York community. In response to the women's having a monthly all-female book club, the men considered starting a book club of their own, but it never took off until someone suggested they form the Big Equipment Club instead. Aside from its humorous name, the idea appealed to the men because they like to work outdoors wielding chain saws and axes. A few have tractors, and there is even a backhoe available for the kind of serious digging that can move a mountain. As the women talked books, the men cleared brush, opened paths through the woods, and built stone walls, and when they ran out of projects of their own, they joined a Habitat for Humanity building project nearby. In companionable groups, it seems the women like to talk, and the men like to do.

Divorce on the Rise

In Japan, newly retired salarymen often go on overseas vacations with their wives, only to return home to a "new Narita divorce." The phenomenon takes its name from the Narita International Airport, outside of Tokyo, where many Japanese wives inform their husbands—whom they rarely saw all the time he was employed—that they will not permit a clinging stranger to become part of their well-established, independent lives. And it's not only in Japan that divorce is on the rise for the over-fifty crowd. In the United States divorce rates for couples past fifty are climbing, with two-thirds of the women doing the walking, and, more often than not, taking the men totally by surprise. What's behind this trend? One AARP study found that the reasons we most often give for separations are that we need freedom, self-identity, and fulfillment. But the truth is that so little research has been done on divorce in late adulthood that the answers must be largely anecdotal.

The decision to seek a divorce is not a casual thing and is usually precipitated by discontentments that have been smoldering for years, ready to erupt when major changes occur. Fifty-year-old women frequently find divorce a stressful conundrum. On the one hand we say we enjoy not having to put up with another person; on the other hand, we frequently become involved in a serious, exclusive relationship within two years afterward. Those of us over sixty who are divorced say we are grateful to have our own identity, which may be why we are wary of marrying again. But divorce is never easy, and a great many of us who go through it suffer from varying degrees of loneliness and depression, aggravated by feelings of failure and concerns about financial vulnerability. When retirement is also in the picture, such feelings of loss are magnified even further. This may be why many couples delay retirement decisions: they see the workplace as a safe haven from marital discord.

> *Among couples between 40 and 70, it is the woman who usually initiates the divorce.*
>
> —AARP survey, 2004

Asking Tough Questions

Rigidity, worry, regrets, lack of courage, and thinking of life as mostly behind us are a few of the things that get in the way of our making healthy transitions. When we get stuck in the past and focus on things like "I should have," "I could have," "I ought to have," it keeps us from moving forward, psychotherapist Mary Beth Kelly told us. Feeling that we are with the wrong person and can't do anything about it shuts down possibilities that we will make good choices in the future. Sometimes our inability to move forward is a result of our being stuck in the expectation that solutions will come to us, rather than finding them for ourselves. Or we may have set ideas about what a good marriage looks like and will not tolerate changing ours, because of what other people will think.

Kay and her husband had been unhappy about their relationship for many years. The signs were all around them. He had another woman, whom he saw regularly. She knew about it but thought that at least they would be with each other in their later years. One day he moved out of the house to end their marriage, leaving her alone and hurt.

Her story compels us to ask ourselves some extremely difficult questions that may rock our boats and pitch us into a sea of unknowns, or set us on a new course together. Kelly says that shake-ups lead to our standing up well for ourselves within our relationship. Even when what we want isn't going to be met with encouragement and support because our partners are in a very different stage of their own lives, it's important that we deal with the things that are always problematic in a relationship—especially the issues of where we are different and how we should navigate those differences.

> *I can understand why a woman in her early sixties might say, "I've had this kind of a life. I don't need him anymore. I want to move on." And she's not necessarily moving on to find a man. She's moving on to find a different kind of life and the freedom and independence that would bring.*
>
> —**Katie**

Raising tough questions reveals much about the structure of our relationships. Can we discuss things that are hard, or do stonewalling, shutdowns, and defensiveness keep the issues and our feelings off the table? Are we able to hash out the differences and hit upon something we can live with, even if it's not ideal? Can we rethink expectations we put upon ourselves, or hold on to as we try to measure up to others' expectations? We are aware that we don't have all the time in the world. Yet we do have the opportunity now—if only we can grab it—to live authentically and express parts of ourselves we subdued when raising kids and bringing home the bacon.

It takes a lot of courage to stand up for ourselves, especially if we've played it safe or haven't practiced establishing our independence. We may find ourselves at a make-or-break point. Is it going to be more of the same feelings—of being de-energized, without adventure or novelty or kindness? Are we ready to face what we don't know? Kelly points out that there is always anxiety about the unknown—but also about what we do know. She says that our willingness to change depends on the levels of anxiety we want to manage and our ability to trust that we'll figure out the next step. "Thinking about how we handled other times in our lives when we were thrown off kilter or didn't get our first choice helps because it allows us to rely on muscle memory to imagine ourselves landing on our feet."

Togetherness Versus Dependency

When Ginny stopped working full-time, she remembers thinking the unspeakable. Since the age of sixteen she had been independent and in charge of her life, but now she worries that retirement will narrow her world to the point where her emotional and social life will be more dependent on her partner. And even though in some ways she looks forward to that, she fears that if she is dependent on him for primary companionship, emotional support, and the daily rhythms of her life, she won't be able to cope if something happens to him. Statistically, he is likely to die or decline at an earlier age than she, and he is already five years older. She feels she is entering dangerous emotional territory without having the cushion of a busy work life to fall back on.

> *I think things that drive me nuts about my husband are magnified now because I see them more. I also think that the things that made me fall in love with him are much more intensified. So there's a deeper intimacy and closeness. I guess that's the nature of the kind of marriage you have: whatever your marriage is gets intensified, for better or for worse, in this stage of life.*
>
> —Lorraine

Over the years we and our partners have worked hard to create a balance between our independence and togetherness. It has become an informal, unwritten contract of how to be a couple. When one or both of us retire, that balance can tip precariously in one direction or the other. Social historian Stephanie Coontz, writing in the *New York Times*, offers a different perspective on marital relationships. She notes that as recently as a hundred years ago, romantic love and togetherness were not the defining goals of a marriage. Rather, most societies considered it "dangerously antisocial, even pathologically self-absorbed, to elevate marital affection and nuclear-family ties above commitments to neighbors, extended kin, civic duty and religion." Coontz suggests that because we have "put all [our] emotional eggs in the basket of coupled love," we neglect important other relationships.

> *I want flexibility in my work and in my relationship too. I want freedom and companionship at the same time. I want to do what I want to do when I want to do it, but I want someone to be there when I need help.*
>
> —**Ginny**

Our current concept of marital togetherness reached a high point during the 1950s, when the nuclear family was touted as the ultimate path to fulfillment. That idea hasn't changed much, except that we added working full-time to our role of caring for our spouses and children. As we lavished attention on our work and on marital relationships, our need for intimacy was satisfied by fewer people. The resulting dependency makes us more vulnerable to loss and isolation and contributes to stressful expectations that our partners can meet all our needs—including our need for a refuge in retirement.

When We Are Needed

One partner's illness or disability can change everything for both. Commitments we made to each other in good times are even more critical when one of us needs support and care. If it is our partner who is dependent on us for help, we try to be there as best we can and put our concerns about our own independence and dream catching on hold. It is a difficult time for everyone involved. Many of us who are faced with this challenge find it enormously helpful to talk with other women who are dealing with similar issues. How we deal with this depends on so many factors that it's difficult to address them even briefly in this book.

Separate Space

Kim is relieved that her husband hasn't retired yet. For eight years she has had the run of their home to adjust to her independent retirement life, with no accountability to anyone other than herself for what she does and when she does it. Even though she loves her husband dearly, if he were home more often she worries that he would breathe down her neck, evaluating how she spent her time. She certainly doesn't want to feel accountable to him. If she wants to do nothing, she knows that's her prerogative.

Virginia, an educator and administrator for the federal government before she retired, is currently among the unretired, having left her career for two years, then taken a different full-time position. She has gone through the retirement process, though, and she advises couples not to leave their jobs at the same moment. "One should go first and figure out some sort of pattern and then have the other see where she or he connects or doesn't." Otherwise, she says, "you wind up being joined at the hip" and doing things that neither wants to do for part of the day.

The relationship between two people will be tested as seldom before when they are suddenly thrust together day and night. Some couples share a common area and wholeheartedly enjoy each other's full-time presence. But many of us need a separate space, where we can be protected from unwanted interference.

In her postcorporate, retirement career, Mandy works from home on a number of different projects, including consulting, teaching, and writing. Her husband, Arthur, recently began to work from home as part of his transition toward full retirement. If anyone had told Mandy that they could both work at home peacefully, she would have been skeptical. But both of them say the experience has been wonderful, albeit with a few minor complaints. They are talkative types, so when they don't get out to see others, they regularly interrupt each other. He is a political junkie and eagerly tells her when there is news. That usually occurs while she is writing, and she must control herself to keep from saying, "That's terrific, but I can't listen to you because I just lost exactly what I was thinking about."

Or he'll yell up to her, "Do you think the dog has to go out?" and she thinks, but does not say aloud, "How should I know, since the dog is downstairs with you?" But she says there are also many days when they have lunch together, which is wonderful, and they are getting along better than ever.

> *At the moment, we're both working out of our home, and, to both of our amazements, it's fun!*
>
> —**Mandy**

Lorraine thinks of her husband as an Energizer Bunny who will never retire. She left her primary career to spend time with her family and on her exercise routine, painting, and serving on the board of a local institution. Although busy, she has been able to get to the point where she can sit and do nothing on occasion. Except that "guilt" pops into her mind, especially when her husband comes home at the end of the day and asks, "What did you do today?" The question is like waving a red flag in front of a bull. In fact, she had a wonderful day but can't bring herself to verbalize that she got up and exercised, showered, had a manicure, and spent two hours at her desk on board work while he went to six meetings and solved ten problems. She recognizes that she has to get over her idea of what it means to be productive, and keep her life private and separate from his. After all, "He didn't know what I did every day that I went to work, so there is no reason for him to know what I do every minute I'm home."

Role Reversion

Retirement influences our decisions about the division of household labor and the power structure of the relationship. Preparing lunch was rarely a chore when we worked outside the home, but now that we're home with our partner, it can default to the one who normally prepares dinner. Or it can come up for negotiation.

Helen figures her husband didn't even realize she had lightened his load of household chores. She had just picked up the household slack, claiming, "I honestly don't mind. I feel that he is working and maintaining us financially, so the least I can do is . . ." Her thought trails off; she picks it up a moment later to say that he has always been a good, sharing person who does a lot around the house and who helped raise the kids. But her hesitation suggests that she is a bit uncomfortable with the lack of sharing of household responsibilities. One wonders whether she lost some confidence and self-esteem during her retirement transition. Perhaps that explains why she reverted to outmoded ideas about how work at home is divided? Of course, if questions about how the living room gets straightened up, the cat litter gets changed, the laundry gets washed and sorted, the dishes get done, went unresolved earlier in our relationships, then they will continue to be bait for conflict.

Conflict Resolution

How easily such things get settled has to do with our abilities to problem solve. When we bicker or fight, hot-button topics like finances or sexual inadequacies or household chores can be red herrings, having more to do with how we handle differences than with the problems themselves. Most couples got through earlier transitions during their time together by engaging in constructive argument delivered with a strong mixture of independence, empathy, and diplomacy. Such a base, and the confidence we gained from successfully resolving past disagreements, improve the odds that we will get through this new stage as well. Couples in newer relationships who have not gone through such tests find themselves less certain about the outcomes.

Another topic seldom acknowledged or discussed is who holds more power in the relationship. Usually, the balance of power evolves over the years, with each partner figuring out ways to accommodate the other while also retaining some influence. It is common for the power balance to alter and even reverse during retirement transitions. Suddenly, decisions frequently initiated by one partner may be taken up and led by the other.

When Mimi was working, she loved earning a high salary and the feeling of independence it gave her. Now that she is retired, it bothers her to be on her husband's health-care plan, which, she realizes, is really stupid, since it is a fabulous plan. Also, he always complained about the money she spent, which she attributed to a common male inclination to get upset over perceptions about how women spend, and to his own personal inclination to be a bit cheap. She would deal with it by refusing to tell him how much something cost and by paying her bills from her personal checking account. But now that she no longer earns much money, she feels just a little bit uncomfortable at the thought that he may think he has nagging rights.

When Mindy stopped earning a salary, she told her husband she couldn't stand the fact that she didn't have any money. He responded, "It's all our money," which made her realize that he was giving her permission to do what she wanted and not feel bad about it. And that was useful to her in one sense, "but it wasn't permission I wanted. He didn't understand that I felt less independent."

Recalibrating the Balance

Wanting too much togetherness is often a problem when both partners are retired. Sue, sixty-two, has had what she describes as a "relatively unstructured life." A mother of five children, she also had the luxury of taking up leading-edge interests, including starting a dance group which became the focus of a documentary film that she coproduced and directed. She feels it has been difficult for her husband of twelve years to find something like a hobby or service work to engage him, "whereas I have a zillion things to do." She complains that he wants to spend all their time together doing what he likes to do, while she has projects that don't especially interest him. "Sometimes I do what he wants, even though it's not what I would choose for myself; sometimes I really like it and it's good for me, even though I wouldn't initiate it myself. And sometimes I announce that I'm going to do something without him, making it clear that I'm not asking for his opinion, because it's not up for negotiation."

Efforts to be flexible and make adjustments are critical if relationships are to work, although too often the flexibility can be all on our part. Frieda's husband had been retired for several years, while she worked full-time at a college and had a million projects going around the house. When she turned sixty-four, he said, "Okay, I'd really like you to retire." She was happy being in a stimulating job with major responsibilities. "Just through longevity I got to be involved in the committees and the running of the school, and I really love teaching." Though reluctant to retire, she could not resist his feelings—he was really lonesome, didn't want to be alone all day when she was so busy, and truly needed her. She had a grand retirement party, and then they went on an extended trip in their RV. "That trip was a good idea because it broke my pattern, which had revolved around the school year—in August work started, in May it stopped, and then I could play." Deliberately taking off when the school year began helped her adjust. But back home she needed more stimulation. So a while later, when she was offered an opportunity to start up a new program at school on a part-time basis, she jumped at the chance. It fulfilled her needs yet still gave her time to enjoy activities with her husband.

> *Four of the most dreaded words to a wife are "I'll go with you."*
> —Sue

Compromise is necessary. A loving relationship usually means communication that accommodates bending on both sides. We have to know when to take a stand about something that is important and when to back down from battles we are never going to win. Newer relationships, especially, have their own dynamics. Greer and Al are highly charged individuals who got together when Greer was in her forties and Al in his fifties. Although very much in love, they lived in separate cities, commuting for weekends and holidays together. Al retired first, and Greer accepted a good job nearby in the advertising field that she loved. But she hadn't worked there very long before she experienced frustrating bottom-line standards that made it a less creative place to work. So she decided to start her own consulting business and work out of their suburban Chicago home. "It turned out to be great because Al and I are each very, very independent. He has his way of running his life and I have my way of running mine." He especially enjoys sailing and other outdoor activities; she loves writing and consulting for select clients. Then one day he announced he wanted to winter in Florida, where he had previously lived, as a corporate executive. Greer's idea of Florida was of a place where people lose connection with the real world. But she was game to give it a try. She says that they found a cute apartment near the east coast and met several people they enjoyed being with, but she became cranky during her first year there; even though she was writing and consulting, she felt retired by virtue of the fact that she was in Florida. Her inner voice protested, "Wait a second. I did what I needed to do to make our lives work. I'm losing my sense of self. I just can't do this." A good friend advised her that she needed to somehow, in her own, sweet way, explain to Al that she was becoming a person he was not familiar with.

> *My husband and I want to retire when we still think we're on top of our worlds. We want to make sure we leave when the time is right and not when we're past our peaks. We keep checking in on each other and have promised to be brutally candid when the time comes. We want to retire on our terms.*
>
> —Catherine

Florida was not the problem. She didn't care where she was or what the weather was like. Rather, she needed to be productive and involved. "I live life in my head. I live life with my friends, and my parents and my daughters. I live life with my work." Al based his life around activities dependent on weather, complaining he was vitamin-D deprived on rainy days. At an incredibly opportune moment, one of Greer's clients asked her to write a book with him. She jumped at the chance, wrote up a proposal, got an agent, revised the proposal, got a publisher, and quickly had a job as an author. "I needed this project because it gave me back my strength. It was an identity I needed. I love the writing, the research, and the intellectual demand that it puts on me, but mostly it gives me back my self, my mojo." And it gave her the strength to tell Al to stay in Florida while she went back to Chicago to finish the book. "He understood completely," she says. But there were times when he asked her to come to Florida to play golf with him, and she could tell by his voice that she needed to bend. Other times, she would put her foot down and tell him, "Look, you're just going to have to be a big boy. I can't do this today." She says that, although he doesn't like hearing it, he deals with it.

Being Together

Alice thinks retirement is harder for her spouse than for her because he was totally defined by his job, while she was driven at work but also had other things to engage her. "I think sometimes he is a little bit adrift. He says he is envious of how I sow seeds so quickly and can jump into whatever comes up. He's much more methodical. He'll make a plan of what he wants to do but then won't do it right away, and when he does it, it's A, B, C, D, and E, and it might be successful, or not."

She says they have always enjoyed spending time together and have also had independent lives. "Even in retirement that's the case. We might eat lunch together if we're both at home. Often, I'm gone more than he is. We take a walk together every morning and are aware of setting up patterns. I'm worried that I won't have time to be by myself." She thinks she's lucky to have a partner who is healthy, and she is aware of that much of the time. "That vulnerability is right there. We've actually asked each other what each would do if the other died. We've allowed ourselves to go over that abyss. Once I asked him if he ever looks at me and sees the older person that I'm going to become. He said yes, and I said, 'And sometimes I see what you will look like when you're eighty.'" She adds that it's kind of shocking and reminds herself to sit up straight, because hunching's a giveaway of old age!

> *I've spent half of my grown-up life by myself and half with somebody and simply prefer being in the company of an intimate person, because it's more fun.*
>
> —**Cynthia**

Judith is married to a man who is fifteen years older than she. Retired, he enjoys staying home, while she works part-time and loves being out and about. When she gets together with friends, she makes a point of inviting him along, although she counts on his saying no. She doesn't consider their separateness a constraint because they have developed an informal ritual that brings them together most days. At 4:15 in the afternoon, he has his own kind of tea ceremony, and if she's not doing something important, she tries to make it home for that. She says, "Now, you must know, I don't like tea. But it's a ritual, and it's our ritual. And it's nice!"

Independently Compatible

We are learning through this process of retirement that sustaining a good relationship doesn't mean we necessarily have to spend all of our time with our partner. When everything is lived together and there's so much closeness, there can be a lack of newness and excitement. Sometimes introducing a kind of separation can put some of that back in the relationship. Even forming friendships with others independently can add spice. Women crave having friends, while most men don't have that urge to the same extent. We can agree to go off in different directions and continue to love, cherish, and enjoy times together.

Beverly grew up living for a time in a single room with her mother and father on the South Side of Chicago. She fought hard to get into a public high school where she could learn and remembers, when the teacher in her first class asked her to diagram a sentence, thinking, "I have no idea how to do this." In high school she made friends with "upper-middle-class black girls" and learned what an SAT was. She went on to a Chicago teachers college and also volunteered with the NAACP, eventually traveling to organizational meetings all over the country on its behalf. After college she discovered that she loved teaching. It was around that time that she was invited to a party in "exurbia," where she met John, a student at the Art Institute of Chicago. They dated, "paying no attention to the fact that we were a mixed couple—we just didn't hear any comments that might have floated around us." They married, and for the next several years, she moved with John as he took college teaching jobs in Dayton, then back in Chicago, and then in New York, where they lived in a loft that she "hated." During this time she taught in primary schools, had a baby, took a master's degree from Columbia's Teachers College, and then went on for a Ph.D. in administration, all the while doing well yet thinking that she couldn't do it. She worked in the New York City school system, where she eventually became a special assistant to the chancellor and served as part of his inner "cabinet." It was a wonderful time for Beverly because she loved making a difference for the kids in the system. But administrations changed, and after several frustrating years, she fell out of love with the board of education and returned to teaching for a few years, got a Fulbright grant to go to Japan for a fabulous month, and waited for her pension to kick in. "To me, retirement meant no more commitments to people telling me what to do."

As a new retiree, Beverly gleefully looked forward to embracing life by visiting museums, going to the theater, taking courses, and learning to belly dance. John too no longer worked, but his idea of heaven was to live in the country and make art. So they both headed to a place where there was a garden to tend and lots of open space. For two years Beverly says she truly tried to like it there. "I put forth as much effort as possible and finally learned the difference between an annual and a perennial plant." But she wasn't cut out for country life, hated bugs, and longed to get back to the city, where the pace was faster and she had things to do any time of the day or night. She asked herself, "Why am I spending time in the country? I'm supposed to be enjoying my retirement, so why am I continuing to do something I dislike?" Her mind made up, she told John that she was returning to the city and would happily visit him in the country occasionally, and that he was always welcome to join her in the city whenever he wanted. "Early in the marriage," Beverly says, "I thought I was doing what I wanted to do, but I think it was because I was socialized to do certain things and follow the rules. I realize now that I did what John wanted. I moved from Chicago to Dayton to New York because of him. I was just going along with the program, and I don't want to do that anymore."

Beverly and John love each other, have been together for more than forty years, and have no intention of splitting. Because they enjoy each other's company, they manage to get together regularly. Gradually, John decided that he likes spending time with Beverly on some of her city adventures, and she has concluded that summer in the country is a pleasant experience in short spurts. Psychotherapist Mary Beth Kelly says, "Sometimes being willing to introduce some kind of separation when neither is rigid and says 'no way' invites the other person on an adventure that can put a sense of excitement back in the relationship."

Togetherness Unbound

When most of us were starting out in a relationship, the word "togetherness" was huge; we were supposed to do everything together, even if one or the other of us didn't enjoy it so much. But now we don't feel as much pressure to be bound together. The retirement transition gives us a new sense of freedom. That means we do things independently of our partners, without feeling the need to ask permission, only to remain courteous and inform them so that they can make their own plans. Sometimes we have a partner who says, "Okay," but sometimes the response is, "But why do you want to go without me?" and we wonder why he seems so dependent on us for companionship. Or he says, "Okay," and takes off on a skiing trip, and we at once feel guilty that we didn't join him and thrilled that we're not holding him back from doing something he truly enjoys.

> *I have a friend who can only get together with her girlfriends when her husband is away. I have another friend whose husband goes off to play golf, but then she goes on safaris to Africa.*
>
> —Judith

In every area of the retirement adventure, we break new ground. And that includes our relationships. We are part of a generation that was immeasurably and irreversibly influenced by the women's movement, which affected how we thought and the things that we did. Even if our marriages were not always perfectly equitable, just the fact that we aspired to equality in marriage has had a major impact on us. Now retirement gives us a renewed reason to reassess what we want our partnerships to look and be like. We want all the many, many good parts to a loving, caring, sharing relationship, and we also want the kind of independence and respect we fought so hard to achieve. This is a wonderful time for us to reimagine the kind of relationships that are possible—and invite our partners along for the ride. It might just be a wild and wonderful one.

PREPARING TOGETHER FOR RETIREMENT

Just as you plan for your financial security and consider things you will want to do when you retire, you need to start a dialogue with your significant other. Here are some things to consider as you begin:

- Speak up. Start talking about your dreams as well as your concerns and open a nonjudgmental conversation so that your partner can do the same.
- Take responsibility for yourself and give your partner space to do the same. Don't offer unsolicited advice or attempt to find solutions for each other.
- Don't leave anything off the table, including financial concerns and how much and what kind of time you expect to spend together, but remember that diplomacy and empathy work better than accusation and blame.
- Analyze all the changes you anticipate facing as individuals and as a couple and prepare to support each other through the most difficult ones.
- Discuss the division of household chores in light of new time structures and at-home patterns.
- Identify how you expect to handle unstructured time if you no longer must be at a job at a particular time. Discuss whether your respective sleep-wake cycles make you compatible for sharing early or late activities.
- Evaluate the difference between acknowledging each other's feelings and making judgments about each other. For example, when you comment that he wants to stay home and not use his time to volunteer, you're judging him. Understanding that he doesn't like being thrust among strangers acknowledges his feelings.
- Don't use absolutes in discussions. Words like "always," "never," and "whenever" signal that it's time for the battle to begin.

- Take a breather if things get tense. It is okay to stop a conversation before it becomes destructive. Calm down and take the time to cool off, but return to the topic several days later and discuss why it is such a hot-button issue.
- Talk with other couples who have gone through a retirement transition to glean insights about the issues and problems they experienced. You'll recognize which issues are relevant to you and which to discard as unique to them.
- Remind yourself that your relationship didn't happen overnight. It unfolded in stages, over time, and needs time to adjust to new events and behaviors.
- If you can't start the conversation, consider going to a professional counselor for a few sessions. This needn't be a long-term process.
- Make a date with your partner to do things together that you both enjoy, such as taking a class, going to a restaurant, biking, or going to the movies. (Planning is essential, and often it is the woman who must do it.)
- Accept limitations. Some changes we experience in retirement are part of aging, and we need to understand and accept them in our partners and in ourselves.

CONCLUSION

How Do I Get the Most out of This New Stage of Life?

Every day our culture reminds us that we are getting older. We get senior discounts at the movies—and enjoy them. We count the years and months until we qualify for Social Security benefits. We get ridiculous birthday cards satirizing aging, which are usually ugly and hateful. And, of course, an AARP membership card arrives through the mail when we turn fifty. And these are the pluses. There are drawbacks galore. Let's not even go there!

We live in a culture that stretches in different directions. On the one end it worships youth; on the other it respects demographics. And that end points directly at us. We have strength in our numbers; and as our numbers grow, so grows our power.

The thing we must learn is how to take advantage of it. Our demographics alone won't give us the power we want. Having power will only start when we accept ourselves for who we are. When others look at us, they may see gray hair, a hearing aid, or the inability to pull all-nighters, and conclude things about what we should or should not do. We all know someone our age who thinks like an old lady as she fusses about everything from the uncomfortable movie-theater seats to her over- or underseasoned restaurant food. We also know many others who are full of youthful activity and vibrancy, even when they have difficult health problems. We get to choose which one we want to be. That can be difficult to do if we accept other people's scenarios for how we should live the second half of our adult lives. Such scenarios usually come with names, such as "needy elder," "greedy geezer," and "dippy granny."

There is nothing left but for us to take charge and show how we want to be judged and defined. It starts as we take a good look at the person we know we are and feel confident about ourselves. We can't do that if we fall victim to negative self-judgments or have any tentativeness about asserting, "I am who I am." It definitely won't happen if we buy into others' limiting ideas of who we should be.

We can't afford to be sissies about getting older. And the fastest way to sissyhood is to deny the fact that we are aging and will have to deal with some dimming capabilities. It's true that we don't look the same as we did twenty or even ten years ago. Some of us think we look better because of firmer muscles earned through workouts. Some of us take pride projecting wisdom with each and every wrinkle. Most of us don't enjoy the sight we see in the mirror. The point is that *how* we look is not *who we are* or *how we feel.*

> *Older women's identities are frequently distorted by misconceptions. The negative social images that flourish with ageing devalues the elderly and their sexuality, rendering this generation invisible and insignificant.*
> —report of the UN secretary-general to the Commission on the Status of Women, forty-third session

There is nothing else for us to do but reject stereotypes in the same ways we resisted earlier ones that didn't fit us. Over the course of our lives, we have been typecast as childlike dependents, as sex objects worthy of catcalls and conquest, and as mothers and nurturers responsible for home and household. We recognized how limiting these roles were, and we worked hard to prove we could make important intellectual, cultural, and physical contributions to society. There's no reason for us to buy into existing images of older women now. No one decrees we must morph into the invisible women so many of us complain about. We do not have to become gray, recessed shadows that are ignored until we suddenly reappear as needy and burdensome.

> *I don't want anyone else's expectations. I'm done with other people's*
> *agendas for me. I have no idea how my life will evolve, but it will be*
> *mine.*
>
> —**Irene**

Tommie's daughter teasingly says she's going to buy her mother a red hat one day, to which Tommie responds, "If she does, I'm outta there!" Tommie has nothing against the Red Hat Society, a national organization of women over fifty who get together for fun and social activities while proudly distinguishing themselves by their red hats. It's just that she doesn't want to be stamped and set apart from others in the mainstream.

Who Will Value Us?

Perhaps we wrestle too much with concerns about being invisible and minimized. Perhaps we've succumbed to negative messages about menopause and aging—about our loss of youth, fading charms, and empty nests—that fixate on atrophy and failure.

It's hard not to, especially when we rarely see older women we can identify with on television and in commercials and films. Mae Laborde's roles are a prime example of the kind of erroneous typecasting that affects us all. Ninety-seven-year-old Mae recently began working regularly as an actor because she is central casting's idea of the perfect grandmother, who spends her time knitting booties and baking cookies. The four-foot-ten-inch-tall, white-haired Mae has appeared in numerous commercials, usually dressed in a cotton housedress and sweater and seated in a wheelchair. Off camera, Mae is very dynamic and quite capable of walking, with the aid of a cane. She couldn't be happier for the attention and extra income earned through her newfound acting career. And more power to her!

> *I'm comfortable in my skin. I can't believe I'm the age I am. I'm full of zest and enthusiasm and don't feel the way some commercials on television show women of my age.*
>
> —**Hannah**

But why would anyone think a ninety-seven-year-old woman represents the ideal of grandmotherhood? Maybe they mean great- or great-great-grandmotherhood? Unfortunately, the frail, elderly, incapacitated grandma image Mae represents on TV is reinforced by the media over and over again. In the meantime those of us who are vital, active, and fully engaged cringe at being so misrepresented. A few of us even go as far as to deny ourselves the title "grandmother" by asking our grandchildren to call us by our first names, or create a sobriquet just so that we won't be confused with a Mae look-alike.

Where's the Disconnect?

Much to our surprise, younger people tell us we are role models for how they want to be when they reach our age. While we think we are in danger of becoming invisible, they see us as confident, knowledgeable, active, caring, capable, and wise. So why is there such a disconnect between their vision of us and our vision of ourselves? Is it that we are trapped inside the kind of ageist attitudes we held against our own parents' generation, which we labeled as placid and wary of change? Sometimes it is difficult for us to reject the very stereotypes we constructed when we were younger, at a time when chants of "Don't trust anyone over thirty" held sway.

Pride of Age

We tell each other we want to be treated with dignity and respect. That we want to be valued for our talents, skills, and wisdom. But being perceived of as valuable by others begins at home. After all, if we aren't able to demonstrate our value, why should we expect others to affirm it? Among the ways we affirm our value are mentoring others, giving ourselves to worthy causes, and nurturing the next generation. We also confirm our value when we fight to make things better and visibly advocate against such things as ageism and other inequalities.

> *To be a role model is to be yourself.*
>
> —Janna

We establish our value when we take pride in our age rather than denying it. The very act of telling our age to others makes several notable statements. It shows that we are proud of who we are, what we know, what we've done, and what we do. Just as important, it establishes a standard against which other people can measure us and measure themselves. Younger people are usually far off in their estimates of what a fifty- or sixty-year-old woman is about. So often when we say we are sixty and others respond "You're kidding! You don't look it!" they are usually genuinely astonished by our looks, energy, and capabilities. Rather than be flattered by the comment, we should realize just how off base they are about what it means to be sixty. It is why we owe it to them to clarify that we are what our true age *looks, and feels, and is like.* If they thought we were too old to climb Kilimanjaro, join the Peace Corps, go back to school, fight for a cause, or run a business, then we owe it to them to tack age onto these activities whenever possible so that they can no longer mistake what it means to be a particular age. Not only that, when we claim our age we give those who follow behind us realistic and worthy models to strive to be like.

> *It's interesting to see oneself mirrored in someone else, particularly if it's a child. That is empowering, to have someone admire your life.*
>
> —Leslie

Betty Friedan wondered about the way society defines age as a "problem." She wrote in *The Fountain of Age* that the more we deny our own age in order to pass as young, the more we give credence to that dread aura of age. And the more we exaggerate that poor, fearful, passive, sick, lonely, helpless, senile image—in order to distance ourselves from it—the more we justify the actual exclusion of people over sixty-five from the work and play and other activities of society . . . But as long as we do "pass" for young, the increasing millions of us who are, in fact, moving vitally through our later years will not alter people's negative image of age. And therefore there *still* will be no image or role model of older people . . . doing useful or enjoyable things.

> *The years that a woman subtracts from her age are not lost. They are added to the ages of other women.*
>
> —Diane de Poitiers

Growth Versus Rigidity

Becky has always wanted to become as mentally and physically strong as she can possibly be. Her idea of transition is even more growth. She's open to all possibilities and explores them as she goes along.

The opposite of such growth is becoming rigid as we get older. Sure, we enjoy being opinionated. And being curmudgeonly is not only fun, it gets attention. But voicing opinions without knowledge can distance us from people who are most important to us. Becky has a friend who thinks any music her grandchildren listen to is crap. Becky rightly advises this woman to open up a connection by listening to their music. If she keeps an open mind, just maybe she'll like it, or at least find some common meeting ground. If she doesn't try, she is in danger of being estranged from the very people she most wants to stay connected with.

During our lives we tend to be either optimists or pessimists about the future, although which one we are is not black-and-white. We are usually optimistic about our own plans, sometimes overly so, expecting that things will turn out well with little evidence to support that supposition except our belief in our competence and ability to control circumstances. One might think that aging would turn us into pessimists, but apparently that's not so. Rather, as we age we tend to focus on happier times and push away memories of bleaker ones. Sometimes our optimism can lead us into trouble, causing us to miscalculate the amount of time and difficulty something might take to accomplish, and sometimes it is self-fulfilling, spurring us on to accomplish difficult projects that a pessimist wouldn't tackle in the first place. Indeed, being optimistic is good for our survival. When we believe that our lives are full of promise, we tend to live longer and accomplish far more than pessimists.

> *I am over the hill in terms of knowing what's current and grabs people now. So my next class is going to be Rap 101.*
>
> —Gabriela

Taking Charge

Samatha says she's always felt a little ripped off by the women's movement. She thinks women have accomplished a lot of things but haven't really changed the world as much as the world has changed them, in terms of how we do things and how we make decisions. That the promise of what women can bring to the workplace and to the world has not been fulfilled. In part it's been because of that closed-door idea: in order to get past the door, we had to be more like the guys than guys. Her hope is that as we become disillusioned and move out of the workplace toward retirement, we will do things differently, instead of fighting tooth and nail to climb up that masculine ladder.

> *Every time I think I am getting old and gradually going to the grave, something else happens.*
>
> —Lillian Carter, mother of Jimmy Carter

Whether she has a point or not, it is clear that we women have enormous strengths that we continually draw upon to survive and ultimately thrive. Perhaps this is the perfect time in our lives for us to use our inherent strengths to reinvent who we are and what society can become. We do see the world differently than men do. We certainly enjoy bonding with one another. To varying degrees we want to nurture and care for others. And we look to have strong relationships based on our values of sharing and caring. These strengths emerge again and again as we reject "the way it has always been." Our power is in our values, and we feel happiest when we can fight for those values.

> *I'm not finished yet. What I'm doing right now is not the be-all and the end-all. Something else is going to come up. I'm going to get involved in something else, and I'm going to be a different person, with a different focus. There are many, many doors I have left to open, even though I have no idea where they are or where they'll lead.*
>
> —Jeanne

We are in the beginning stages of redefining retirement as an extraordinary period when we have opportunities to make changes that will profoundly impact the next generation. In this way we are returning to the very best of what it means to be an elder in society, as we challenge the limitations society has imposed on that role. We are extremely fortunate to be able to lead the way. We also have time on our side. All we need is the determination to go out and do it. The best part is that we also have the life experience, the self-confidence, and the wisdom to make lasting changes.

ACKNOWLEDGMENTS

So many people were essential to making this book a reality. It never would have happened at all if it weren't for the women in TTN, whose initial questioning, explorations, and imaginings of a new world for women over fifty helped stir my thinking. But it was the encouragement of my ever-supportive husband, Werner; my son, Denny; and my longtime friend Barbara Burn that set me off on what became a two-year adventure, and they were there to help me get the project through the heavy-lifting phases. Each of them listened as I vented, and contributed important insights at all the right moments. They have my love, gratitude, and appreciation.

And without doubt I am beholden to TTN cofounders Christine Millen and Charlotte Frank for enthusiastically embracing this project from the beginning. I am especially obliged to them for their confidence in my efforts to write and to manage TTN's first book through the publishing process. I am also grateful for the valuable thoughts and comments they offered throughout each stage of the book. And special thanks in particular to agent Ellen Levine of Trident Media Group, who understood the book's potential from the start and worked tirelessly to help it take form and find a loving home. Her friendship, support, and commitment have been crucial.

Once the book was under way, I enjoyed (in all the best senses of the word) the wonderful insights and personal stories of the fabulous women who generously gave their time for interviews. I am especially obliged to Mona Kreaden, TTN's national chapter leader; Arlene Reiff and Janet Mandelstam, cochairs of TTN's San Francisco/Bay Area chapter; and Binnie Fry, who heads up TTN's capital-area chapter, for their assistance in introducing me to so many fascinating women.

Also, I am ever grateful to David M. Hudanish and Lawrence E. Jacobs for their backbreaking legal labors, and to psychoanalyst Laurence J. Gould and psychotherapist Mary Beth Kelly for sharing their psycho-smarts. Thanks too to Betsy Werley, executive director of TTN, for reading an early draft of the manuscript and providing astute comments, and to TTN members Anita Lands, Deirdre Aherne, Marcia Fox, Ann Michell, Glenda Rosenthal, and Susan Zigouras for their helpful contributions. And special thanks to TTN-er Nancy Bowles, who proved herself a most able and committed researcher as she uncovered valuable information for the Resources section.

From the beginning, Karen Murgolo, editorial director of Springboard Press, and editor Michelle Howry were enthusiastic supporters who contributed their vision to what the book could be. I am indebted to them and to my wonderful editor, Natalie Kaire, and copyeditor, Katharine Ochsner, whose keen comments helped to make the book that much better.

Thank you all.

Gail Rentsch

APPENDIX I

About TTN

The Transition Network (TTN) is a national community of women over fifty, run *by* and *for* women who are thinking about the next stage of their lives.

TTN is many things, including:

- A gateway for information and education about life choices, satisfactions, concerns, and relationships.
- A community of peers offering camaraderie and support, good conversation and ideas, a network of contacts and resources, and a variety of small-group activities.
- A catalyst for exploring paid and nonpaid work opportunities and developing new talents, new careers, and new ways to volunteer.
- A voice for our generation consisting of pathfinders who seek to change society's images and institutions regarding women over fifty.

TTN was founded in New York in 2000 by two extraordinary women, Christine Millen and Charlotte Frank. They sought to create a movement through which women could reimagine retirement, which they envisioned as a series of transitions—bridges—that would lead from one career to another, from employment to volunteerism, from acceptance to advocacy, and from isolation to community. The organization has a national membership, with active chapters in New York City; Boston; Chicago; San Francisco and the Bay Area; Washington, DC, and Virginia; Houston; Denver; and the greater New York areas of Long Island and Westchester, and other chapters are in formation.

TTN chapters hold regular general meetings where leading experts, who are often TTN members, speak on a range of topics of interest to women over fifty, and members have a chance to meet, network, have fun, and form friendships. In addition to these regular meetings, each chapter develops various events for its members, which may include docent-led historical and art tours, workshops, wine tastings, and meetings with artists and authors.

At the heart of TTN are peer groups that meet regularly, usually monthly. These small groups of some eight to twelve women connect to discuss topics of mutual interest, share experiences, and enjoy friendship.

In addition, the TTN Web site is an online community where members can network, engage in conversations, share opinions, and find useful information.

TTN also is committed to volunteer work that engages the professionalism and passions of its members. From the beginning, TTN members have worked with many worthy organizations to provide expertise and services these organizations wanted but could not otherwise afford.

And, finally, TTN is committed to overthrowing negative images of age in our culture and to raising its voice in support of new options for older women. An annual Pride of Age event honors women who go public with their ages and thus become role models demonstrating that vitality exists at all ages. TTN also promotes the value of the older worker and has joined forces with other organizations in order to fight age discrimination in the workplace. And TTN is actively developing a support system—a caring community—that will allow women to live independently in spite of health problems or temporary disabilities.

TTN is recognized as a leading social innovator by Civic Ventures, a San Francisco–based group that is reframing the debate about aging in America, as well as by Ashoka: Innovators for the Public, a global organization dedicated to investing in social entrepreneurs and the organizations they lead, in order to support solutions for society's most challenging problems.

To learn more about TTN and to sign up for the TTN monthly newsletter, go to www.thetransitionnetwork.org.

APPENDIX II

Start a Peer Group

Peer groups are the heart of the TTN experience. Described as *circles of connectivity,* peer groups generally consist of approximately eight to twelve women who meet once a month at members' homes. The peer group provides a small interactive setting where members discuss problems and exchange ideas within an environment based on compatibility and trust. Each group has its own coordinator, as well as a representative to the larger organization. Women join peer groups for a variety of reasons, beginning with the need for intellectual stimulation and including the opportunity to make new friends, have fun, and explore relevant issues. Some TTN peer groups focus on issues surrounding retirement. Some are aimed at pursuing specific interests, such as books, health issues, or starting a business, while others are solely recreational. In the peer group Salon, women gather to discuss important issues of the day such as immigration and global warming. Another group, Singles in Suburbia, is committed to creating a positive singles community in a world where couples dominate. In still another group, members explore the world of travel, share experiences, and plan new trips, often with one another.

The three kinds of peer groups are:

- *General transition discussion groups.* These focus on a range of issues that women experience as they move through the work-to-retirement continuum. Examples of issues covered in such groups are defining a new persona or identity; constructively using unstructured time; separating from professional colleagues; opening new doors; taking risks; measuring success; and managing change.

• *Issues-oriented discussion groups.* These focus on specific topics and can cover almost anything, including women who work at home; women with (or without) partners; woman entrepreneurs; political and social issues; and books.

• *Social-activities groups.* These are for members that enjoy the company of like-minded women in pleasure-oriented pursuits. Examples of such group activities include theater-, film-, or concert going; museum expeditions; gourmet networking; poker playing; choral singing; fiber-arts creation; hiking, biking, or boating trips; fitness motivation; and travel.

By starting a TTN peer group in your area, you will meet an amazing variety of women your own age. All you need to start is a few good women.

For more information, go to www.thetransitionnetwork.org.

RESOURCES

Compiled by Nancy Bowles

GENERAL	
http://www.aarp.org/	The AARP and the AARP Foundation are *the* leading organizations for programs, initiatives, and information that support the interests and needs of people over fifty. Browse the site and use its search functions to mine the wealth of information available there.
http://www.aoa.gov/	The Administration on Aging, part of the Department of Health and Human Services, provides health and community services for older Americans.
http://ssa.gov/	The official Web site of the U.S. Social Security Administration
CAREER	
http://www.aarp.org/money/careers/	Provides advice on job hunting and job retention and promotes change in workplace attitudes to benefit older workers
http://www.aarp.org/research/work/agediscrim/	AARP research reports on age discrimination
Achieving the Good Life After 50: Tools and Resources for Making It Happen	By Renée Lee Rosenberg (New York: Five O'Clock Books, 2007)
http://www.boardnetusa.org/	Helps people identify nonprofit-board opportunities in their home city

http://www.bridgestar.org/	Provides high-level job postings and group meetings in some cities to help people in the for-profit world move into the nonprofit world
http://www.careerbuilder.com/	Useful for searching for full- and part-time, consulting, and freelance jobs; also provides career-related advice and further resources
http://www.careerjournal.com/	Web site of the *Wall Street Journal.* It offers useful articles about finding and maintaining jobs and the employment situation in general.
http://www.careernews.com/	Weekly news service of articles and tips about job hunting
http://www.craigslist.org/	This online network of communities in the United States and other countries provides classified advertising in a variety of categories, including items for sale, services wanted or available, housing, and so on. It also has job postings for full- and part-time work.
http://www.dinosaurexchange.com/	A U.K.-based site that acts as an intermediary between retired people with experience and employers who need them
http://www.diversityworking.com/	A job-posting Web site for employers seeking cultural diversity in the workplace, including the older worker, defined here as over forty. Search for "mature worker."
Don't Retire, REWIRE! 5 Steps to Fulfilling Work That Fuels Your Passion, Suits Your Personality, or Fills Your Pocket	By Jeri Sedlar and Rick Miners (Indianapolis: Alpha Books, 2003)
http://www.eeoc.gov/facts/qanda.html	Here, the Equal Employment Opportunity Commission briefly describes employment-discrimination laws, including the ADEA—the Age Discrimination in Employment Act of 1967—and prohibited employer practices.
http://www.enrge.us/	The Employment Network for Retired Government Experts is a free job site for retired government workers who want to work full- or part-time or as a consultant in the for-profit world.
http://www.entrepreneur.com/	Information for those who have, or wish to start, their own business; includes some guidance on franchises
http://www.execsearches.com/	Job site for executives in the nonprofit sector

http://www.franchise.org/	International Franchise Association; provides basic information and links to over twelve hundred franchises
http://www.franchising.com/	Provides guidance for establishing a franchise, and industry descriptions of franchises, as well as examples of available franchises
From Making a Profit to Making a Difference: Careers in Nonprofits for Business Professionals	Tips on how to launch a new career in nonprofits, by Richard M. King (River Forest, IL: Planning/ Communications, 2000)
http://www.gofreelance.com/	A freelance-work exchange connecting employees and employers
A Guide to Careers in Community Development	Information about and advice on how to break into the field of community development, by Paul Brophy and Alice Shabecoff (Washington, DC: Island Press, 2001)
http://www.guru.com/	A well-regarded network for freelance job seekers
http://hotjobs.yahoo.com/	One of the largest job-search Web sites
http://www.inc.com/	For entrepreneurs, with lots of specific information for small to midsize businesses
http://jobsearch.about.com/	Provides links to job-listing and job-search Web sites for full- and part-time work; includes advice on composing résumés and cover letters, along with many useful samples
http://www.linkedin.com/	A network like My Space for adults, with a business focus
http://www.monster.com/	One of the largest and best-known job-search Web sites
http://www. multiculturaladvantage.com/	Offers articles, job opportunities, and resources for professionals from diverse backgrounds
http://www.nptimes.com/	*NonProfit Times* is a newsletter covering the nonprofit sector, including job openings. Available in print and on the Web.
http://www.philanthropy.com/	The *Chronicle of Philanthropy* Web site provides news, trends, training opportunities, and jobs in the nonprofit sector.
http://www.quintcareers.com/ mature_jobseekers.html	Offers useful links for career and job searching; includes a section on changing careers and career coaches

http://www.retiredbrains.com/	Connects retired adults with employers interested in hiring experienced people; provides many useful links, from how to find a franchise, to free access to industry publications, and more
http://www.retirementjobs.com/	Lists job opportunities for people over fifty—full-time, part-time, and consulting—as well as board-seat openings
http://www.rileyguide.com/	A comprehensive source of information on job hunting and résumé writing, with valuable links to job-posting sites and more
The Savvy Part-Time Professional: Tips on How to Land, Create, or Negotiate the Part-Time Job of Your Dreams	By Lynn Berger (Sterling, VA: Capital Books, 2006)
http://www.score.org/	The Service Core of Retired Executives provides advice to small businesses on all aspects of managing a business. The Web site offers information and lists specialty-business counselors' contact information.
http://www.seniors4hire.org/	Lists job openings for people over fifty
http://www.snagajob.com/	Lists part-time hourly jobs and includes information for people fifty and over
http://www.wetfeet.com/	Provides industry, company, and job profiles, including salary information, some available free and some by subscription
http://www.womenatworknetwork.com/	A placement forum and network for professional women seeking various work arrangements, including permanent full- and part-time jobs, and consulting and project assignments
http:www.workforce50.com/	Lists full-time, part-time, temporary, and volunteer job openings for people over fifty
Working After Retirement for Dummies	By Lita Epstein (Indianapolis: Wiley, 2007)
http://www.yourencore.com/	A job site sponsored by many top corporations that links senior talent with corporate opportunities

ENRICHMENT/LIFESTYLE

http://www.aarp.org/about_aarp/aarp_foundation/	Within the AARP Foundation, the Women's Leadership Circle works to promote philanthropic resources that recognize concerns of older women and encourage programs to improve the lives of those in this group.

http://www.coachfederation.org/ICF/	The site of the International Coach Federation, an organization of personal (life) and career coaches, is useful for understanding what to look for when selecting a coach and also how to locate one.
http://www.lifeplanningnetwork.org/find-consultant.htm	The Life Planning Network is a community of professionals from diverse fields that provides a broad spectrum of life-planning services and resources.
http://www.oasisnet.org/	A national nonprofit educational organization that offers programs in the arts and humanities, and on wellness, technology, and volunteer service, to older adults seeking to continue personal growth and provide service to the community
http://www.outwardboundwilderness.org/	Promotes personal growth; has a few programs for active mature women
http://www.thirdage.com/	Offers tips, tools, blogs, and more on health, relationships, money, work, beauty, fun, and classes for people over fifty
http://www.womensenews.org/	A news service covering topics relevant to women of all ages

FINANCE

http://www.citibank.com/womenandco/	Targeted toward helping women understand financial and securities topics and how to plan for their financial comfort and independence (requires a small annual membership fee to use certain financial services, including a financial-inventory worksheet)
Don't Run with Your Retirement Money: Understanding Your Resources and How Best to Use Them	A pithy, clearly written guidebook on the primary financial resources for retirement income, by the Actuarial Foundation and the Women's Institute for a Secure Retirement (WISER)
http://www.fpanet.org/	The Financial Planning Association Web site provides guidance about financial planning and assistance in finding a financial planner.
http://www.howstuffworks.com/	Search in the Money section for explanations about business, credit and debt, economics, and financial planning.
It's More Than Money, It's Your Life! The New Money Club for Women	By Candace Bahr and Ginita Wall, the cofounders of the Women's Institute for Financial Education (WIFE) (Hoboken, NJ: Wiley, 2003)
http://www.pathtoinvesting.org/	Sponsored by the Foundation for Investor Education

http://personal.fidelity.com/	Fidelity's Retirement Resource Center offers valuable information as well as personalized plans for reaching your goals. Find these and other useful services by clicking the Retirement & Guidance tab.
http://www.smartmoney.com/	The *SmartMoney* magazine Web site regularly covers retirement planning. Search for articles in the Personal Finance section. It also covers information about health and health insurance.
The Wall Street Journal *Complete Retirement Guidebook: How to Plan It, Live It, and Enjoy It*	A look at retirement, with solid information about becoming financially prepared, by Glenn Ruffenach and Kelly Greene (New York: Three Rivers Press, 2007)
http://www.wife.org/	The Women's Institute for Financial Education provides all types of useful financial information and "A Man Is Not A Plan" bumper stickers.
http://www.wiser.heinz.org/portal/	The Women's Institute for a Secure Retirement provides information to assist women of all ages and income levels in preparing for financial independence.
Women & Money: Owning the Power to Control Your Destiny	Offers a five-month "save yourself" plan, by Suze Orman (New York: Spiegel & Grau, 2007)

HEALTH

http://www.cdc.gov/aging/	The Centers for Disease Control is responsible for public health and providing health-related information. The section on aging addresses health concerns of the older person. The site also offers immunization information for travelers.
http://www.4women.gov/	A U.S. government site with information about women's health
http://www.helpguide.org/index.htm	A collaboration of the members of the Rotary Club of Santa Monica and the Center for Healthy Aging, this Web site offers free information on many topics of interest to seniors.
http://www.mayoclinic.com/	Among the many medical topics covered are seniors' health and women's health, in the Live Well section.
http://www.medicare.gov/	The primary location for official information on Medicare—about signing up, the different plans, and what is covered
http://medlineplus.gov/	A useful site that directs you to information to answer health questions; provided by the National Library of Medicine of the National Institutes of Health

| http://www.medscape.com/home | Part of WebMD, this site provides professional clinicians with current medical reports but is also accessible to the consumer (free registration). |
| http://www.nih.gov/ | The National Institutes of Health site is a good source of information about medical conditions and diseases. Be sure to check out the section on senior health. |

LIFELONG LEARNING

http://www.elderhostel.org/	One of the largest travel/education programs for people fifty and over. The Elderhostel Institute Network acts as a resource and communication channel for lifelong-learning institutes (LLIs) and encourages the development of new LLIs.
http://www.hilr.harvard.edu/	The Harvard University Institute for Learning in Retirement offers peer learning and study groups; membership is limited to former academics and professionals.
http://www.newschool.edu/irp/	The Institute for Retired Professionals at the New School is the grandmother of peer-learning programs around the country.
http://www.seniornet.org/	A network of older adults who wish to communicate through online discussion groups; provides access to tutorials about computer use and online courses covering a variety of topics
http://www.uclaextension.edu/plato/	The PLATO (Partners in Learning Actively Teaching Ourselves) Society is part of the UCLA extension program.
http://www.unca.edu/ncccr/	The University of North Carolina–Asheville Center for Creative Retirement provides those of retirement age with opportunities to continue learning and working, and has a college for seniors.
http://www.usm.maine.edu/olli/national/	The Osher Lifelong Learning Institutes National Resource Center, based at the University of Southern Maine, provides information on effective educational programs for older learners. Use this site to find an OLLI program near you.

NETWORKING

| http://www.eons.com/ | A Web site and blog community for those over fifty; includes brain games to promote mental acuity, a "LifeMap" to share with family and friends or go public with, and much more |

http://www.facebook.com/	Anything on the Internet can be viewed through the eyes of people you know and trust. This site uses the wisdom of crowds—mostly trusted friends—to pull in helpful information, including information on topics you might not have thought to ask about.
http://www.meetup.com/	An Internet-based community that links people with similar interests who then meet in real time
http://www.olderwiserwomen.com/	A women's online forum for exchanging experiences about growing older and improving others' perceptions of the older person
http://www.owl-national.org/index.htm	The Older Women's League is a national organization—with local, state groups—interested in research, education, and advocacy activities concerning women as they become older.
http://www.redhatsociety.com/	A social organization primarily for women over fifty with an emphasis on having fun
http://www.thetransitionnetwork.org/	A national organization in which women over fifty explore issues relevant to growing older, exchange ideas, and find friendship and new ways to enjoy and add meaning to their lives
TRAVEL	
http://www.50plusexpeditions.com/	Offers trips to areas such as the Arctic, Patagonia, and Laos; for active adults over fifty
http://www.eldertreks.com/	Provides adventurous and off-the-beaten-path trips for people fifty and over
http://www.grandtrvl.com/web/guest/home	A tour agency offering luxury trips for grandparents and grandchildren traveling together
http://www.homeexchange.com/	One of many programs for domestic and global home exchanges
VOLUNTEERING	
http://www.1-800-volunteer.org/	A national database supported by the Points of Light Foundation listing nonprofit jobs
The Boomers' Guide to Good Work: An Introduction to Jobs That Make a Difference	By Ellen Freudenheim, with Civic Ventures; available in PDF at http://www.civicventures.org/guide/
http://www.civicventures.org/	A think tank and catalyst for engaging people over fifty in the community through volunteer opportunities, paid work, and recognition programs

http://www.experiencecorps.org/	Experience Corps, located in twenty-one cities, prepares people over fifty-five to assist and mentor elementary school students who are having difficulty learning to read.
http://www.habitat.org/wb/	An international program through which women and girls volunteer to build homes for those in need
http://www.idealist.org/	Action Without Borders provides a forum through which individuals can connect with communities and organizations in the United States and globally that seek to fill full- or part-time paid or volunteer jobs.
http://www.pointsoflight.org/	The Volunteer Center National Network helps connect individuals with specific programs in local volunteer centers.
http://www.reserveinc.org/	ReServe Elder Service was established in New York City to go beyond volunteerism by linking older workers with experience and skills, with stipend-paying jobs that serve a beneficial purpose.
http://www.seniorcorps.org/	The Retired and Senior Volunteer Program (RSVP), part of the Corporation for National and Senior Service, encourages volunteerism among older adults.
http://www.volunteermatch.org/	Helps potential volunteers find roles, and organizations recruit volunteers

VOLUNTEERING ABROAD

http://www.crossculturalsolutions.org/	This program emphasizes the importance of experiencing and learning about the culture of the communities in which volunteers are placed.
http://www.globalcrossroad.com/	Provides vacations combined with volunteer work in countries in Africa, Asia, and Latin America; also partners with Teaching English as a Foreign Language (TEFL) institutions
http://www.globalservicecorps.org/	An international nonprofit volunteer organization providing service-learning opportunities in Thailand and Tanzania for people worldwide
http://www.globalvolunteers.org/	A nonprofit organization with well-established programs around the world in which people of all ages volunteer services. Volunteers pay fees to cover on-site housing and make a small donation to the program.

http://www.i-to-i.com/	This British volunteer travel organization has volunteer programs, internships, and (minimal) paid work in Eastern Europe, Latin America, and Asia.
http://www.peacecorps.gov/	The Peace Corps was established in the early 1960s to train volunteers to work in and assist peoples in developing countries. The Peace Corps' many programs are available for older workers.
http://www.volunteerabroad.com/search.cfm	A source for finding study, work, and volunteer opportunities in Europe, Asia, Latin America, and Africa; also links with TEFL institutions and U.S. and overseas schools with foreign-language programs
Volunteer: A Traveler's Guide to Making a Difference Around the World	By Charlotte Hindle, Nate Cavalieri, Rachel Collinson, Korina Miller, and Mike Richard (Oakland, CA: Lonely Planet, 2007)
http://www.volunteerinternational.org/	The international Volunteers Program Association is an alliance of nonprofit organizations that provides information and explains requirements to those who wish to volunteer for work abroad. (Joining the group requires paying a fee.)
http://www.volunteersforprosperity.gov/	A clearinghouse for volunteer opportunities, this federal program encourages U.S. professionals to use their skills to improve economic, educational, and health conditions in other countries.

BIBLIOGRAPHY

AARP Women's Leadership Circle Study: General Population. January 2006.

Adams, Gary A., and Terry A. Beehr. *Retirement: Reasons, Processes, and Results*. New York: Springer Publishing, 2003.

"Age Bias and Employment Discrimination." Center on Aging and Work/Workplace Flexibility at Boston College. Fact sheet, February 2007.

"The Age Explosion: Baby Boomers and Beyond." *Harvard Generations Policy Journal* 1 (2004).

"The Aging of the U.S. Workforce: Employer Challenges and Responses." Ernst & Young, LLP, ExecuNet Inc., and the Human Capital Institute Survey, 2006.

Ameriks, John, Holly B. Fergusson, Anna B. Madamba, and Stephen P. Utkus. "Six Paths to Retirement." Vanguard Center for Retirement Research, vol. 26, January 2007.

Anthony, Mitch. *The New Retirementality: Planning Your Life and Living Your Dreams*. 2nd ed. Chicago: Kaplan, 2006. First published in 2001 by Dearborn Financial Publishing, Inc.

Armour, Stephanie. "Many Workers Sitting Pretty After Buyouts." *USA Today*, August 16, 2006.

Armstrong-Stassen, Marjorie, and Sheila Cameron. "Factors Related to the Career Satisfaction of Older Managerial and Professional Women." *Career Development International* 10, no. 3 (2005).

Ashoka. "What Is a Social Entrepreneur?" http://www.ashoka.org/fellows/social_entrepreneur .cfm.

Azar, Beth. "Little Evidence that Old Age Causes Work Deterioration." *APA Monitor*, American Psychological Association, July 1998.

Bastien, Stephen. "12 Benefits of Hiring Older Workers." *Entrepreneur*, September 20, 2006. http://www.entrepreneur.com/humanresources/hiring/article167500.html.

Bauer-Maglin, Nan, and Alice Radosh, eds. *Women Confronting Retirement: A Nontraditional Guide*. New Brunswick: Rutgers University Press, 2003.

Begley, Sharon. "Confusion Over Dementia." *Wall Street Journal*, April 28, 2006.

———. "Old Brains Don't Work That Badly After All, Especially Trained Ones." *Wall Street Journal*, March 3, 2006.

———. "The Upside of Aging." *Wall Street Journal*, February 17, 2007.

Belenky, Mary, Blythe Clinchy, Nancy Goldberger, and Jill Tarule. *Women's Ways of Knowing: The Development of Self, Voice, and Mind.* New York: Basic Books, 1986.

Bender, Keith A., and Natalia A. Jivan. "What Makes Retirees Happy?" Issue in brief, Center for Retirement Research at Boston College, no. 28, February 2005.

Berkowitz, Gale. "UCLA Study on Friendship Among Women." 2002. http://www.anapsid.org/cnd/gender/tendfend.html.

Block, Sandra. "Working Longer to Live Better: Women's Top Retirement Strategy Often Is to Stay on the Job." *USA Today*, September 14, 2006.

Block, Sandra, and Stephanie Armour. "Many Americans Retire Years Before They Want To." *USA Today*, July 26, 2006.

Bond, James T., and Ellen M. Galinsky. "The Diverse Employment Experiences of Older Men and Women in the Workforce." The Center on Aging & Work/Workplace Flexibility at Boston College, no. 2, November 2005.

"Boomers at Midlife." AARP Life Stage Study, wave 3, 2004.

Bornstein, David. *How to Change the World: Social Entrepreneurs and the Power of New Ideas.* New York: Oxford University Press, 2004.

Brandon, Emily. "Working Can Boost Your Health, Keeping You Active and Sharp." *U.S. News & World Report* 140, no. 22 (2006).

Brewster, Mary Kim. "Entering and Exiting the Corporation: A Developmental Study of Women Executives at Midlife." Dissertation submitted to the graduate faculty in clinical psychology, the City University of New York, 1998.

Bridges, William. *Transitions: Making Sense of Life's Changes.* 2nd ed. Da Capo Press, 2004.

Burby, Liza N. "Finding Yourself in Retirement." *Newsday*, January 13, 2007.

Burica, Barbara A., Simone G. Schaner, and Sheila R. Zedlewski. "Enjoying the Golden Work Years." In *The Retire Project Perspectives on Productive Aging.* Urban Institute, May 2006.

"The Business Case for Workers Age 50+: Planning for Tomorrow's Talent Needs in Today's Competitive Environment." A report for the AARP prepared by Towers Perrin, December 2005.

Butler, Robert. "Dr. Robert Butler Discusses Aging Workers." Interview. *Morning Edition*, NPR, July 13, 2005.

Calvo, Esteban. "Does Working Longer Make People Healthier and Happier?" Issue brief, Center for Retirement Research at Boston College, February 2006.

Carey, Benedict. "The Fame Motive." *New York Times*, August 22, 2006.

———. "A 'Senior Moment' or a Self-Fulfilling Prophecy?" *New York Times*, July 18, 2006.

Caudron, Shari. "On the Contrary: Fleeing Corporate America for More Meaningful Jobs." *Workforce Management*, October 1998.

Charness, Neil. "Older Worker Training: What We Know and Don't Know." AARP Public Policy Institute, 2006.

Chen, Yung-Ping, and John C. Scott. "Phased Retirement: Who Opts for It and Toward What End?" In-brief research report. AARP Public Policy Institute, January 2006.

Cohen, Gene D. *The Creative Age: Awakening Human Potential in the Second Half of Life.* New York: Avon Books, 2000.

Colonia-Willner, Regina. "Older Managers Can Learn the Best New Tricks." Study, American Society on Aging. http://www.asaging.org/at/at-201/study.html.

Coontz, Stephanie. "Too Close for Comfort." *New York Times*, November 7, 2006.

"Couples Filing for 'New Narita Divorces.'" *Financial Express*, Tokyo, January 27, 2006.

Coutu, Andréa. "Surviving Feast or Famine Consulting Work Cycles." *Consultant Journal*, June 8, 2006. http://www.consultantjournal.com/blog/surviving-feast-or-famine-consulting -work-cycles.

Coy, Peter, with Diane Brady. "Old. Smart. Productive." *BusinessWeek*, June 27, 2005.

Critchley, Robert K. *Rewired, Rehired, or Retired?* San Francisco: Jossey-Bass/Pfeiffer, 2002.

Csikszentmihalyi, Mihaly. *Flow: The Classic Work on How to Achieve Happiness.* Revised and updated ed. London: Rider, 2002. First published by Harper & Row in 1992.

Cullen, Lisa Takeuchi. "Not Quite Ready to Retire." *Time*, February 19, 2006.

Daniel, Lisa. "Courting Senior Workers." *Staffing Management*, Society for Human Resource Management, July–September 2005.

Deiss, Kathryn J. "Steal a Base or Stay Safe?" *ARL Newsletter*, January 4, 1999.

Diebel, Mary. "'Brain Drain' Coming With Wave of Retirements." *Seattle Post-Intelligencer*, February 13, 2006.

"The Divorce Experience: A Study of Divorce at Midlife and Beyond." AARP, 2004.

Donkin, Richard. "Why We Need to Hire Not-So-Fresh Blood." *Financial Times*, January 26, 2006.

"Dramatic Decline in Disability Continues for Older Americans." U.S. National Institutes of Health, May 2001.

Dunleavey, M. P. "The Money Myths We Inherit from Mom." moneycentral.msn.com, 2006.

Dychtwald, Ken, Tamara Erickson, and Bob Morison. "It's Time to Retire Retirement." *Harvard Business Review*, OnPoint, 2006.

Edmondson, Brad. "Working Wonders." *AARP*, November/December 2005.

"Enjoying the Golden Work Years." Data and policy brief, Retirement Project Perspectives on Productive Aging. Urban Institute, May 2006.

Enright, Elizabeth. "A House Divided." *AARP*, July/August 2004.

Epstein, Lita. *Working After Retirement for Dummies.* Indianapolis: Wiley, 2007.

Erikson, Erik H. *The Life Cycle Completed.* New York: Norton, 1982.

Essick, Kristi. "Job Sites Grow for 55-Plus Crowd." *Wall Street Journal*, July 3, 2006.

"Facts About Age Discrimination." U.S. Equal Employment Opportunity Commission, 1997. http://www.eeoc.gov/facts/age.html.

Felt, Susan. "Don't Call Me Grandmother: Boomers Adopt New Monikers." Gannett News Service, May 22, 2007.

Fierman, Jaclyn. "Do Women Manage Differently?" *Fortune*, December 17, 1990.

Fisher, Anne. "How to Plug Your Company's Brain Drain." *Fortune*, July 19, 2006.

Fisher, Patty. "Baby Boomers Living in Past About Aging." *Mercury News*, October 30, 2006.

"Free Agents: The World of Independent Contractors." AARP, 2004. http://aarp.org/money/ careers/selfemployment/a2004-06-14-freeagents.html.

Freedman, Marc. *Encore: Finding Work That Matters in the Second Half of Life.* New York: PublicAffairs, 2007.

———. "Life Begins at Sixty-five." Civic Ventures, 2006.

———. *Prime Time: How Baby Boomers Will Revolutionize Retirement and Transform America.* New York: PublicAffairs, 1999.

Freedman, Marc, and Phyllis Moen. "Money & Management." *Chronicle of Higher Education*, April 29, 2005.

Freudenheim, Ellen. *The Boomers' Guide to Good Work: An Introduction to Jobs That Make a Difference.* San Francisco: Civic Ventures, 2005.

———. *Looking Forward: An Optimist's Guide to Retirement.* New York: Stewart, Tabori & Chang, 2004.

Friedan, Betty. *The Fountain of Age.* New York: Simon & Schuster, 1993.

Friedberg, Leora. "The Recent Trend Towards Later Retirement." Issue in brief, Center for Retirement Research at Boston College, series 9, March 2007.

"From the Age of Aquarius to the Age of Responsibility: Baby Boomers Approach Age 60." Pew Research Center, December 2005.

"The Future of Retirement." HSBC Global Forum on Ageing and Retirement study, Oxford University's Oxford Institute of Ageing, May 2007.

"The Future of Retirement: What the World Wants & What Employers Want." USA report, HSBC Future of Retirement Global Survey, 2006.

Gale, Sarah Fister. "Phased Retirement." *Workforce Management*, July 1, 2003.

Gardner, Marilyn. "Making Marriage Work After Retirement." *Christian Science Monitor*, August 30, 2006.

———. "More Women Decide to Extend Careers." *Christian Science Monitor*, January 4, 2006.

Generations Policy Initiative and the Harvard Institute for Learning in Retirement. "The Age Explosion: Baby Boomers and Beyond." *Harvard Generations Policy Journal* 1 (Winter 2004).

Gianturco, Paola, and Toby Tuttle. *In Her Hands: Craftswomen Changing the World.* 2nd ed. PowerHouse Books, 2004.

Gibbs, Nancy. "Midlife Crisis? Bring It On!" *Time*, May 16, 2005.

Goldberg, Elkhonon. *The Wisdom Paradox: How Your Mind Can Grow Stronger as Your Brain Grows Older.* New York: Gotham Books, 2005.

Goodman, Ellen, and Patricia O'Brien. *I Know Just What You Mean: The Power of Friendship in Women's Lives.* New York: Simon & Schuster, 2000.

Gould, Laurence J. "A Political Visionary in Mid-Life: Notes on Leadership and the Life Cycle." In *Group Relations, Management, and Organization*, edited by Robert French and Russ Vince. New York: Oxford University Press, 1999.

Gowans, Ann. "Working Migration Fits Retiring Boomers' Needs." *Columbia Daily Tribune*, October 2, 2006.

Grainge, Zoe. "Age Concerns." *Utility Week*, September 15, 2006.

"Graying Japan: The Downturn." *Economist*, Tokyo, January 5, 2006.

Green, Penelope. "When Mates Don't Match." *New York Times*, January 11, 2007.

Greene, Kelly. "Avoiding the Volunteer Trap." *Wall Street Journal*, April 24, 2006.

Griffin, Nancy. "Goldie Hawn." *AARP*, March/April 2006.

Grifith, Victoria. "Happiness in Life's Minutiae." *Financial Times*, December 3, 2004.

Gross, Jane. "Aging at Home." *New York Times*, February 9, 2006.

———. "Alone in Illness, Seeking Steady Arm to Lean On." *New York Times*, August 26, 2005.

Gubser, Michael, and Kristina Gryboski. "The Role of Grandmothers in Developing Countries." AARP, May 2006. http://www.aarp.org/research/international/perspectives/may_06_gubser_grandmother.html.

Gurchiek, Kathy. "Older Employees Prompt New Work, Retirement Trends." *HR News*, December 15, 2005.

Gutner, Toddi. "Still Working and Loving It." *BusinessWeek*, October 16, 2006.

Hamilton, Joan. "Woman of the Year." *Town & Country*, January 2006.

"Happy 150th Birthday: A New Era Looms for Old Age." Reuters, 2006.

Harder, Arlene. "Family Routines and Rituals Reinforce Family Rules." Support4Change, 2002. http://www.support4change.com/stages/generation/rules/rituals.html.

Heilbrun, Carolyn G. *The Last Gift of Time: Life Beyond Sixty.* New York: Dial Press, 1997.

———. *Writing a Woman's Life.* New York: Norton, 1988.

Heim, Pat, and Susan Murphy, with Susan K. Golant. *In the Company of Women: Turning Workplace Conflict into Powerful Alliances.* New York: J. P. Tarcher/Putnam, 2001.

Helmuth, Laura. "The Wisdom of the Wizened." *Science*, February 28, 2003.

Helyar, John. "50 and Fired." *Fortune*, May 16, 2005.

Herbert, Trish. "There Are Only Eight Inches Between a Halo and a Noose." *Vital Aging Network*, 2006.

Hively, Jan M. "Know and Grow: The Market for Older Adult Education." *MACAE Journal*, December 2003.

Hochschild, Arlie Russell. *The Time Bind: When Work Becomes Home and Home Becomes Work.* New York: Metropolitan Books, 1997.

Hoffman, Ellen. "A Course in What Next?" *BusinessWeek*, July 24, 2006. http://www.business week.com/magazine/content/06_30/b3994408.htm.

Holt, Jim. "You Are What You Expect." *New York Times Magazine*, January 21, 2007.

Hounsell, Cindy, and Pat Humphlett. "The Female Factor." WISER (Women's Institute for a Secure Retirement), September 2005.

Huffington, Arianna. "Would Things Be Any Different if Women Ran Corporate America?" HuffingtonPost.com, May 14, 2003.

Huget, Jennifer. "After the Rat Race, What Next?" *Washington Post*, December 5, 2006.

Huggins, Charnicia. "Dog Walking Helps Seniors Meet Exercise Goals." *Reuters Health*, October 5, 2006.

Ibarra, Herminia. *Working Identity: Unconventional Strategies for Reinventing Your Career.* Boston: Harvard Business School Press, 2003.

"Ideal Retirement Job Scenario." Retirementjobs.com survey, November 2005.

"Is a Franchise Right for You?" AARP, 2004. http://aarp.org/money/careers/selfemployment/a2004-05-14-franchise.html.

"Is Contingent Work Becoming a Preferred Option?" *HRFOCUS*, January 2006.

Jacobs-Lawson, Joy M., Douglas A. Hershey, and Kirstan A. Neukam. "Gender Differences in Factors That Influence Time Spent Planning for Retirement." *Journal of Women & Aging* 16, nos. 3–4 (2004).

James, Estelle, Alejandra Cox Edwards, and Rebecca Wong. "The Gender Impact of Alternative Social Security Policies." Policy brief, University of Michigan Retirement Research Center, July 2006.

Johnson, Richard W. "Do Spouses Coordinate Their Retirement Decisions?" Issue brief, Center for Retirement Research at Boston College, July 2004.

Johnson, Richard W., Gordon Mermin, and C. Eugene Steuerle. "Work Impediments at Older Ages." Urban Institute, May 2006.

Johnson, Richard W., and C. Eugene Steuerle. "Promoting Work at Older Ages: The Role of Hybrid Pension Plans in an Aging Population." Pension Research Council Working Paper, 2003.

Kadlec, Daniel J. "The Marathon Generation." *Time*, June 18, 2006.

———. " 'Me Generation' Becomes 'We Generation.' " *USA Today*, August 3, 2006.

Kendall-Tackett, Kathleen A., ed. *Handbook of Women, Stress, and Trauma.* New York: Routledge, 2004.

King, Marsha. "Elderly Seek to Grow Old Together, Form New Support Groups." *Seattle Times*, May 1, 2006.

Kitchen, Patricia. "Networking: Professional Women Team With Others for Support and Social Activities." *Newsday*, January 14, 2006.

Kluger, Jeffrey. "The Surprising Power of the Aging Brain." *Time*, January 8, 2006.

Kolata, Gina. "Old But Not Frail: A Matter of Heart and Head." *New York Times*, October 5, 2006.

———. "A Surprising Secret to a Long Life: Stay in School." *New York Times*, January 3, 2007.

Kroke, James, Jr. "Breaking Free." *Across the Board*, January/February 2005.

Landman, Beth. "Wagging the Dog and a Finger." *New York Times*, May 14, 2006.

Lansford, J. E., T. C. Antonucci, H. Akiyama, and K. Takahashi. "A Quantitative and Qualitative Approach to Social Relationships and Well-Being in the United States and Japan." *Journal of Comparative Family Studies*, 36 (2005).

Layard, Richard. "Happiness: Has Social Science a Clue?" Lecture delivered at Lionel Robbins Memorial Lectures at the London School of Economics, 2002–03.

"Leaders in a Global Economy: A Study of Executive Women and Men." Families and Work Institute, Catalyst, Boston College Center for Work & Family, [2000–2003].

Leland, John. "Trouble Transitioning? Just Hire a Coach." *New York Times*, April 11, 2006.

Levine, Suzanne Braun. *Inventing the Rest of Our Lives: Women in Second Adulthood.* New York: Viking, 2005.

Levinson, Daniel J. *The Seasons of a Man's Life.* New York: Knopf, 1978.

Levinson, Daniel J., and Judy D. Levinson. *The Seasons of a Woman's Life.* New York: Knopf, 1996.

Lewis, Leo. "Retirement Cruises Put Marriages on the Rocks." *The Times*, February 22, 2006. http://www.timesonline.co.uk/tol/news/world/asia/article733374.ece.

"Life Expectancy in G-7 Industrialized Nations May Exceed Past Predictions, Study Suggests." U.S. National Institutes of Health, June 14, 2000.

"Living Longer, Working Longer." MetLife Mature Market Institute study, 2006.

"The LLI Movement Across College and University Campuses." Elderhostel, February 14, 2007. http://www.elderhostel.org/ein/ilrmovement.asp.

"Looking at Act II of Women's Lives: Thriving and Striving from 45 On." AARP Foundation Women's Leadership Circle study, with Roper Public Affairs, April 2006.

Lopez, Steve. "Getting Paid to Act Her Age: 97." *Los Angeles Times*, December 17, 2006.

Lyman, Rick. "Report Foresees No Crisis Over Aging Generation's Health." *New York Times*, March 10, 2006.

Magee, Marc. "Boomer Corps: Activating Seniors for National Service." Policy report, Progressive Policy Institute, January 2004.

Mahoney, Sarah. "The Secret Lives of Single Women." *AARP*, May–June 2006.

Manheimer, Ronald J. "Older Adult Education in the United States: Trends and Predictions." North Carolina Center for Creative Retirement, University of North Carolina–Asheville, 2002.

Marano, Hara Estroff. "The Reinvention of Marriage." *Psychology Today*, January/February 1992.

Mermin, Gordon B. T., Richard W. Johnson, and Dan Murphy. "Why Do Boomers Plan to Work So Long?" Discussion paper 06-04, Urban Institute, December 2006.

Merrill Lynch New Retirement Study, May 2006.

Moen, Phyllis, ed. *It's About Time: Couples and Careers.* Ithaca: ILR Press, Cornell University Press, 2003.

Moen, Phyllis, William A. Erickson, Madhurima Agarwal, Vivian Fields, and Laurie Todd. "The Cornell Retirement and Well-Being Study: Final Report." Ithaca: Bronfenbrenner Life Course Center, 2000.

Moen, Phyllis, and Patricia Roehling. *The Career Mystique: Cracks in the American Dream.* Lanham, MD: Rowman & Littlefield, 2004.

Morrison, Ann M., Randall P. White, and Ellen Van Velsor. "Executive Women: Substance Plus Style." *Psychology Today*, August 1987.

Munnell, Alicia H. "Policies to Promote Labor Force Participation of Older People." Issue brief, Center for Retirement Research at Boston College, January 2006.

Munnell, Alicia H., Francesca Golub-Sass, and Anthony Webb. "What Moves the National Retirement Risk Index? A Look Back and an Update." Issue brief, Center for Retirement Research at Boston College, January 2007.

Munnell, Alicia H., and Natalia Jivan. "What Makes Older Women Work?" Issue brief, Center for Retirement Research at Boston College, September 2005.

Munnell, Alicia H., Steven A. Sass, and Mauricio Soto. "Employer Attitudes Towards Older Workers: Survey Results." Issue brief, Center for Retirement Research at Boston College, June 2006.

Nelson, Brittne, and Katherine Bridges. "Preparing for an Aging Workforce: A Focus on New York Employers." AARP, November 2005. http://www.aarp.org/research/work/employ ment/ny-workforce.html.

"The New Agenda for an Older Workforce." White paper, Manpower, 2007.

"New Face of Work." MetLife Foundation and Civic Ventures survey, 2005.

Newhouse, Margaret, with Judy Goggin. "Life Planning for the 3rd Age: A Design and Resource Guide." Civic Ventures, 2004.

"Older Women Workers, Ages 55 and Over." Women's Bureau, U.S. Department of Labor, March 2007.

Patchett, Ann. *Truth & Beauty: A Friendship.* New York: HarperCollins, 2004.

Perle, Liz. *Money, A Memoir: Women, Emotions, and Cash.* New York: Henry Holt, 2006.

Platman, Kerry. "Age Myths Must Be Confronted." *Occupational Health*, April 2006.

Price, Christine A. "Retirement for Women: The Impact of Employment." *Journal of Women & Ageing* 14, nos. 3–4 (June 2002).

"Professional and Executive Temps: Knights in White Collar." hr.com, December 6, 2004.

Rapoport, Rhona, and Lotte Bailyn. "Relinking Life and Work: Toward a Better Future." Report to the Ford Foundation based on a research project in collaboration with Xerox Corporation, Tandem Computers, and Corning, 1996.

Rath, Tom. *Vital Friends: The People You Can't Afford to Live Without.* New York: Gallup Press, 2006.

Rayasam, Renuka. "Your Marriage May Profit From a Little Less Togetherness." *U.S. News & World Report*, June 12, 2006.

Raymo, James, and Megan Sweeney. "Work-Family Conflict and Retirement Preferences." UCLA Center for Population Research, June 2005.

"Reinventing Aging: Baby Boomers and Civic Engagement." Harvard School of Public Health, MetLife Foundation Initiative on Retirement and Civic Engagement, 2004.

Reio, Thomas G., and Joanne Sanders-Reio. "Combating Workplace Ageism." *Adult Learning* 11 (1999).

"Retirement Only a Breather." Putnam Investments study, December 8, 2005.

"Retirement Planning in the 21st Century." National Endowment for Financial Education. May 26–28, 1999.

Roberts, Sam. "51% of Women Are Now Living Without Spouse." *New York Times*, January 16, 2007.

RoperASW. "Baby Boomers Envision Retirement II—Key Findings." Survey of baby boomers' expectations for retirement. AARP, May 2004.

Rose, Barbara. "Baby Boomer Brain Drain: Retirement Saps Work Force." Knight Ridder Tribune News Service, May 3, 2006.

Rosener, Judy B. "Ways Women Lead." *Harvard Business Review*, November–December 1990.

Roth, Peggy. "What Happens to a Couple in Retirement?" Council for Relationships, September 20, 2004. http://www.councilforrelationships.org/articles/retirement_9-20-04.htm.

Sahadi, Jeanne. "He Said, She Said: Retirement Ideas Differ." *CNN Money*, April 17, 2007. http://www.money.cnn.com/2007/04/17/pf/retirement/fidelity_couples_survey/index.htm.

Schwartz, Felice N. "Management Women and the New Facts of Life." *Harvard Business Review*, January–February 1989.

Sedlar, Jeri, and Rick Miners. *Don't Retire, REWIRE! 5 Steps to Fulfilling Work That Fuels Your Passion, Suits Your Personality, or Fills Your Pocket*. Indianapolis: Alpha Books, 2003.

Seligman, Martin E. P. *Authentic Happiness: Using the New Positive Psychology to Realize Your Potential for Lasting Fulfillment*. New York: Free Press, 2002.

Sheehy, Gail. *Pathfinders*. New York: Morrow, 1982.

———. *Sex and the Seasoned Woman: Pursuing the Passionate Life*. New York: Random House, 2006.

Simmons, Beverley A., and Myra J. Betschild. "Women's Retirement, Work and Life Paths: Changes, Disruptions and Discontinuities." *Journal of Aging* 13, no. 4 (2001).

Smith, Jim. "Seeking the Unretiring Sort: Volunteer Groups Look to Baby Boomers to Fill Gaps in Their Ranks." *Newsday*, October 14, 2006.

"Spirituality and Aging." College of Arts and Sciences at the University of Missouri–Kansas City. http://cas.umkc.edu/casww/sa/spirituality.htm.

"Spirituality and Religion Among Americans Age 45 and Older." *AARP*, October 2004.

Stein, Howard F. "Letting Go of Who We Were: The Triad of Change-Loss-Grief in Organizational and Wider Cultural Life." *Organizational & Social Dynamics*, 2006.

Stern, Stefan. "Don't Get Fooled Again—You're Not Too Old for the Job." *Financial Times*, December 5, 2006.

Sternberg, Esther M. *The Balance Within: The Science Connecting Health and Emotions*. New York: W. H. Freeman, 2000.

Stier, Max. *Are You Experienced? How Boomers Can Help Our Government Meet Its Talent Needs*. Policy Series. Civic Ventures, 2007.

"Study Challenges Image of Depressed Widows." Reuters. March 15, 2006.

Sullivan, Marianne. "Female Entrepreneurs Win Notice for Taking Risk." Women's eNews. January 27, 2005. http://www.womensenews.org/article.cfm/dyn/aid/2162.

Sutton, Charlotte Decker, and Kris K. Moore. "Executive Women—20 years later." *Harvard Business Review*, September–October 1985.

Taylor, Shelley E., et al. "Biobehavioral Responses to Stress in Females: Tend-and-Befriend, Not Fight-or-Flight." *Psychological Review* 107, no. 3 (2000).

Tergesen, Anne, and Mark Morrison. "Getting Psyched to Retire." *BusinessWeek*, July 24, 2006.

Tobias, Sheila. *Overcoming Math Anxiety*. Revised and expanded ed. New York: Norton, 1993.

Trafford, Abigail. *My Time: Making the Most of the Rest of Your Life*. New York: Basic Books, 2003.

"Training and Reskilling Practices of Healthcare Organizations." *AARP*, March 2007.

The Transition Network. "Survey." October 2005. http://www.thetransitionnetwork.org/about.asp.

Treat, Stephen. "Prepare Your Marriage for Retirement." MSNBC, March 15, 2005. http://www.msnbc.com/id/7187691/.

"Trend: Graying of Small Business." TrendTracker. January 2004. http://www.trendtracker.blogspot.com/2004/01/trend-graying-of-small-business.html.

Tyre, Peg. "Learning to Adapt." *Newsweek*, June 19, 2006.

"Update on the Aged 55+ Worker: 2005." AARP Public Policy Institute, April 2006.

U.S. Census Bureau. *Statistical Abstract of the United States*, 2007.

Vandervelde, Maryanne. *Retirement for Two*. New York: Bantam, 2004.

"Voluntarism Among Older Adults." Fact Sheet at the Center on Aging & Work/Workplace Flexibility at Boston College, January 2007.

Wallis, Claudia. "The New Science of Happiness." *Time*, January 17, 2005.

Wellner, Alison Stein. "Tapping a Silver Mine." *HR*, March 2002.

Winston, Norma A., and Jo Barnes. "Academic Women and Retirement." *AABSS Journal*, 2003.

"Women Are Redefining Power." Study of women's attitudes toward power, Simmons School of Management, March 15, 2005.

"Women Are Willing to Take Business Risks." *Boston Business Journal*, September 10, 2004.

Woolf, Linda M. "Gender and Ageism." Webster University, 1998. http://www.webster.edu/~woolflm/ageism.html.

"Working After Retirement: The Gap Between Expectations and Reality." A Social Trends Report, Pew Research Center, September 2006.

"The Working Retired." Putnam Investments study, December 8, 2005.

Zissimopoulos, Julie, and Lynn A. Karoly. "Work and Well-Being Among the Self-Employed at Older Ages." AARP research report, February 2007.

Zuboff, Shoshana. "The New New Adulthood." *Fast Company*, August 2004.

INDEX